THE GOD QUESTION

A Catholic Approach

Francis R. Smith, S.J.

PAULIST PRESS
New York/Mahwah

Library of Congress Cataloging-in-Publication Data

Smith, Francis R., 1934–
    The God question : a Catholic approach / Francis R. Smith.
      p. cm.
    0-8091-0418-0 (cloth)
    1. Theology. 2. Catholic Church—Doctrines. I. Title.
BX1751.2.S483 1988
230'.2—dc 19
                                                88-2470
                                                  CIP

Published by Paulist Press
997 Macarthur Boulevard
Mahwah, N.J. 07430

Printed and bound in the United States of America

CONTENTS

Section II: The God of Jesus

CHAPTER V: THE SOURCES OF OUR KNOWLEDGE
            OF JESUS OF NAZARETH

CHAPTER VI: THE REIGN OF GOD IN THE PREACHING
             AND ACTS OF JESUS OF NAZARETH

ACKNOWLEDGEMENTS

This book was a long time in gestation. It certainly contains the ideas and in some cases even the very words of other theologians. Readers familiar with theology will recognize the influence of Lonergan, Rahner, and Walter Kasper. Special debts are owed to *Neues Glaubensbuch*, Herder, 1975 (English edition, *The Common Catechism*, Seabury, 1975), Part I (originally the work of Paulus Englehardt) for the formulation of the "God Question" in Chapter 3, and to Ben F. Meyer's *The Aims of Jesus*, SCM Press, 1979, for the argument pursued in Appendix 5, "The Aim of Jesus."

I wish to especially thank two people without whom this book would never have been written: Ethel Johnston, who miraculously "processed" page after page of scrawl into the printed word, and Lovene Wood, who encouraged me to think about a book, typed large parts of the earliest drafts and made helpful comments about style and content. Anne Kearney made helpful editorial comments. My thanks are also due to Rita Lossett and the Carmelite sisters of Santa Clara for their assistance in the final stages of production. Finally I thank the many descendants of J. Phillip Bannan, for their generosity to this enterprise and to Santa Clara University.

PREFACE

This book originated as a text for an introductory course in Catholic theology. The task was threefold: (1) To introduce students who had minimal theological background to theology; (2) To expose them to the central questions and sweep of theology; (3) To lead them to a preliminary synthesis from which further theological questions could be addressed. Given the task, the choice of topics had to be strategic. The topics of the ten chapters are the result of years of negotiations between what the author thought was important and what first-level students signaled they needed to know.

In time the emerging text came to be used on a second level, principally in a christology course. The christological chapters raised questions that required further treatment. The appendices are largely the result of this further demand.

Classes of students do not fall neatly into *only* beginners or *only* advanced. Some first-level students raised advanced questions. Some advanced students had skipped more fundamental questions. It seemed reasonable to offer both levels in the same book and let teachers and students take what they needed.

Accordingly, this book is designed to be used on a number of levels. The chapters treat some main theological questions and are designed to take a first-level student from a consideration of what theology is, to theological synthesis; that is, to a genuine, if preliminary, *logos* about *theos*—human discourse about God. The appendices treat questions that may or may not be deemed worth pursuing by individual teachers or students, but in any case were not essential to the main task of the book. In both chapters and appendices the principal source has been the biblical witness, read from an historical-critical perspective, from within the Catholic doctrinal tradition.

Part I:
ASKING THE QUESTION

Chapter I

THEOLOGY

INTRODUCTION—THEOLOGY IN AN AMERICAN CONTEXT

An introduction to theology aimed at the American reader must begin by acknowledging the peculiar history of theology and the study of religion in the United States. Before the Revolution theology played a prominent role in the curricula of young American universities, most notably at Harvard and Yale. But these institutions were founded under religious auspices. With the Revolution, the separation of church and state, and the spread of state-supported public institutions, theology fell from favor in much of American higher education. Schools of theology were prominent in many of the older prestigious American private schools, but for the most part theology was relegated to that special institution called the seminary.

This historical data helps illuminate the distinctive nature of theology. The American colonies were largely founded along religious lines. Not surprisingly one of the major concerns of the educational institutions they spawned was reflection on the Christian faith from a specific denominational point of view. This "inside" look at the Christian faith is the theological viewpoint. Because of the principle of separation of church and state, however, public institutions could not permit such an approach to religion. While schools of theology are not uncommon in the great state universities of Europe and Canada, theology had no place in American public higher education. And for a long time public institutions did not consider religion a topic of study at all. Partly this is because of the distinctive nature of American Christianity.

From the very beginning Americans have had sharply diverging attitudes toward religion. For many of the founding fathers, especially Thomas Jefferson, the genius of the American political system, the only true religion was a "religion within the limits of reason alone." For

Jefferson the God to be worshiped was not the mysterious "Yahweh" of Abraham, Isaac and Jacob but "nature's God." A religious orientation is evident in the American Constitution, but it is the religion of eighteenth century deism. On the other hand, many American Christians, especially on the frontier, swung to the opposite extreme. What became characteristic of much American religion was not rationalism but emotionalism, fundamentalism, the path of uncritical faith. Two sharply divergent approaches to being religious were present in American culture during its formative years. The result was that a truly reflective approach to religion from within, or even as a human phenomenon to be studied "from without," had little place in the institution characteristic of American academia, the state-supported institution.

In recent years the benign neglect of religion by American academia has given way to the emergence of the discipline called "religious studies." Many institutions acknowledge that religion is a significant human phenomenon, the neglect of which is inconsistent with the ideal of comprehensive knowledge that the university aspires to. Thus the "religious studies," that is, the history of religion, the sociology of religion, the psychology of religion, and related disciplines, have taken their place beside the more familiar subjects. These "of" disciplines apply the tools of the various "human sciences" to the phenomenon of humanity as religious. Just as psychology studies men and women from the point of view of behavior, and sociology examines them as a collectivity, the religious sciences study us as religious.

How does theology differ from "religious studies"? Both in theory and practice it is impossible to clearly distinguish religious studies from theology. They are on a spectrum. With regard to methodology, most scholars in religious studies acknowledge that to remain completely "outside" the phenomenon of religion is to cut oneself off from adequate understanding of it. There must be some sort of "entering in," some sort of participation in a religion to understand it. In the study of religion, at least, "objectivity" can be a hindrance. But when one "enters in," adopts a sympathetic stance, or takes an "insider's" view, one proceeds down the spectrum toward theology. The theologian, on the other hand, by profession, leans toward the religious studies end of the spectrum because he or she seeks to be *critical*. The word "critical" is not meant in a negative sense here. Theology is "critical" in that it seeks to give reasons for its assertions. Within its acknowledged starting point, a specific religious commitment, it critically argues its case. With those preliminary clarifications, we can now analyze more closely just what theology is.

THE WORD

Given the history of religion in America, it is not surprising that the word "theology" means different things to different people. For some people it is synonymous with religion. For others it is equivalent to mythology. Words are not just precise denotations of particular concepts or things; they also carry many connotations. They carry layers of meanings, meanings that embody value judgments and attitudes. So while it is legitimate, because it is inevitable, that the word "theology" carry different meanings for different people, it is important to understand *what* meaning a given speaker attaches to it.

So we must begin by defining "theology" as it is understood in this book. Let us start with its etymology. "Theology" derives from the Greek words *logos*, speech, and *theos*, God. Theology is human speech about God. It is not God's speech about God; it is not God's *self-revelation*. Nor is theology *doctrine*. It is not what a *community* says about what it believes. Rather, theology is the *reflective activity* which believers engage in when (usually as members of a community) they wish to fathom further what God has revealed and their community has expressed. Theology is part of one's response to God's self-revelation. It has its beginning in the need to *understand* religious beliefs. In a way, all believers are theologians because reflection on the content of revelation is integral to its reception. This is the beginning of theology. Let us further define theology by talking about its "object" and its "subject."

THE OBJECT OF THEOLOGY

Theology is a distinctive human endeavor. While in a way every believer is willy-nilly a theologian, "theology," in its strict sense, designates not just any reflection by believers on what they believe. It is an intellectual activity of a certain level and type. In this book theology designates what *religious* people do when they *reflect systematically* and *critically* on what they believe. In the strict sense, theology occurs when reflection on what is believed achieves a certain intellectual level. In the Middle Ages theology was called a "scientia," an organized, coherent body of knowledge. Conceded its starting point, a believer (its "subject"), and its goal, a transcendent God (its "object"), theology is critical and coherent. Like all bodies of knowledge it must respect the canon of verification, it must give evidence for its statements (be critical). *Within its own rules,* theology does this. But "its own rules" make it distinctive among intellectual disciplines. Why?

Let us talk first about the "object" of theology. If theology is reflection on what is believed, then the object of theology is simply the object of faith. But the object of Christian faith is a transcendent God. By definition, then, the object of theology is *mystery.* The Christian God is a creator God, but is not part of what is created. God "transcends" the finite, created world. The problem, then, is this: the object of theology, *theos,* will always exceed, not just by degree but *in kind,* the subject of theology, the reflective believer's finite capacity to understand.

Is that a problem unique to theology? Isn't it true that all intellectual disciplines move toward a mastery of their data but never reach their goal? Yes. But one must recognize that other disciplines, in principle if not in fact, *can* master their data. Their fields are not mysteries in principle, but merely in fact. In principle, the human mind is capable of understanding the finite world. The data are infinite not in the sense that they transcend human understanding but in their variety and quantity.

The object of theology is different, because it is mystery in principle. By God's very nature, God *must* "transcend" the world. If God were part of the world, God would be comprehensible. But then God would also be finite and so would not be God. So the object of theology, God, is, and must remain, a *mystery.* As we will see, God is not the opaque mystery of unintelligibility, but the mystery of superabundant meaning, the mystery of infinite love.

THE SUBJECT OF THEOLOGY

If the preceding paragraphs create an impression that theology is unique among fields of study, those following on the *subject* of theology will intensify that impression. The distinctiveness of theology is reflected in the ambivalence of our culture toward it. What is the source of this ambivalence? Theology claims to be intellectual, but it is suspect in the intellectual community. If theology is what *believers* do when they become reflective, then it presupposes faith. It *begins* by holding something to be true. This seems to contradict the norms of genuine intellectual activity. In an intellectual pursuit, is not truth what one arrives *at,* rather than what one begins *with?* Should not one proceed from an "objective" starting point in the search for truth? How can anything that is *already believed* respect the demands of intellect for objective, verifiable reasons?

THE SOCIOLOGY OF KNOWLEDGE

One could, of course, point out that the notion that the intellectual life begins from a purely objective standpoint is an oversight. *All* inquiries proceed from previous knowledge or assumption. In fact, sometimes the positions are held so firmly or the assumptions so unconsciously that only with great difficulty can one even become aware of one's presuppositions. Furthermore, *all* human beings are believers, for no one can critically establish one's worldview, and all inquiry presupposes the existence of a worldview.

This is one of the insight's of the *sociology of knowledge.* Everyone, simply to survive, is socialized into a culture, a process that involves being given that culture's worldview. Affirming or rejecting the adequacy of it is a long and probably endless task. And even when one embarks on a critique of an inherited worldview, one must employ elements of the very worldview being critiqued.

The insights of the sociology of knowledge have minimized the distinctiveness and therefore the suspect character of theology's approach. However, the distinctiveness should not be eliminated. It is better for theology to clearly acknowledge its uniqueness. Theology *is* different. It begins in faith and it heads toward mystery. The medieval theologians expressed this when they defined theology as *fides quaerens intellectum.* It is *"faith seeking understanding."* This does not conflict with our earlier definitions but merely emphasizes the unique starting point of theology. Theology presupposes a commitment. We usually think of a commitment resulting *after* knowledge is acquired. In theology the commitment initiates the process. The believer seeks to understand more deeply what he or she believes.

It is clear that the uniqueness of theology stems from the nature of its ground which is faith, and the nature of its object, the mystery that sustains but must, by that fact, transcend us. In the next chapter we will discuss faith more thoroughly. But first we must clarify the nature of theology by distinguishing (but not separating) theology from religious studies. The difference lies in the *operational* presence of faith.

THEOLOGY AND RELIGIOUS STUDIES

As we said, academia recognizes that religion is a significant human phenomenon, and like any human phenomenon it can be studied in an organized, critical manner. So one can study the history of religion, the sociology of religion or the psychology of religion. The data of these disciplines is humanity as religious. The tool of study used in these disciplines is a critical analysis that seeks to understand mankind in a certain way—in its historical development, in its behavior as groups, in its behavior as individually motivated, but as religious.

It would appear that religious studies approaches religion from the "outside." That is a valid initial characterization. Outstanding studies of religious tradition have been completed by scholars who do not believe in the truth claims of those traditions. Nevertheless, many scholars recognize a dilemma here: Religions are ways of life. They embody what is of ultimate concern in people's lives. They pervade daily life in ways that can only be experienced and are not accessible to the neutral observer. How can one adequately understand such a phenomenon if one does not experience it oneself? This dilemma indicates that identifying religious studies with a purely "outside" approach and theology with a purely "inside" approach is an oversimplification. Neither a purely outside nor a purely inside approach is adequate. A scholar studying a religion purely from the outside will always remain at a distance from the heart of that religion. On the other hand, a believer who never adopts a reflective, even a critical attitude toward his or her religion runs the risk of not integrating it into the rest of his or her life, especially if, in other areas, reflection and critical thinking *are* cultivated. And so outsiders have to venture inside and insiders have to stand outside. This leads us to the conclusion that religious studies and theology are not separate but distinct— like the ends of a spectrum. Religious studies and theology are not two radically different disciplines. The terms designate approaches to religion in which *faith* plays a varying role. Religious studies does not explicitly guide its study by a faith commitment. Its map of the phenomenon, its key questions, are questions anyone could ask. They are historical, sociological, and psychological. One cannot answer these questions by appealing to faith statements. Although the student of a particular religion cannot fully understand it without participating in it, nevertheless, he or she "controls" the effect of sympathy, and does not let it substitute for empirical data.

In contrast, theologians consciously and explicitly reflect from within a religious tradition or faith commitment. Theological questions are not merely historical, sociological, or psychological questions. It is true that, more and more, theology is using the religious studies disciplines which give it a greater "objectivity," and lead to new ways of understanding. But when theology asks its own proper questions, it must verify its answers with properly theological data. In the end this data is supplied by faith because it is data of God's self-revelation. The object of theology is not men and women as religious but God as self-revealing. Only if mystery reveals itself to us will we be able to say anything at all about it. Theology must respect the nature of its subject and the nature of its object. It is the human effort to understand and articulate what the transcendent mystery has revealed of itself. It is true or false depending on its fidelity to that revelation which can only be known in faith.

Nevertheless, Catholic theology has always conceded that even theology cannot be purely an insider's view because no one is purely an insider. The medieval phrase *fides quaerens intellectum* describes the major theme of theology. But the phrase is turned around, and the minor theme is revealed. Theology is also concerned with *intellectus quaerens fidem*—understanding seeking faith, or better the grounds *why* one believes. Here the believer becomes an outsider. He or she acknowledges that he or she is a human being and that conscience requires that there be an accounting for one's faith commitment. The nature of that accounting will be discussed in Chapter II.

The willingness of theology to take a look from the outside and the lessons learned from the sociology of knowledge have helped soften the resistance of academics to seeing theology as an intellectual discipline. Many courses taught in theology departments tend toward the religious studies end of the spectrum, while some courses in state universities could qualify as theology, for they are taught by people who come from the faith tradition being reflected on or by people sympathetic to that tradition. They are taught with a scholarly objectivity and an acknowledgment of their presuppositions. The movement from one end of the spectrum, religious studies, is being matched by a movement from the other end, theology.

CONCLUSION

This chapter has discussed theology in an introductory way and in a narrow context—the world of the university, and indeed, the American university. The desire of theology to find respectability in that milieu is understandable. It is important for both theology and the university that theology have a place in higher, even secular higher education, and if it is to be there, it must meet the general ground rules of academic pursuits. But it should not be overlooked that academic theology is open to the charge that it is "ivory-tower," divorced from experience, (theoretically) "correct" but not "true" (to life). The academicization of theology must be recognized for what it is, a type of theology. There have been, are, and will be different types.

Theology cannot forget that it is reflecting faith. We will see in the next chapter how comprehensive that term, faith, is. Theology has its roots in lived faith experience and is the reflective component of that experience. As a component of faith, it seeks to clarify, direct, and critique the life of faith. Even in its most speculative moments theology begins in faith and seeks to guide the practice of faith.

Thus theology grows out of prayer, worship, community, but also life's daily struggle lived in a concrete situation. In turn, it seeks to guide life in the daily struggle. The roots of theology in the concrete situation and its practical application is especially emphasized by "liberation theology," which defines theology as "reflection on the practice of the faith in the light of the word of God." It is *liberation* theology because the concrete situation of this reflection is one of perceived oppression. It is theology "from the underside of history." The reader will find in Appendix 1 an introduction to this important development in the history of theology.

Chapter II

FAITH

INTRODUCTION

If theology proceeds from faith, a correct understanding of faith is indispensable for a sound theology. The strengths and weaknesses of theology, its peculiarities, its status as knowledge, its capacity to be critical and systematic, the verifiability of its conclusions and the success of its application to life—all will stem from the nature of faith. And theologies differ to a great extent because they differ in their definitions of faith.

The history of theology confirms the centrality of the concept of faith. How a tradition understands faith exhibits fundamental values cherished in that tradition. But one must expect also that, precisely here, an overstressing of a cherished value can appear. What in fact has a *number* of components may be reduced to *one* component.

One can see something of this in the way the two major western Christian traditions have approached the question of faith. In nineteenth century Catholicism faith was presented in the theological manuals as "assent to revealed truths." Today we would say that such a view represents a contraction from the richer biblical and patristic notion of faith. But precisely as a contraction it illustrates the distinctive Catholic approach to faith and the cherished value behind it. Faith is a form of *knowledge*. The mind has a role to play in faith.

In Protestantism, the opposite pole can sometimes be observed. The nineteenth century Danish Lutheran philosopher Sören Kierkegaard liked to quote Tertullian (third century) when asked why he believed in Christianity: *"Credo quia absurdum est."* "I believe because it is absurd." When one examines Kierkegaard's writings, however, one sees that what is really at stake is the cherished Protestant value of *trust*. Faith is *more than* knowledge. The will has the crucial role to play in faith.

If the extremes of the two traditions have a common defect, it is

11

that each fails to view faith as the response of the whole person. Faith *is* more than knowledge; it is a personal relationship with God. That relationship is belief *in* God (trust). But this trust in God is based in personal *knowledge,* in God's self-revelation, and in a full, human response, one that involves the mind.

TOWARD A CATHOLIC CONCEPT OF FAITH
A MINIMALIST NOTION OF FAITH

Everyone has a faith. Just to function on a daily basis, each person must have a framework, a worldview, a "horizon." As we are faced with questions and decisions, what enables us to answer and decide, even to perceive objects in the world around us, is our ability to "locate" new data within a framework. That framework is a "faith" because we did not generate it ourselves; rather we absorbed it from our culture. While this framework appears to us to be self-evident and universal, it is to a large extent culturally conditioned. And we do in fact continually modify it to make better sense of our experience.

RELIGIOUS FAITH

But in normal usage "faith" designates not just any worldview but one that assumes that human life is ultimately meaningful and not absurd. Here faith takes on a more specific meaning. It indicates *one* of the paths a person can choose when he or she asks if there is any ultimate ground or meaning to human life. A properly religious faith would answer affirmatively and locate that ground in a "transcendent" reality. That is, the meaning of human life is grounded in a reality which is not part of the world. Later we will see that such a faith entails that the meaning of our lives is ultimately a gift from something which has—in contrast to us—self-generated meaning.

Not everyone affirms a transcendent source of meaning. Many people, probably more than in previous ages, deny such a source. They believe there is no transcendent ground of meaning, but that all possible meaning is *immanent* in human life.

For everyone, our *initial* answers to these questions are based on our inherited worldviews. But most people at some time in their lives face a crisis. We are forced to consider seriously the validity of our assumptions, our inherited faith.

For a person to affirm any faith, since it is precisely a belief, some-thing not really self-evident and obvious (this is the core of the "crisis of faith": what seemed self-evident no longer appears so), a *readiness to believe* must continue. There is a painful paradox here. In a crisis of faith one wants to "ground" faith, to rationally justify it. But one can go only so far in grounding faith, for a thoroughly grounded faith is a contradiction in terms. Ultimately, a "mature" faith, one that has been affirmed after questioning, whether religious or otherwise, is the result of a *decision*. That is, it is more than merely a *judgment*. A judg-ment terminates rational inquiry. Given reasons, one makes a judg-ment, more or less probable depending on the persuasiveness of the reasons. A faith is never merely the result of a reasoning process. It "leaps" beyond a judgment. It does not leave reasons behind, but it is not simply an affair of reason. Reasons can be assembled to point to the ultimate meaning or meaninglessness of the world. But in the end, one *chooses*. The grounds for the choice may seem very obvious and the choice easy. Then again they may not. It may be like love at first sight or a long, difficult but committed marriage. In either case it is ultimately more than a judgment; it is on the order of choice, decision, will, love.

Any mature faith is a decision to see the world in one way or the other. It is a moral act, an act of conscience that engages not merely the mind but the whole person. Religious faith is the decision to see the world not as meaningless but as having more meaning than one can wrap one's mind around. Religious faith is the decision to see the world as rooted in self-generating meaning. It is the decision to put one's possibilities for meaning in a transcendent source that is its own ground of meaning. One enters into a relationship in which meaning is a *gift*. Religious faith is the decision to *en-trust* oneself to an absolute (self-generating) meaning, to a transcendent personal absolute.

CHRISTIAN FAITH

A look at *Christian* faith shows us more clearly what faith involves. One way to put it is to say that Christian faith is an authentic, consci-entious response of the whole person to Jesus Christ as the historical manifestation of the transcendent personal absolute. Christian faith recognizes the absolute in that historical person, and claims that in Je-sus Christ, the self-revelation of transcendent meaning is definitively completed.

FAITH AS A GIFT

As based on God's self-revelation, faith is a gift, because genuine self-disclosure is always a free gift of self. What is more difficult to see is that just as this self-revelation of God in Christ is a gift, so is our response. The revelation creates the response. This is not as strange as it sounds. In all relationships that are genuinely loving ones, there is an exchange of self. It is this mutual giving of self that creates the relationship. Between persons with differing capacities for love, the giving of self enlarges or even creates the capacity in the less loving to reciprocate. Between the transcendent and the immanent, the infinite and the finite, the creator and the creature, *all* of the response of the beloved has its source in the lover.

FAITH AND REASON

If faith is a response of the whole person, it cannot be an arbitrary decision. It would not be a truly human act to believe simply because one wished or needed to believe something. Faith must have its reasons. But religious faith is not merely a form of knowledge either. It is a commitment to a *personal* absolute. It is not merely believing *that* such an absolute exists. It is a believing *in,* or better, it is believing God. Faith is a personal relationship with transcendent personal meaning which has revealed itself. The offer is an offer of self, of love. And the only adequate response is love. Faith as the act of entrusting myself to that which offers itself to me is love.

If faith is love, one need not articulate all the reasons why one believes for the faith response to be an authentic human act. As Pascal said: "The heart has reasons which reason does not know." Authentic faith is not unreasonable, but its rationality is the rationality of love.

As love, faith is not "verified from without." It is *self-authenticating.* It is authenticated in the living of it, as all loves are. One cannot believe against one's conscience, but, all things considered, it is not unreasonable to leap or jump or fall into love, anticipating "verification" of the "reasonability" of that act in life itself.

CATHOLIC FAITH

We have been giving a general account of faith, religious faith, Christian faith. Let us now look at some characteristically (although not exclusively) *Catholic* notions about faith.

FAITH IS ECCLESIAL

Faith brings one into union with others who believe. It forms communities. The core of the early Christian community was a common faith in the Resurrected Christ. The present day Christian believes *because* others have believed and are believing. While faith is believing God speaking to us in the depths of our being, we mediate, articulate that speaking to one another.

The *ecclesia*, the community of believers, is the *carrier* of the good news of God's self-revelation in Christ. The historical self-disclosure of God continues to be present in human history through the community which has been called together for precisely that purpose by the Spirit of the Risen Christ. In salvation history God is revealed to be Father, Son, and Holy Spirit. The Church is the result of that self-revelation and bears witness to it. To believe its message implies union with it.

THE EFFECT OF FAITH

We have already pointed to the first effect of faith. It results in a community of believers. What is its effect on individuals in that community? If faith is a response of love to love, we must expect faith to have a *transforming* effect. At least in comparison with the Reformation tradition, Catholicism has stressed this characteristic of faith. The Reformers tended to emphasize the disruptive effect of sin on human nature. One suspects that they were trying to safeguard a genuine Christian principle that the practices of late medieval Catholicism had obscured, namely, that salvation is a gift. Portraying the consequences of Adam's sin as a severe wounding of human nature stressed the inability of men and women to save themselves, thus reinforcing the necessity of God's salvific action. The gratuity of salvation *is* a fundamental Christian principle. The Reformation principle *sola gratia*, grace alone, intends to safeguard the character of salvation as love by ensuring that salvation could not be earned.

But what effect does love have? It can make fundamental changes in people. Indeed, its presence or absence in the life of an infant affects the eventual personhood of the infant. Even mature persons are changed by love.

The First Letter of John alludes to this transforming effect of love in its statement that the believer *already* has "eternal life" (5:11). God's love has a divinizing effect, with the result that the real believer will be a lover as God is. In this light the controversy of the sixteenth century over "faith or works" as the mechanism of salvation appears to be based on an oversight. If faith is love, the only real indicator of the presence of faith would be the presence of love. Indeed, they would be the same thing. "Works" would be faith in operation.

Because faith is the acceptance of love, faith that does not issue in deeds—in love—is not authentic faith. Nothing has been transformed or divinized in a life that professes to believe and center itself on God, but is a self-centered life.

FAITH AS "PRAXIS"

If faith is the response of the whole person to God's love, and if love can only be truly accepted by a return of love, faith is not merely being loved, but loving. One comes to faith in loving; one deepens one's faith in loving. We do not first believe and then love. We do not come to know God and then love. We come to know God as the deepest dimension of our loving. We do not find God and then, as a consequence, love as God loves. We find God in participating in what God is doing, loving.

"Praxis" is a word commonly used in theology today to signal the recognition of the primacy of action over reflection ("theoria"). This can be overdone. Activity (for the Christian: loving) without reflection is blind and can cease to be truly loving. Reflection unrooted in participation in what is being reflected upon never comes to grips with reality and, as such, is simply untrue. This seems especially true with regard to the question of faith. If I demand that faith be preceded by exhaustive reflection I will not come to faith. If I love and reflect on the deepest meaning of my action I open myself to God. How could it be otherwise? Can I demand of God that the relationship observe my terms? Or is not the crucial step that I become willing to enter it on God's terms?

THE FREEDOM OF FAITH

If faith is a gift, if we believe because God actuates in us a power to believe, if we love because we are loved, are we still free? Gifts, including the gift of love itself, can be refused. Rejection of love is irrational, but we do it. We know that the only adequate acceptance of love is a reciprocation of it. Given the widespread avoidance today of entangling commitments, it is hardly surprising that faith is not thriving. We know what it entails.

But when we accept love, when we believe, are we not generating our acceptance of that love ourselves? Not on the deepest level. On the analogy of a child's love for its parent, faith, love of God, is a *response*. Just as the parent's love for the child awakens love in the child, God's love for us empowers us to respond. But love does not coerce. Love does not extort but creates love.

There is another sense in which faith must be free. It must be the result of a *free decision*. Faith cannot be the conclusion of a rational proof. It cannot be imposed by reason. If God is offering love, our response must be love. Faith is not the mere adherence to certain truths. Faith is adherence to a person. It entails risk, commitment, and surrender. While it may not go against reason, it must venture beyond it. But then personal relations always do.

THE FAITH OF NON-BELIEVERS

The response of faith may be something we do from our earliest days. Or it may happen later in our lives. This leads us to assume that God's offer of love comes at different times to different people. It is more accurate to say that we become *aware* of the offer at different times. The offer, because it is God's love, is coextensive with one's life. When we accept, we accept what has always been there. God is love, or better yet, God *is* loving. Accordingly, the offer is always in place simply because it is God's nature to love.

For the same reason God's love does not discriminate. The Catholic tradition has consistently rejected the contrary view. Against the ninth century theologian Gottschalk and again in the sixteenth century when John Calvin proposed the doctrine of "double predestination," that is, that God decrees, antecedent to our chance to respond, that some are saved and some are damned, Catholicism rejected that view and clearly affirmed that God's love embraces all persons. This is a difficult problem, for, just as clearly, Catholicism affirms that salvation is a response to grace, that faith is necessary for salvation. This raises an interesting question: Is it possible that non-believers believe, that the unfaithful have faith?

In Catholic doctrine there is room for such a view, which we will discuss at length when we come to the question of the attitude of Catholicism toward the non-Christian religions. But a brief discussion is called for here. Catholic doctrine does not say that a person can be saved without faith, which we know by now would be impossible. Faith is the loving response to God on our part. To say that faith is dispensable for salvation is to say that that loving response is dispensable. One cannot have a loving union without a loving response.

So the real question is this: Can a person respond lovingly without formally recognizing to whom he or she is responding? The Second Vatican Council answered yes. We will see later that the principle behind this position is both Catholic and biblical, but some reasons can be given here.

Faith is a response to God's self-disclosure. According to Catholic doctrine, such a response can take place before one ever encounters revelation as "objective" revelation, in the form of Christian preaching. Indeed, it must. It is precisely the witness of God's Spirit that enables one to *recognize* the truth of objective preaching. This inward illumination that empowers one to believe has no objective content in itself, yet it is clearly the beginning of God's self-disclosure. It is sometimes called "transcendental revelation," the, as yet, contentless orientation of a person toward God through God's call. This is what enables us to accept the objective revelation of God in Christ as mediated by the Church in history, or what is sometimes called "categorical revelation." In light of this the question becomes: Is it possible that a person could be responding to God's call but that because of cultural, historical or personal reasons does not recognize in the Church's preaching the one who is calling?

Appendix 1:

WHAT IS LIBERATION THEOLOGY?

On the eve of Vatican II, John Courtney Murray wrote an essay called "Is It Basket Weaving?" (*We Hold These Truths*, pp. 175–196). The "It" in the title was life, existence, and, by extension, Christian existence. Murray was recalling an early form of the Christian life—that of the monks of the desert. The story goes that in the morning the monk would weave a basket; in the afternoon he would unweave it; the next day he would start over. The image is transparent. True Christian existence is a patient waiting for the world to come. This world is passing away. Nothing done here has lasting value. Let us turn from the illusory seductions of this world. Let us live in patient hope, uninvolved in a fallen world, waiting for salvation. Murray called this "eschatological Christianity."

Murray pointed out that in the history of Christian existence there was a strong counter-trend. He called this "incarnational Christianity." Here the arena of Christian existence was not the desert but the city. The "incarnational" Christian took the world seriously, affirmed its value. Sometimes the "incarnational" Christian overvalued the world. A "sacred canopy" was draped over contingent worldly realities, wars, politics, philosophy. Individuals claimed divine commissions to govern; nations claimed they were God's chosen instruments for the salvation of history.

Murray thought these two tendencies, the eschatological and the incarnational, were *both* part of an authentic Christianity. True Christian existence does not eliminate either but holds them in *tension*. His own judgment was that, in the period called modern history, Roman Catholicism had been in a markedly eschatological period. He anticipated and urged a new engagement of Christianity with a now "secularized" world, a movement of Christianity toward a more incarnational stance in order to redress what he believed to be an imbalance.

Everyone familiar with Christian history is aware that this tension is the fundamental paradox of Christianity. At the heart of it lies what Walter Kasper calls "a probably insoluble problem" (*Jesus the Christ*, p. 242), the fundamental problem of the biblical religions, namely that there is a Creator and there is creation; there is Being and there are beings; there is the Infinite and there is the finite, and the latter is real, autonomous, and radically dependent on the former. How do they interact? It is not surprising that the history of Christianity is a constant tug-of-war between two poles.

The existence of tension and the necessity of paradoxical language to capture it does not mean that every answer, either in theory or practice, does a good job of maintaining the tension. Vatican II was an admission by the Catholic Church that there was an imbalance in its theology and practice.

It is not an oversimplification to say that Vatican II was, as such, an attempt to make the Church and its message relevant to the world. "Aggiornamento," updating, but also engagement, relevance, effectiveness, incarnation, were its program. This program has its dangers, but it is not a novelty. The separation of religion from culture is a recent phenomenon. Indeed, what Vatican II was calling for was a resumption of the traditional role of Christianity as a shaper of culture, but in a new mode: not by domination but by service.

In the modern age a process has occurred called secularization. An emancipation of humanism from its Christian origins has taken place. The division of Christianity in the sixteenth century removed a common basis for culture and society, with the result that religion turned inward. Concepts originally rooted in the Gospel, the concepts of law, freedom, conscience, and their incarnation in structures, sought a new non-religious, or even anti-religious embodiment.

For a long time the Church saw the danger of the trend, not only to itself, but to western culture. But it would see only one solution: restoration, return to the pre-modern synthesis of religion and culture. This led, especially in the nineteenth century, to a war between Catholicism and modernity, to a retreat of the Church within walls, to a Catholicism concerned about preserving its identity rather than a Catholicism performing its age-old role of sowing the seeds of the Gospel in the culture of its time.

Vatican II was a new positioning of the Church vis-à-vis the world. The autonomy of the natural order, the sacredness of individual conscience, on the one hand, but the origin of the world in God, the rootlessness of values

without God, the self-destructiveness of a humanism without any genuine absolute—Vatican II struggled toward an affirmation of the world and the contribution that it needs from the Gospel to be truly itself. The paradox of Vatican II is that never had Roman Catholicism so endorsed the autonomy of the world yet so acknowledged its own mission for the transformation of the world.

Under the inspiration of Vatican II the bishops of Latin America, in 1968, at Medellín, Colombia, took the steps that would signal the most dramatic response to the proposals of Vatican II. They presented the traditional Christian concept of salvation as liberation—from all that oppresses. Medellín was both a product of and a source of "liberation theology."

So what is "liberation theology"? In the ground-breaking work that gave this movement its name, A Theology of Liberation (Spanish edition 1971, English: Orbis, 1973), the Peruvian priest, Gustavo Gutierrez, defines theology as "critical reflection on the practice of the faith in the light of the Word of God." It is fundamental to liberation theology that there is a "dialectic"—a continuing interaction between theory and practice—in the lives of those who theologize. But practice comes and, indeed, came first. Liberation theology did not set out a program which was then implemented. It grew out of, was reflection upon, what was already happening.

What was happening? Even in the 1950's some Latin American churchmen were beginning to question the effect of Roman Catholicism on the ordinary people of Latin America. As the living conditions of most Latin Americans worsened relative to the first world and indeed, to the growing wealth of local "elites," a number of people began to ask if, indeed, Latin American Catholicism wasn't just what Marx said all religion is—an opiate, something which focused the believer's attention so radically on the next life that it rendered him or her passive before the problems of this life. They began to ask: Had the very proper concern of Roman Catholicism with salvation after death resulted in an unbiblical depreciation of this world? This was not systematic thinking but very practical—action oriented—unscholarly reflection in limited circles.

In Argentina and Uruguay middle class university students and priests began to organize and in some cases cooperate with Marxists in attempting to influence what they thought were unjust structures. Generally this took the form of a socialist solution to Latin America's problems and took a political path. In extreme cases Catholic laymen and laywomen and priests (the most

famous was the Colombian priest Camillo Torres) actually became guerrillas. In Chile the "Christians for Socialism" movement, in Argentina the "Priests for the Third World Movement," were leftist but not guerrilla groups. Generally these currents rejected the idea that Latin America could follow the path to development that Europe and North America had, but they were on the fringe of a Catholicism marked more for its piety and concern for the other world than activism and this world. Events in the worldwide Church soon changed this.

Both John XXIII, in *Mater et Magistra* (1961) and *Pacem in Terris* (1963), and Paul VI, in *Populorum Progressio* (1966), and a key document of Vatican II, *Gaudium et Spes* (1965), had attempted to deal with questions arising from the lack of "development" in the third world. *Gaudium et Spes* recognized that there was a link between the development of the first world and the underdevelopment of the third world (#9). At Medellín the bishops of Latin America adopted this analysis of the situation, but they also recognized that the inequalities within Latin American societies and between Latin America and the first world were at least partly due to the way Christianity had been preached. Accordingly, and this is to be understood against Catholicism's previous alliance with the Spanish and Portuguese colonizers and then later with the upper classes of the Latin American countries as they became independent, the bishops at Medellín made an "option for the poor," that is, they committed themselves to assist in the liberation of the oppressed. They presented the traditional Christian concern, salvation, as liberation, not merely from sin and death, but from *everything* that oppresses men and women. Medellín was both a product and a source for liberation theology, the heart of which is that the Church must ally itself with the poor in their attempt to liberate themselves from whatever oppresses them. In 1971 the thinking of Medellín won wider acceptance in the Church when the Synod of Bishops in Rome declared:

Action on behalf of justice and participation in the transformation of the world fully appear to us as a constitutive dimension of the preaching of the Gospel, or, in other words, of the Church's mission for the redemption of the human race and its liberation from every oppressive situation. (*Justice in the World,* intro.)

This sentence (especially the word "constitutive") and what it means, especially in the practical order, have since become a subject of controversy. But it is not an exaggeration to say that thousands of laymen and women, Church workers, catechists, religious women and men, priests and bishops have suffered arrest, imprisonment, torture, exile and death because they believe what that statement says is true. The reality of Latin American Catholicism's option for the poor is undeniable. On the other hand, even within Latin American Catholicism, and certainly in the Vatican, there is concern that, in terms of John Courtney Murray's analysis, an overly eschatological Christianity is being replaced by an overly incarnational Christianity.

I said above that Medellín and liberation theology were influences on each other. However, they cannot be identified. In particular, liberation theology has adopted more of "Marxist social analysis" than Medellín did. When the liberation theologians (and Medellín) saw the mission of the Church as participating in the liberation of men and women from all that oppresses, they had to ask what caused the oppression. Is it the work of unscrupulous, powerful individuals or groups? Or is it "structural," that is, is it built into the system of economic, political, and social relationships which help to make Latin America what it is? They found ready to hand the analysis commonly accepted by the Marxist intellectuals of Latin America. Contrary to the philosophy of the Alliance for Progress and, in general, the views of many first world economists who believed that the underdeveloped world would develop by repeating the experience of the developed world—industrialization, capital formation, free trade—Latin American Marxist (and non-Marxist) analysts said that the southern hemisphere cannot develop through participation in the worldwide market economy. The financial, technological and political power of the developed world will always insure that the third world will remain a source of raw materials and a market for products, but never a competitor in the world economic scene. This is "dependency theory," widely accepted by Marxists, liberation theologians and, indeed, other economists. The corollary of this economic thinking is a position on the politics of the region, namely, that any given Latin American country will be controlled by the group in that country which benefits from this arrangement. But as dependent and falling further behind, the country itself will become, at least relatively, impoverished and more dependent. Investment by the first world in such countries will be for the first world's benefit, and more and more of the undeveloped world will be mortgaged to the first world. The national economies will be hostage to the notoriously fluctuating prices of natural resources and crops. Agriculture will turn to more efficient corporate farming from small farm

worker holdings and from raising food for local consumption to cash crops that appeal to the international market.

The question whether the economic analysis employed by liberation theologians is correct cannot be answered by recourse to the liberation theologians themselves, for they simply present it as the best available analysis. Nor do they delay long on what they think is the solution to the problem: an indigenous, nonaligned socialism. It is the capitalist market system that holds the underdeveloped world in bondage. To take itself out of that system and hope for growth and just distribution of wealth, the third world must have another economic system.

One can see the next question coming. This would probably not be a peaceful process. Is liberation theology a theology of revolution? How can a Christian theology endorse violence? Does liberation theology simply end up cooperating in the replacement of one oppressive elite by another?

On these concrete questions there is no common position among the liberation theologians, and there is some evidence that those who early-on endorsed, always reluctantly, the inevitability of violence have backed off from that in recent writings. But in classic liberation theology there is a consensus that the Marxist analysis is the best available analysis of the fundamental problem. This bothers Church authorities and is their biggest single objection to the school. The charge is that Marxist analysis is so inevitably intertwined with Marxist "ideology," by which Church authorities mean the whole Marxist system, that using *any part* of it will result in a corruption of Christianity. Since it is a matter of debate even among Marxists whether Marxism is a "metaphysics" or just a "canon of interpretation" without metaphysical implications, this point becomes the center of controversy.

But, as theology, liberation theology does not rise or fall with the question of the use of Marxist analysis. It rises or falls with three other questions: (1) What is theology? (2) What did Jesus mean by the Kingdom of God? (3) What is the Church's role in the coming of the Kingdom? Question #2 will be addressed at length in this book. Question #3 is beyond the scope of this book. Our discussion of liberation theology here will conclude with a discussion of liberation theology's answer to Question #1.

Christian theology, like the faith it reflects on, has had a history. Certain elements are constants, others are variables. As theo-*logy* it is always *logos*—human speech. As *theo*-logy it is always about God. As *reflecting faith* it does this from *the concrete situa-*

tion of the believer. This is not to say that the theologian does not try to escape being imprisoned in the cultural situation he or she is living in. It does mean that no theologian exists outside of a given historical situation.

In the first millennium of Christianity the leading theologians were bishops and monks. The theology of the "Fathers" and the early Middle Ages is often called "theology at the *prie-dieu*," theology done on one's knees. It was a prayerful, contemplative, listening, which produced theology as *sapientia*–wisdom. The personal, even mystical, contact of the theologian with God was the touchstone, although this theologizing always took place within the centuries-long tradition of Christian belief.

In the high Middle Ages, with the emergence of the universities, theology became more "public," critical, coherent, scientific, not so much *sapientia* as *scientia*, in the sense of an organized, publicly held, and rationally disputed body of knowledge. It was "theology at one's desk" and theology in the lecture hall. Philosophical systems were employed as its language. Something (coherence, verifiability, accountability, rationality) was gained, something (contact with personal religious experience, the life of the Spirit, mysticism as a source) was in danger of being lost. As sources, the public data (Scripture and tradition) were given appreciably greater weight than the private data (personal religious experience).

Before we address the question of how liberation theology fits in this history of theology, it is helpful to point out that Christian *spirituality* also has a history and that there is a reciprocal causality between spirituality and theology. The period of the monks of the desert was relatively short-lived. The eremitical life (hermit monks) was succeeded by the cenobitical life (hermits coming together to eat and pray) and, in turn, by the conventual life (monks living together). In time some monks undertook to go out from the monasteries to minister. What is common to the monastic spirituality is that the primary locus for finding God is a special "religious" environment. If the monk goes into the world, he brings what he has found in contemplation in that religious sphere and "expends" it in the "worldly" sphere. Monastic theology would not generally look to the world as a source for understanding God but as a place which was to be the beneficiary of the wisdom found in contemplation.

In the high Middle Ages not only did theology become more secular, but so did spirituality. Orders embracing the "mixed life" (of contemplation and action) began to emerge (the Dominicans, the Franciscans).

Typically their two leading theologians defined theology as a *scientia*. For Thomas Aquinas theology was a *scientia speculativa;* its object was principally God (S.T. I, q. 1, art. 4 Sed contra). For Bonaventure it is a *scientia practica;* theology has its object the doing of the good (1 Sent. prooem, q. 4 resp.). One could say that for Aquinas the contemplative component remained *the* theological component. Bonaventure was on the way to integrating activity into the theological enterprise.

In spirituality, at least, Ignatius of Loyola, the founder of the Jesuits, marks a significant new phase. Ignatius did not separate contemplation and action. Contemplative moments were not different times from active moments but intensification of the awareness of God which was to be the habitual state of mind of very active people. There was no priority of contemplation over action but an interpenetration of contemplation and action. God's will (and therefore God) was "discerned" and acted upon in the concrete situation. God was not found in a special religious sphere and then "brought into" a worldly sphere, but was encountered precisely in the events of history, whether personal or communal.

Just so, in the light of the history of theology, liberation theology is a significant new departure. It has new proposals about the "subject" of theology, the "object" of theology, and the "sources" of theology.

If the *subject* of theology in patristic and early medieval times was the pray-er, and for medieval and modern theology the professor, the subject of theology for liberation theology is the oppressed, individually and as groups ("base communities"), and those in solidarity with the oppressed. The thesis of liberation theology is that the Gospel of Jesus Christ is first and foremost good news for the poor. Jesus himself made a "preferential option for the poor," it was the poor who understood what he was saying, and it was the poor who responded to him, comprising the new people of God. (That the poor have a special "sensus fidei," an instinctive sensitivity to the Gospel, is affirmed by the so-called "comprehensive" evaluation of the proposals of liberation theology by the Congregation for Divine Faith, *Libertatis Conscientia*, #98–99.) The poor, thus, have a privileged theological position for the liberation theologians.

The *object* of theology for liberation theology is an extension of the nuance contributed by Bonaventure. In the foreground of liberation theology is not the Being of God but the practice of faith as response to God. There is possibly a danger here. Sooner or later, explicitly or implicitly, theo-

logies are the result of their ruling conception of God. A theology which concentrates on the practice of the faith runs the risk of being controlled by an unexamined and possibly erroneous conception of God. Theology is reflecting faith. Faith is not a human product but a response to God revealing. Everything is rooted in God's self-revelation. Theology must explicitly address this at some point, and "praxis" must be rooted in the doctrine of God which results.

On the other hand, faith is not mere theoretical knowledge of God. Liberation theology reminds us that faith is discipleship, lived out in concrete conditions. A theology which did not reflect this would be not merely sterile. It would not be true in any genuine biblical sense.

Finally, liberation theology looks not only to personal religious experience, Scripture, and tradition as *sources* for theology but, paralleling modern spiritualities, looks directly at the concrete situation to find God. As the Old Testament prophet found God in the threats of annihilation at the hand of enemies, so liberation theology finds God in the aspiration of the oppressed for liberation. In classical theology the concrete situation raised questions which Scripture and tradition answered. In liberation theology faith questions the concrete situation, and Scripture and tradition guide the search for answers which emerge from the situation itself. Theology proceeds through a dialectic of theory and practice. Practice is not merely a consequence of theory but a partner in the theological dialogue.

The warrant appealed to for such a theological method is the biblical tradition itself, the history of Israel's search for liberation and especially the historical practice of Jesus of Nazareth. In the course of this book we will be implicitly examining the proposals of liberation theology on these points. One must keep in mind, however, that no one who has not experienced the situation of the poor can adequately judge these proposals.

What has been the net effect of the liberation theology movement on Catholic theology? It is undeniable that theology is subject to fads. Who reads the "death of God" theologians of the 1960's today? But liberation theology seems to be different. For one thing it grows out of the genuine biblical and orthodox Christian mainstream and does not begin by rejecting ages-old Christian doctrine. Second, while holding on to the tradition, it seeks to revitalize it by appeal to the "historical praxis" of Jesus of Nazareth. Third, men and women inspired by it live heroic lives.

Chapter III

THE SITUATION OF FAITH TODAY

If theology is grounded in faith, then the relevance and meaningfulness of theology rises or falls with the existence of faith. But is faith even possible today?

THE THESIS OF SECULARIZATION

> What can be affirmed, and what also can be easily shown with the help of some statistics is this, namely, that faith in a personal God, in a God who reaches into history, and in a God who hears and answers man, is in the western world nowadays no longer the self-evident, all-embracing framework according to which the majority of society thinks, acts, and organizes life (Heinrich Ott, *God*, John Knox Press, 1974, p. 10).

Parallels to the above statement abound in theological writing of the last thirty years. Put more succinctly, the statement says this: Modern men and women are "secularized."

What does this mean? It is a widely held opinion in contemporary theology that a fundamental change has taken place in western society. Past societies were formerly theo-centric, or God-centered. A person living in such a society was born into a culture that oriented him or her toward God as the ground and goal of human life. Socialization, the process of learning to live in a culture, involved the absorption of society's belief in a "transcendent." Along with such a belief, one was given the means to express it, a rich system of symbols involving ritual, signs, and religious vocabulary. One was also given norms of behavior, norms which were unquestionable because they were "God-given."

The thesis of secularization maintains that all this has broken down. We are no longer born into theocentric communities that provide us with both an orientation to the transcendent and the language and norms to express the meaning of this orientation. Instead we are born into cultures that orient us from the beginning toward this world (Latin: *saeculum*), an orientation which renders traditional symbols of the transcendent meaningless. Moreover, we are born into a world that, rather than providing us with ready-made norms of behavior (*heteronomy*), demands of us that we set our own norms (*autonomy*). The secular person is said, then, to have three characteristics: he or she is preoccupied with *this world* ("the here and now") and unconcerned with the transcendent; he or she finds religious symbols *meaningless;* and finally, such a person acknowledges no other norm of behavior beyond that which is *self-imposed.*

Discussion of the thesis of secularization centers on two questions: (1) Is it true, and, if so, to what extent? (2) If the thesis is true, what has caused the phenomenon of secularization? Among those theologians who think the thesis has some validity, there is a common explanation of the phenomenon. Modern science and technology have "demystified" the surrounding world. The pre-scientific worldview allowed the mysterious world of nature to mediate God's presence to us. But science has allowed us to approach the once "numinous" natural world as an object of examination and manipulation. It is no longer a sacrament of the creator but a system running according to its own laws. Furthermore, because of technology, we no longer even experience nature. We set it aside in "parks" and "wildernesses" to remember what it was like, because we have overlaid the natural reality with a technological culture that screens nature from us. The result is that the place where people used to find God, the world of nature, is no longer available to us, and the experience it mediated to us is lost. We live in a rational, technological world that reflects *its* creator, the human species.

But we must not overlook the first question. There is considerable debate on the validity of the thesis. Major sociologists regard it as a vast and dangerous oversimplification. Most concede that there has been "a secularization of institutions" or of "outward forms." Major components characteristic of modern culture—corporations and unions, the military, government, education—are not influenced by religion the way their counterparts, say, in the Middle Ages, were. But on the question of whether there is a corresponding "secularization of consciousness," there is considerable dispute. What people *think* is difficult to measure in any case, and there are no sociological studies of medieval consciousness. As a matter of fact, contemporary surveys consistently point to the *perdurance* of religious consciousness in some form rather than its disappearance. They also point to the fact that to perdure religion must constantly adjust to new situations.

It seems clear that at least this is true: As Heinrich Ott says, the existence of the transcendent is far more questionable for us than for our ancestors. God is not self-evident for us. But then one must ask: Is it good for God to be self-evident? To put it another way: Does the thesis of secularization really point to the fact that in each new epoch of its journey humanity must rediscover God?

CRISIS/KAIROS

The Greek root of our word *crisis* means to judge, to discriminate. The word *crisis*, then, designates a moment of decision, not necessarily a deteriorating or negative situation. Another Greek word, *kairos*, denotes a moment of unusual opportunity, a moment when life offers more than ordinary possibilities. If there is a *crisis* of faith today, the first response of faith should be to ask: Is the crisis also a *kairos*?

THE CRISIS/KAIROS OF CATHOLIC FAITH

It is time to be more specific. An introduction to Catholic theology cannot be content with a discussion of Christian faith in general.

In our discussion of faith, we pointed out that at times individuals undergo crises of faith. The question we wish to address here is: Is the Catholic community undergoing a crisis of faith?

There are, indeed, symptoms of a crisis. Mass attendance among Catholics is down from about seventy-five percent to about fifty percent; vocations to the priesthood and religious life have slumped dramatically, and large numbers of priests and religious have left those forms of ministry; divorce has become more common among Catholics than ever before; there is continuing dissent between various groups of Catholics and Church authority; the distinctiveness of Catholicism is challenged by many.

But, as I pointed out, crises are not necessarily bad. Indeed, a crisis can be a time of accelerated growth, integration and maturity. One would thus hope to see, if the crisis is a *kairos*, besides symptoms of decline in the Catholic community, symptoms of vitality as well. And there are such signals: the greater participation of lay people in Church life; a renewed interest in Scripture; greater vitality in the liturgy; new religious congregations and forms of Church service; the number of Catholics, especially women, pursuing higher studies in theology; the higher level of Catholic scholarship, popular writing, and preaching; the commitment of the Church to having a voice in issues of justice (often at the price of alienating its own membership); an openness to truth coming from outside Catholicism; greater interest in prayer and deeper religious experience; the implementation of the principle of collegiality by national conferences and synods of bishops.

In both the symptoms of decline and vitality, one can see validations of elements of the thesis of secularization. It is not merely that individuals are becoming more secular; Catholicism *itself* is becoming more secular. Recent Church teaching consistently commits Catholicism to the task of human development and "integral liberation," that is, not only from sin but whatever dehumanizes us. Moreover, Catholicism has recognized the need to rejuvenate its symbol system by liturgical and theological renewal. Finally, while Catholicism continues to struggle with the question of the bounds of legitimate autonomy, there is no doubt that many individual Catholics exercise a more responsible, less mechanical, adherence to Church teaching than previously, and that parts of the Church, especially in the third world, are seeking to make the Gospel meaningful to their respective cultures.

Over and above what the thesis of secularization offers, is there another way to understand what is happening in Catholicism? Although theology and faith are not the same thing, they are inevitably intermixed. One cannot have faith without at least implicitly having a theology because faith necessarily seeks some sort of conceptual expression. Theology articulates faith. If this is so, can we understand the *Catholic* crisis better by examining what has happened in recent Catholic *theology?*

THE EFFECT OF THE EMERGENCE OF HISTORICAL CONSCIOUSNESS ON CATHOLIC THEOLOGY

The thesis of secularization sees a "geologic shift" in the consciousness of men and women. While most theologians acknowledge the shift, not all find the secularization thesis the most apt way to analyze what is specific in the *Catholic* crisis. Secularization affects everyone; what explains the *Catholic* crisis? Many prefer to speak of a change from "classical" to "historical" consciousness. In understanding recent developments in Catholic theology this analysis does seem to offer more light.

According to this view, the turmoil in Catholic theology in recent years is the result of a change in the "horizon" of theological thought, a change which is rooted in a corresponding general shift in the way we think.

For centuries, Christian theology was elaborated in the intellectual context of the Greek, "classicist" mentality. The Greek mentality had its own complexity, but the following generalization can be made: The Greeks viewed the world as relatively *static*. They presupposed order in the cosmos, the *fixed identity* of beings within the cosmos, and the *fixed relationships* among these beings. Theirs was a mental outlook that organized reality in categories derived from the observation of a relatively stable world, a world of unchanging natures or essences that are clearly distinguished from each other. In this world-view, "man" had a unique place: He was the summit of the cosmos, but he was at the same time a part of it. In fact, this was a reflection of ancient man's actual situation. He lived much more *in nature,* dominated by nature, than we feel ourselves to be. Man's glory was that he could master this world with his *mind;* knowledge was his goal. There was a *logos*—a rationality—immanent in the world, and man could find it. He attempted—through reflection and contemplation—to penetrate its secrets and the problems of his own place in it. He sought to discover and elaborate the values, and the culture based on these values, that flowed from his own essence or nature and the natural world around him. *But he never realized the extent to which he could change nature.* According to Plato, he could penetrate beyond the physical world where essences or natures are constantly struggling with the effects of materiality, to the ideal world, which was thought to be the real world because it is the world of pure, *unchanging* essences. It was real precisely *because it did not change.* For Plato man learned the truth precisely by transcending the temporal, changeable world—by moving from the shadow to the reality, from the world of natures materialized to the world of ideal natures. We see here an identification of true being with unchanging being, of truth and *lack of change.*

Moderns have inherited the Greek commitment to rational inquiry, but there are many differences between the way the Greeks thought and the way we think. We are not convinced that the order or reality is unchanging. We know the natural world is much more fluid and dynamic than that which the Greeks observed. We have come to wonder whether there are really radical breaks in nature like that between inorganic and organic, or between what is merely sensitive and what is also reflective, even between a world of matter and a world of spirit. We see the world not as an hierarchically fixed cosmos, but as a *process.* But more importantly, we do not see ourselves as situated solely in a world of nature. Contemporary men and women are acutely conscious of their power not merely to *discover* meaning—the meaning of a world of nature that they are a part of—but also to *create* meaning. They do not picture themselves as situated within a world of nature and a culture that is part of nature. They realize that they create as much meaning as they discover, that cultures are not part of nature, that they do not drop out of heaven or flow automatically from the essence of "man," but that they are human creations. Cultures are created by groups of human beings. Precisely how much freedom is present in the creation of a culture is a matter of dispute. Nevertheless, the tremendous cultural differences we observe illustrate that they are human creations, and the fact that we create our own environment, our own milieu, reveals that *our nature is open-ended,* not fixed. It is a self-transcending nature; it goes beyond itself. It is precisely *"human nature"* to create meaning, to create "worlds." And in the exploitation of this capacity to create meaning, we have come to realize that even our own identity is in our hands, that to some extent we are called to enter into our own *self*-creation through our capacity to create meaning.

So runs the thesis of "the movement to historical consciousness." Men and women, in reflecting on what they have done, see that they are not a fixed point in a natural landscape, but creators of their own identity. They realize that the proper place to situate themselves is not in a world of fixed and abstract essences, or in the world of nature, but in a world that is much more fluid, dynamic, and open-ended—a world where men and women (and not impersonal natural factors) act as the dominant forces. This is the world of *history.* Here history is not seen as something accidental to reality, something that merely happens on the surface of a stable world of changeless essences. Rather, history is the real world, and it is also a world that men and women create. Our capacity to generate meaning is a capacity to generate history, and in the process we are called upon not merely to discover our identity, but to *give* ourselves an identity. The world is not "out there" waiting to be discovered; it is *in* us waiting to be created. And in this capacity to create our world, we have a capacity for, and a task of, participating in our own self-creation.

The corollary of this self-understanding is the awareness that we are "essentially historical." History is the all-embracing inescapable context of everything we do and are. Our languages, our values, our achievements, even our hopes are historical. Furthermore, all our reflection is historical—it takes place in definite historical contexts and is given expression in historically conditioned ways. As a result, our grasp of truth and expression of it are historically conditioned. Thus if we are going to express truth in differing historical contexts, we must be willing to change the way we express it; and if it is going to be true for us, it will have to be rediscovered again and again. For us truth has a greater fluidity than for the Greeks.

What is the importance of this for theology? Theology, especially Catholic theology, was elaborated in the context of a self-understanding of humanity much closer to the Greek view than the modern view. There was an underlying assumption of the fixity of nature and of human nature and a definite bias against the historical character of human existence. Revelation was thought to be the *timeless* statement of *timeless* truths. Today revelation is understood as God's communication of *himself* to us *where we are—in history*—and it is mediated to us by historically conditioned means. In this way God does not merely reveal timeless "truths" to us but *enters into our creation of meaning* and the self-creation that goes on in that process. Revelation, the ground of theology, is itself a continuing historical process.

Recent Catholic theology reveals considerable acceptance of the thesis we have been discussing. It saw that it had a good reason to do this despite the obvious dangers. Through its increased interest in the historical aspect of Scripture, it came to the realization that Scripture presents God as engaged in an historical dialogue with Israel, in the Old Testament, and as a personal presence in history in the New. The word of God to man "historicizes" itself, culminating in "the Word made flesh," an historical person. Thus, in the biblical view, revelation itself is essentially historical, and theology as reflection on revelation partakes of its historical character.

As rooted in faith, theology presupposes hearing what God has said. But God, in order to speak to us, must speak to us where we are. And since we are historical, God has spoken to us in history. The Letter to the Hebrews reads:

> In times past, God spoke in fragmentary and varied ways to our fathers through the prophets; in this, the final age, he has spoken to us through his Son whom he has made heir of all things and through whom he first created the universe. This Son is the reflection of the Father's glory, the exact representation of the Father's being, and he sustains all things by his powerful word. When he had cleansed us from our sins, he took his seat at the right hand of the Majesty in heaven (Heb 1:1–3).

Contemporary Catholic theology draws two important consequences from the historical character of revelation:

1. *Scripture,* as the record of God's speaking to us, cannot be treated
   as a series of timeless propositions. The development and historical
   context of revelation in Scripture must be taken seriously. If the
   author of a given book had a different sort of consciousness than
   we do, we must take that into account. In the past, Catholic theologians tended to use Scripture as a source book for "proof texts."
   Today, they use a number of methods including the "historical-critical method." That is, they take seriously the specific historical origin of each book of the Bible.
2. The *transmission* of revelation involves the *historicity of doctrines.* Doctrine—the articulation by the community of what it believes God
   has said to it—is affected by the historical situation in which it is
   formulated. This may mean that, even to say the same thing that
   we said before, we may have to say it in different words. It means
   further that doctrine "develops"—that new understandings of old
   doctrines may be possible, provided they do not contradict the intended meaning of old doctrines—as the situation of believers
   changes.

We have been speaking of the underlying causes of recent
changes in Catholic theology. But even what we have said so far merely
touches the surface. The necessity of a new "hermeneutic" (a method
of interpretation) for Scripture and doctrine in Catholicism is a result
of something more profound. A new hermeneutic addresses the question of *how to rephrase an answer.* Why do we need to rephrase the answer? It can only be because the question has changed. Let us return,
then, to the question that *all Christians* face today, the most fundamental question of faith, "the God question." In our discussion we will am-
plify and expand what we have said here concerning the change in
consciousness that we are experiencing.

THE GOD QUESTION TODAY

I. *Introduction: The Necessity and Limits of a New Answer*

Like any other intellectual endeavor theology tries to answer questions. The difficulty is that behind theological questions lurk other
questions which are more than merely intellectual. Perhaps the basic

theological question is: What is the meaning of life? But that is not only an intellectual question. It is an existential question. It engages a man or woman at all levels and in the totality of life. If there is an answer, theology cannot provide it. It can merely point, in its own way, where that answer might be found.

Theology tries to point to these answers from the point of view of reflective faith. It is commonly assumed that unlike the rest of life faith does not change. But there is a crisis. The traditional formulations of the answer do not speak to us as well as they used to. If faith is to provide real answers, it must change, for real questions change. We have come to acknowledge that there is a great deal of truth in the position that "human persons are essentially historical." Their ultimate concerns may be fundamentally unchanging, but history forces us to live out these concerns in different situations. So the questions change. And the answers to be real answers must respond to the changed form of the questions.

On the other hand, because it is reflective *faith* that is pointing to the answer, that is, the answer is rooted in a response to God's self-revelation, the new answer must be in continuity with the old. If it is really theology, reflection on what God has revealed, it is tied to what has been revealed. So any new formulation has to acknowledge that to be truly the answer of faith it cannot be a wholly new invention.

II. *The God Question Today: Nature or History?*

What seems to be the problem is that our basic question has changed. The old answer would work otherwise. What is the new question? Well, the crisis is deep enough to say it is the fundamental question—the question about God.

The basic question that any statement of faith tries to answer can be called "the God question." This question used to be asked in a way in which the word "God" actually appeared in the question. So the Hebrews asked "Is God merciful?" or "Is God on our side?" Luther's question was: "How can I find a gracious God?" In the eighteenth and nineteenth centuries the rationalist philosophers asked "How does one prove God exists?" But for a long time now people have tired of those *ways* of asking the question. Yet they still ask the question; only its form has changed. Anyone who thinks a little about his or her life asks this question secretly. It often appears in a hidden form or with other questions. "Has life any meaning?" "Is life absurd?" These are ultimately questions about "God," because they seek an ultimate context, an ultimate meaning, an ultimate ground. They seek to know whether there is an active, ultimate ground which one can interact with, relate to, be addressed by, be responsible to, depend on, and in an ultimate way. When one asks what, at least in the western tradition, we mean by "God," we mean what would be implied by an affirmative answer to these questions. Such questions are really questions about "God." But why do modern men and women not ask directly about "God"? Why is the question about God hidden in these other questions? Because in our time there has been a major change in the way we ask about God. The fundamental question has changed. Those questions looked for "God" *in nature*. We look for "God" *in history*.

There seem to be two main ways of asking the God question. One can ask about God in the context of *nature* or in the context of *history*. Is part of the crisis that we are moving from one way to the other? Catholic theology today, and it is hardly isolated in this, believes that the place where men and women today must ask about God is not nature but *history*, and that has changed the God question. What does this mean?

For the vast numbers of people who ever lived, and probably perhaps for a majority of our contemporaries, the "place" where the God question is asked is in the natural world. For eons human beings have been tied to the natural world, radically dependent on it, threatened by it. Its rhythms, its power, its fertility, its capriciousness were part of their lives. Religions reflected this. The great ancient and largely abandoned religions were "nature religions." And even when the religions which explicitly claim a revelation of God not primarily in nature and nature's forces but in history, and in a personal God directly addressing us, emerged, even then and in those traditions "God" continued to be thought of as someone standing behind nature, acting primarily in nature, reflected by nature. Nevertheless, a person influenced by *biblical* religion will be more predisposed to look for God in *history* rather than in *nature*. Is that taking hold in our time?

It is not simply a question of finally doing justice to biblical religion. The God question, the question about the ultimate meaning of human life, can hardly be asked by contemporaries except in the context of history. It is not that we are not closely bound to nature, that we float above nature in a special atmosphere of our own making called history. No—we know that we are part of nature, that we depend on it, are still somewhat at its mercy. And if we are religious, we still see God as the giver of the good things when we receive nature's gifts. And when disaster strikes, sickness, suffering, death, we try to find God in those experiences. But the fact is that, for *western men and women*, this has become more difficult when compared with our ancestors or even other contemporary people. Why? Precisely because of our *success* in subjugating nature, and therefore in changing our relationship with nature. We do not experience nature as an abundant yet hostile power, but as something unlimited and creative which we can mold. It is not divine; it is just raw material for our creativity. Nature is in the process of being transformed by human science and technology. It no longer reflects God, but humankind itself. More of this and its consequences later.

There is another factor that compels us to ask the God question in the context of history—that is where our biggest problems lie. Western men and women can feed themselves; they no longer ask whether nature is going to be benevolent. But they are asking more and more if our domination of nature is becoming a destructive exploitation. Moderns, by dominating nature, are absorbing it into our own history. We are beginning to ask whether the promise of science and technology is not going to turn into a curse, ending in the destruction of both nature and ourselves. So we perceive a threat but not from nature. "We have found the enemy and he is us."

There are two views of *the role of technology* in this dilemma. No one today sees it as an unequivocal good. The nineteenth century belief in inevitable progress, based on science and technology, is dead. Indeed, some people see technology itself as an evil. It is the genie released by the sorcerer's apprentice, a genie that refuses to return to the bottle, a reality created by humanity but which now is going to dominate its creator. In a way analogous to the ancients' view of a fate ruling their lives, some contemporaries see the scientific-technological world as a "second-order fate," a mechanism created by humanity but now relentlessly moving toward domination of human history. However, most people view technology as something that can be good or evil depending on how it is used. But they fear that we will not rise to the challenge of using it for good.

III. *Summary and First Statement of Our Question*

Contemporary western men and women experience a feeling of threat in the face not of nature, but history, the area where human beings act. We are asking whether our control of nature is going to end up as destruction of nature and ourselves. Rather than asking whether nature is benevolent or hostile to us, we are asking if nature can survive us and therefore if we ourselves will survive. The possibilities raised by our technological progress force us to ask the question about meaning in the context of history. The power of evil, and an evil that seems man-made and therefore not merely to be overcome by better technology, is most clearly revealed in the sphere of history, and it impels us to ask the God question in a new way: *Does history have a future?* What is meant here by "history"? We do not mean the science, the record of, and interpretation of, the events of the past. We mean *the events themselves,* the interaction among people in space and time. It is the meaning of these events that we are concerned with. And so we will ask the question about God, in however way we ask it, in the context of these events. If we are looking for God, we will look for God as a God giving meaning to history. In saying this, we are not saying that the former ways of asking about God are illegitimate. It is simply that history is contemporary humanity's problem, and so any answer to the God question which ignores that context will simply not mean anything to us.

FIRST ATTEMPT AT AN ANSWER

The question then arises: Does Christianity really speak of a God who is relevant to our present question? Some idea of the God of Christianity might help. Anticipating what we will say later, we can say that a genuine view of the Christian God yields the following picture:

The God of Christian faith is not a nature god manipulating natural forces. Nor is the Christian God a manipulator of history. Most importantly God does not take away from us our responsibility for history. From the Christian point of view the question is *whether we stand alone* with our responsibility or whether there is someone who is above the world and yet at the same time in it and *who shares our responsibility.* Believing in the God of Christianity means relying on God's presence in the world and on our ability to give meaning to history because we have received meaning from God. The God of Christianity does not deprive us of our responsibility for history, nor dispute our right to it. On the contrary, God gives us courage to act in history because God wants to achieve our salvation within history through our acceptance and exercise of our responsibility for history.

If that is the God we are looking for, and if that is the God of Christian faith, perhaps Christian faith has an answer for contemporary men and women. But is it true that the Christian God is a God who "wants to achieve our salvation within history"? Is not God's goal "the salvation of souls with him in heaven"? An answer to these questions can only emerge in the course of this entire book, but a preliminary answer can be offered when we look at other proposals for finding meaning in human life.

IV. *Another Proposal*

It is especially the spread of *Marxism* that challenges Christians to rethink what they mean when they say God is found in history. Religious people are not the only ones who look for the meaning of human existence in history. That is precisely where Marxists look. Sometimes Marxists and Christians have been able to agree on short-term programs to affect history, but there remain fundamental questions. If it is true that, in the Marxist view, the meaning of history is derived *exclusively from man's activity* and from the *potentialities of matter*, there remains a fundamental incompatibility. If Marxism is a metaphysics then and not merely a "canon of interpretation," there seems little hope for cooperation. While both Christians and Marxists think *"eschatologically,"* that is, they look forward in *hope* to a good world in the end, to a (successful) culmination of history, their understanding of how this would happen would differ radically.

Nevertheless, the Marxist challenge has spurred a number of Christian thinkers in the twentieth century to clarify what Christianity hopes for, and what the relationship of human action is to what man hopes for. This has helped to sharpen the contemporary God question. In the 1920's and 1930's, in Protestantism, there was the debate between *Karl Barth,* who believed that what God is doing is addressing a call to the individual who then allows himself or herself to be called away from the world and its sinful structures, and *Paul Tillich,* who thought God was calling man to the struggle to renew society. Tillich seems to have seen the question better. In Catholicism, in France, against an older reactionary Catholicism which still had not accepted the French revolution, more progressive Catholic thinkers, inspired by the Jesuit paleontologist and philosopher *Teilhard de Chardin,* and aware of the challenge of Marxism, began to say that faith should act as an impulse not only toward personal private goodness but toward affecting the structures of the world. This line of thought was resisted in Catholicism but then cautiously adopted in an official way at Vatican II.

Today, in both Protestant and Catholic theology, we see developments along this line of thought, in "political theology," in "liberation theology," and indeed in official documents. The common view of these theologies is: Faith should impel us to take responsibility not only for our own souls but for the world itself, that it is an incomplete faith unless it does, and as incomplete faith it risks becoming no faith.

The question is: Is this consistent with biblical faith? Is this not remaking the God revealed in Jesus Christ in the image of what *some* contemporary Christians *want* God to be? While there is a danger of excess in this turn, there seems to be solid grounds for this new orientation in the Bible itself. An examination of the biblical grounds for this "turn toward the world" would look this way.

NEW BEGINNINGS: A MORE WORLDLY CHRISTIANITY?

BIBLICAL ORIGINS OF CHRISTIAN FAITH

It has often been pointed out that Abraham, the father of biblical faith, experienced God in history. In this he was different from his contemporaries, who found God in nature, and so the religions that flow from him are different, in that they too look for God primarily in history. The Old Testament, the New Testament, and the Koran all emphasize the *faith* of Abraham in finding God, and that faith was a looking for God in current events. Faith in a God who acts in history was *the* way, the *sine qua non* of finding meaning. In fact, in the Bible there is an Abraham theology, that is, a theme running through Scripture in which *having faith like Abraham* is the key to finding God. The Yahwist, one of the theologians responsible for the Pentateuch (the first five books of the Bible), used Abraham in this way to say for his own contemporaries (tenth century B.C.) that one cannot hope to find God otherwise. In Genesis 12:1–4 the Yahwist portrays Abraham as a person capable of making a *new historical beginning*. But this faith is not a new interpretation of the world; it is a new way of living in history.

When Israel, four centuries after Abraham, under the leadership of Moses, found itself free from slavery in Egypt, it interpreted that event from the point of view of the memory—of Abraham's faith. In fact, it interpreted all its history, or was asked by the *prophets* to interpret it so, as something the key to which was faith, unconditional trust in the God of Abraham as someone who would stand behind new beginnings. It did this in the face of the most despairing historical conditions.

If biblical religion is true, if it is in some way not just *an* answer to the meaning of human life, but in some way *the* answer, it seems that it can be such only if those who believe in it allow it to become the inspiration of a *new beginning*. Is that what is happening to us now, that we seem to be being forced by history to rediscover the essence of our own religion? The key seems to be not that faith will provide us with a new interpretation of history but that *it will enable us to act differently*. The meaning we are being forced to seek is not a theory about the world or history but a ground for acting. The God question for us is not a question of a new interpretation which will allow us to stand back from history and say, unconcernedly, we know where it is going. Rather faith today must be what it was for Abraham, a new source of strength for action. But there is a problem—Christians are not disposed, *precisely by our Christian past*, to accept the challenge of new beginnings. Why is that?

A PROBLEM: THE DEFINITIVE NATURE OF THE REVELATION IN CHRIST

What is a Christian? One way to put it, in a minimal way to be sure, would be to say that a Christian is one who sees the promise made to Abraham, that through his faith all the nations of the earth would be blessed, realized in the person of Jesus of Nazareth.

For Christians Jesus is the Christ, the Messiah, the anointed one, the fulfillment of all the promises. In Jesus God's definitive act to save us occurs. But that belief, or the way that we have believed in Christ, has had an unfortunate effect on Christians. Precisely because we believe that Jesus is the final word of God to us, we look for no new revelation. It is true: Jesus *is* all that can be said. We believe that this is God's Son, God's perfect self-expression, God's definitive word to us. But speaking this way can also be terribly misleading. In fact the New Testament and later history show that again and again, for some reason, Christians and others have been dissatisfied with the notion that revelation is closed. This is a healthy dissatisfaction if it is a rejection of the position that Christianity is merely a concern for what happened in the past. How could we ever come to a definitive understanding of such an abundant *mystery?*

But another reason for this dissatisfaction may lie in the essential aspect of our faith as faith in the God of history. It would be very surprising if God, who all during the time of preparation was continually calling God's people to new beginnings, now, in the culminating call to faith, stopped calling us to a new beginning. If Christian faith is biblical faith, it is *always* enacted in new beginnings made while trusting in God's guidance. Faith itself cannot be thought of as closed or drawing to a close. It has no final form. It is, of its essence, openness to God's call. This does not contradict having normative beliefs. They guide us on our way. But beliefs are not themselves the object of faith; they are guides to understanding where to find the object, which is God.

Strangely, Christians have no difficulty accepting the need for openness to God's call as *individuals*. They accept that to be a Christian involves *metanoia*, conversion, a willingness to hear God's call. But they find it hard to extend this principle to the Christian *community* itself. Yet if Christian community stops seeing God's world in the history around it, if it mistakes its signposts for its destination, it runs the risk of not being biblical. God does not speak to men and women in a series of statements so that faith is holding onto the right statements. God reveals himself to us in Jesus, as one who will be found if we are willing to take a risk, and make a new beginning, and who mysteriously stands beside us as we take the risk.

In this context we can see the importance of Christian belief in the resurrection of Jesus. What does it mean to believe that Jesus rose from the dead? At least this: Believing in Jesus' resurrection, the Christian knows that God has accepted the world and that the world can be transformed. The resurrection is key because it says that faith must envision the possibility of radical transformations—really new beginnings—the transformation of human beings and therefore of matter. If we believe this as a real possibility, we can derive real courage to act. What we accomplish *now* is the stuff of a *permanent* transformation. New beginnings of a radical sort become feasible with this hope.

A SECOND PROBLEM: THE NEW TESTAMENT—WHAT DOES IT SAY ON OUR QUESTION?

You would think the *New Testament* would have something to say on this. It does to the extent that it urges people to constant new beginnings, to *metanoia*, conversion. On the other hand, the New Testament merely shows people setting out on new beginnings in *their* historical situation (especially against the two concrete problems of the early Church: (1) whether one had to first become a Jew to be a Christian, and (2) what was the meaning in the delay of the parousia, the return of Jesus). It is worth noting that to these two problems faith eventually gave shocking, *new* answers. But the point is that the questions which are so important to the Christian of today were not envisaged by the New Testament. The factors which shape our current historical situation were unknown: science, technology, world politics, the struggle for liberation of all types. The result is that it is impossible to simply consult the Bible and repeat isolated statements as though they answer our questions. *But* an answer *without* the Bible at its core would not be a Christian answer. We must examine the *central content* of the biblical message again and concentrate in our search on its meaning for our own times. A truly *biblical* faith must in a real sense go constantly beyond the Bible, make a new beginning, *in order to be faithful,* to *remain biblical.* The Bible itself insists on this in its insistence on the role of "the Spirit of truth." The biblical message is not that God is "back there," but that God is present, and can be found again in each new historical situation by people who, like Abraham, are willing to make a new beginning. It is precisely the biblical promise that God will be there for people who turn to God for new beginnings. If people are unwilling to make a new beginning, God will not be found.

A THIRD PROBLEM: GOD, HUMAN LOVE, AND COMMUNITY

We turn now to an apparently unconnected line of thought. Western men and women, simply because of our history, have a certain pre-understanding of God. All human understanding takes place in one or other tradition. It is often possible to observe, in discussing the question about God, how much we all bear the impression of the western tradition of faith in God. In the west people think of God as someone who is *concerned about them*—and that has not been a necessary conception of God everywhere and at all times. In the western tradition one is not primarily dealing with the god of the philosophers, a ground of being, but the God of the Bible, the God with a name, Yahweh, a God who can be addressed. Our understanding of God is profoundly influenced by the Bible and so we ask about a God that we can have a personal relationship with—not a "Supreme Being" who is simply the principle behind the world, but a God we can talk to, who speaks to us and invites us to respond. This is our pre-understanding of God, and any God which is going to make any sense to us will be a God found where there is speaking, dialogue.

Now it appears that our pre-understanding of God and what we as westerners think about *meaning* converge. Meaning for us is found in the process of accepting and being accepted, loving and being loved. Really the question about meaning *at its deepest level* is the question about God: Is there, in and beyond all *human* relationships, a relationship involving the whole of one's life? Is there a relationship which would continue even if *human* meaning cannot be established? Finally, is the God of the Bible possibly the other party to this relationship? Christian theology presents the God of the Bible, the God revealed in Jesus Christ, as the possible answer to the question. But first a problem arising from the side of modern man to accepting the God of the Bible must be dealt with. The reason is that if the God of the Bible is the answer to the question of meaning, then the whole question about God is wrapped up with the question of personal love—because the question of meaning and the Christian answer to the question of meaning are about a personal love that gives meaning *despite all*. And the fact is: personal love in our society is under some peculiar pressures that might make acceptance of the biblical God difficult.

We are becoming increasingly aware that people who have been deprived of love as children are often incapable of loving later in life, or at least severely hindered in their capacity to love. If people are not looking for love (and the condition of finding it is the capacity to give it), and if love is meaning, they will not even be looking for God because they are not looking for meaning. But it may be true that today there are growing numbers of people who have not experienced acceptance by and turning toward another person in childhood or whose experience of this is very inadequate. A brutalizing environment without love is often the cause of this, but it also happens that parents who apparently give their children a great deal of love and allow them unlimited opportunities as *consumers* may in fact be denying them the possibility of being accepted by and turning toward one another. To simplify radically: the source of our capacity to be an "I" who can turn toward a Thou is the environment that we know as children. This environment is under threat. Our upbringing is often excessively authoritarian or excessively permissive.

What is the effect of this on the question about meaning and the question about God? A child brought up in this way will not experience the radical, unconditional affirmation that seems to be necessary for him or her to love. He or she will rather experience it as a confrontation, as repression, or as unconcern. Furthermore, this fundamentally ambiguous experience of *authority* will inevitably be transferred to every encounter with other authorities.

In the western tradition, the content of the word "God" is closely associated with the content of the word "authority." It is hardly surprising that God is experienced as an authority, strong or weak as the authorities of our youth may have been, but in either case not an authority with which one had a real *dialogic* relationship. God will be experienced as another authority that refuses to be questioned, as a repressor, or as unconcerned because too permissive. People grow up and naturally question authority. They gradually dissociate themselves from the authority which they have a bad experience of and in the process dissociate themselves from God.

The situation is complicated by the fact that in the Christian tradition the authority of God is linked with the name "Father," and the image and role of the father have become very ambiguous in contemporary society. Many men need to compensate in the home and family for the meaninglessness of what they experience at their place of work. Often a father cannot transfer to his children a positive attitude toward society because he does not have one himself. And as a father his share in the upbringing of the children is often limited to sanctioning the mother's intentions, those which have been fulfilled, but most especially those which she has not been able to carry out. This is the "father as enforcer." The image of father cannot help but affect the image of God as Father—an unpredictable and repressive figure is anticipated.

These changes are not just the result of moral failure—*they are the result of changes taking place in society,* especially of industrialization and specialization. They do complicate the question of God.

A FOURTH PROBLEM: OUR PRESUPPOSITIONS

We have shown that for the Christian Gospel to retain its power it must be willing to adapt. Because the hearers of the Gospel live in different historical, cultural, political, and economic situations, there is and must be a continuing reinterpretation of the Gospel. For the Gospel to be for each succeeding generation what it was for the first generation of Christians, a message of salvation and redemption, it must be continually re-presented in such a way that it addresses genuine concerns.

But there is an obvious problem. In adapting to each new situation the Gospel runs the risk of being distorted by the new context. This is what Jürgen Moltmann has called the "identity-relevance problem." If the Church proclaims the Gospel in a traditional form, it preserves the clarity and unambiguousness of its message (its "identity"). But it runs the risk of not being heard (not being "relevant"). It does no good to insist on one side of the tension at the expense of the other. If the Gospel is distorted by any context, it becomes a merely human word. It has been "reduced" to what that context can handle. On the other hand, if the Gospel is thought to be a static thing, a truth frozen in amber for all time, which cannot be reinterpreted for varying situations (reinterpretation happens, after all, right within the *New Testament*), it runs the risk of ceasing to be, in fact, a word of salvation.

How do we avoid sacrificing "identity" for "relevance"? One thing we must do is examine our own presuppositions. Presuppositions form a worldview which to a great extent determines what can count for us as true. Yet worldviews are largely unexamined. They are so familiar to us that we accept them as obvious. But do we not have an obligation as thinking human beings to examine the worldview out of which we inevitably operate but which in fact we unconsciously inherited with the rest of our culture? Especially if we are going to adapt the Gospel to contemporary minds, should we not examine contemporary presuppositions?

Rudolf Bultmann's description of the chasm between the worldview of the community which produced the Gospels and the contemporary worldview is famous and probably accurate. In the early Christian community, as well as for many others of that time, the divine and the mundane intermingled and formed one whole, one cosmos. This cosmos was envisioned as three-storied (heaven, earth, hell), with what happens in the middle story being constantly affected by the forces of the other two stories. Accordingly, natural causes were not given their full value; the divine and the infernal were given the major role in earthly events. Not yet aware of the true causes of things, first century men and women mixed divine and worldly, understanding the divine in a worldly way and the worldly in a divine way. They saw miracles and supernatural causes where we would see natural causes. They looked for divine intervention to save them. According to Bultmann, the timeless truth that this "mythological" view embodies is that we are not in control of ourselves or our destiny. Perhaps it says more than that.

According to Bultmann, the contemporary view, in contrast to the mythological view, treats the world as possessing its own inner rationality. Both the natural and the human sciences seek insight into the immanent objective structures of the physical and social world. They positively exclude the hypothesis of the supernatural in their search. Furthermore, they exclude questions which would require such an hypothesis. As members of a culture formed by science and technology, we regard the world in a worldly way. We expect it to run, in both its natural and historical dimensions, according to its own immanent laws. It is a closed system. What it has been, what it is, and what it will be are givens of its initial potentialities. They may unfold in an evolutionary way, but there is no room for "intervention" from without. Human wisdom is not to expect the entrance of non-worldly forces into the cosmos to transform it. We are to seek mastery in a responsible way of natural and historical forces.

Bultmann did not subject the contemporary worldview to a critique, but he should have. If his description is correct, it is merely the popularization and diffusion of the view of reality pioneered in the philosophy which emerged in the eighteenth century in response to the growth of science (the Enlightenment). Here it is sufficient to point out that the Enlightenment so exalted human reason that "the principle of subjectivity" triumphed. Reality's possibilities cannot exceed what human reason can comprehend. Furthermore, it is not merely human reason's reach which becomes the limit of reality. It is *how* human reason understands in terms of grouping similars (analogy) or by subsuming particulars under general categories (universalization), by ignoring the unique and concentrating on the general. We know now that this has limitations even in the natural sciences, but it is especially when it becomes an unconscious presupposition of our view of history that we have a problem. History becomes a natural process. Freedom, human or otherwise, is not taken into account. Ernst Troeltsch showed that the historical writing which emerged from the Enlightenment in the nineteenth century and which aspired to "objectivity," that is, to be free of any presuppositions, was in fact operating under unconscious presuppositions which prevented it from being able to deal with the very factor that makes history what it is and which lifts it above a merely natural process, namely, freedom. Freedom involves the unique, the underivable, the *novum*. To deal with history by a method which aspires to imitate the natural sciences is to distort it. Insofar as historiography starts from the assumption of the similarity in principle of all events, it perceives everything according to analogy and presupposes that the future can never truly transcend the past. That is, there can be a natural unfolding of what was present potentially from the beginning (a "closed system"), but there is no room for the truly new, a transcendence of the past by the future due to something entering history from without (an "open system"). All history's potentialities are present from the beginning. Hope is placed in a physical, social, moral evolution as a process immanent from the beginning in reality as it first comes to be.

There is a fundamental clash between this view of reality and that of the people who wrote the Bible. It is not because evolution is incompatible with the Bible. The Bible is not a science text. But it has a fundamentally different worldview. For the Bible the cosmos is an "open system," that is, one open to transcending itself through participation in God's creative activity. The biblical concept of *creation* is much more than the view that God creates a physical world out of nothing. Even some philosophers of the Enlightenment held that. The biblical view is that God is continually creating, that the act by which the physical cosmos was created is merely the condition of the possibility of further creation, the creation through creatures' cooperation with God's activity which is history. This is where the biblical mind and the Enlightenment part company, and it is important if the contemporary mind is merely the popularization of the Enlightenment's philosophy.

Theologically, to hold for a closed system is questionable. It amounts to saying that God, who brought the world out of nothing, by that fact loses power to take it to a higher level. It can never be more than what it was at the beginning. It says that God has stopped creating.

A closed system is questionable from a philosophical point of view, also. It asks us to account for all that is, intelligent life, freedom, love, new persons, by reference to the potentialities of matter alone. That view is itself the result of the very presuppositions we are examining.

Existentially, too, a closed system is unsatisfactory. We experience ourselves as constantly seeking to transcend our own impotence. We acknowledge our limitations and aspire to go beyond them. We *hope*. But hope for transcendence is illusory if "this is all there is."

Rudolf Bultmann accepted the inevitability of the contemporary view. He did not think it needed a critique. Instead, he called the worldview of the biblical peoples "mythological." Yet he was himself the victim of a myth. No doubt there are mythological elements in the ancient worldview, but when we ask what is the basic difference between that view and our own, is it so obvious that the present view (as described by Bultmann) accords with the evidence better than the ancient view? What is the basic difference? The modern view is that the cosmos is a closed system. Remarkable as it is there is nothing new under the sun. It is simply the unfolding of what was there *in potentia* in the beginning. But is what we have now adequately explained by the potentialities of matter (to say nothing of its very existence)? It is especially the phenomenon of human freedom that is difficult to explain. How is freedom contained in the potentialities of matter? It is more logical to hold with those who deny that there is freedom than to attribute its existence to the mere evolution of matter.

In contrast the biblical view reconciles the data better. It recognizes two inescapable facts which we cannot deny without denying our humanity. We feel responsible, and we refuse to relieve ourselves of responsibility. In doing so we acknowledge that in some sense we transcend mere blind physical causality. The second fact is that our freedom is surrounded by limitation. On the one hand we acknowledge our responsibility; on the other, we acknowledge our inability to exercise our freedom in a consistently responsible manner. Our situation is accurately captured in the ancient myth of Sisyphus. Doomed to roll a large rock up a hill, Sisyphus did not possess the stamina to get it to the top. But every time it rolled back to the bottom, his humanity impelled him to try again. If that is our situation, is it so unreasonable to look for signs that we are not alone with the human task? We have freedom. Where did it come from? Is there a freedom that stands ready to sustain our freedom? There is a Catch-22 here, of course. If we do not think of the cosmos as open to the influence of a transcendent freedom, we will not look for signs of its presence. And if we do not look, we will not find.

One thing is clear. A radical difference in Christianity results from the choice of worldviews. A worldview which sees the cosmos as a closed system running according to its own immanent laws can tolerate nothing really new. The God who created it out of nothing cannot take it to a higher level in an event like the resurrection. Jesus' own proclamation of the coming of the reign of God, the eschatological event, must be demythologized. The traditional claims of Christianity about Jesus himself become intolerable, for they speak of a personal presence of the transcendent God in history and the cosmos.

The question is: Is it *reasonable* to demand that reality be only what the human mind can comprehend? Is it not more reasonable to see ourselves as encompassed by mystery and ask if that mystery is speaking to us?

REVIEW/SUMMATION

We are, each of us, mysteries to ourselves. We experience ourselves as having the desire to be happy but that we are dependent on others for our fulfillment, for meaning. We are dependent on others for love, and we know that without love we cannot be happy. We know that without love it will be hard for us to be human, to grow, to keep from stagnating. We will be enclosed, self-centered, incapable of going beyond ourselves, to "transcend" ourselves. Love seems to be a *sine qua non* of a vital, expanding human existence, for happiness, for meaning. There is another proposal about human happiness, of course. It does not consist in *being something*—it consists in *having things*. Sometimes fulfillment as *being* and fulfillment as *having* get mixed up. We seek to fill ourselves with things. Or we seek to possess someone, to demand their love. This is self-defeating, of course. Love which is not given freely is not love. It is, and must be, a gift for it to fulfill us.

But even the greatest of loves are vulnerable. Happiness is fragile. As Mac Sledge said in the movie *Tender Mercies*, "it can't be trusted." You think you've got it and tragedy strikes. A tire blows and a car leaves the road. A young mother gets cancer and all efforts fail to stop it. A marriage sours, parents become enemies, children disappoint. A young man is drafted and dies in a faraway, senseless war.

No one is untouched by tragedy. We are reminded every day of our finiteness. Try as we might to be happy, joyful, even ecstatic as we may be at times, we experience every day our limitations, our frustrations, and the disappointment of our hopes. Our desire for happiness seems to be infinite; the ability of life to satisfy that desire seems to be finite. We are a passion, an appetite. But are we, as Jean Paul Sartre said, "a useless passion" that can yearn but yearns in vain?

Or is life a mystery? Is the infiniteness of our yearning a sign that we are involved in a genuine mystery, something that can't be fathomed, not because it *lacks* meaning, but because it *possesses more* meaning than we can comprehend? At any rate, even when love comes our way we know it is vulnerable, capable of dying, being abused, perverted. And even when it is joyous there is a melancholy to it—for it itself creates a desire for more love, deathless love. In short, we humans seem to be appetites for *infinite* love. Is there such a thing?

But it's not merely that I want happiness for myself. How could I be happy in a world of misery? I want others not to have to suffer, not to be oppressed, not to live lives of grinding poverty, ignorance, and abuse. I do not want this to happen to my loved ones. But would I be happy *if it were happening to anyone?* Would I be happy in a private little corner of a world? Would I be happy where I am powerless to help those who need help, where my desire to love more fully, even to love those I do not know, can only encounter constant frustration because I cannot actualize my love? Is the infinite yearning not only for *my* happiness but for *our* happiness—in the widest extent possible? But is that not a useless dream?

Finally, what are we to make of death? When I was young, I felt as though I would live forever. And now most of my life is gone. What is the point? Am I just "dust in the wind," a match flaming briefly in infinite darkness? Will my loves die with me? If so, what have they really meant?

Yet I *hope* in the face of my own lack of freedom, my selfishness, my inconsistency, my inability to love, I hope to be free and loving. In a world rent by oppression and injustice, poverty and war, I *hope* for freedom, justice, peace. In the face of death I *hope* for the permanence of my loves. Are these vain hopes, or are they evidence that my little mystery is part of an infinite mystery that urges me to hope?

These questions are the God question, the question that human beings are to themselves, the question they constantly are asking. What are they asking when they ask these questions? It seems to me they seek to know: *Is* there a love which stands unconditionally behind human loves, bears them up, sets them free—gives them depth, extension, and perdurance that they could not otherwise have?

This is the way I would say we ask today: Does God exist? It is not a theoretical question. It is simply the question of human existence.

Part II:
LOOKING FOR AN ANSWER
THE BIBLICAL GOD

INTRODUCTION

We have framed the contemporary God question in terms of whether there exists a transcendent source of love that will empower and sustain us in our desire to love unconditionally. Is there an unconditional love in which we can participate?

It is important to note that if such a love exists, it can only be known if it chooses to reveal itself. Love can only remain love if it remains a free gift and a free *self*-disclosure. Moreover, it can only really disclose itself if it is accepted, for love can only be known by being accepted, by a return of love. In other words, while reason can direct us to a principle behind the existence of all else, the God question asks much more: Is there self-generating love, and has that love disclosed itself in an act of love? We do not wish to disparage the philosophical search for a ground of being. It has its place. We merely wish to acknowledge that theology cannot (because faith cannot) be satisfied with the "God of the Philosophers," but must seek the God who can only be known if he chooses to reveal himself. The reason is simple: faith in God is more than merely knowing *that* God exists. It is response to God, dialogue with God, and love of God. It is the response of love to love—not the discovery of an objective, neutral fact.

Christian faith claims that this source of love exists and has revealed itself in the history of Israel and definitively ("eschatologically") in Jesus of Nazareth, the Christ. For all Christians the normative account of this revelation is enshrined in the Old and New Testaments. In the light of them we seek God in the events of our lives. This brings us to a central concern of contemporary Christian theology, the nature of our constitutive writings. To know the God who has been revealed in history, and whom we wish to encounter in our history, we spontaneously turn to the accounts of that revelation. This raises a crucial question. What is the nature of these accounts, and how should we read them?

We will approach this classic theological question, one of the most debated in Christianity today, through another one. Is it only in Israel and Christianity that God has been revealed? We will ask, first, what Catholicism holds on this question. Secondly, we will ask if Catholicism's answer is really biblical. In the process we will come to (1) a better understanding of the contemporary Catholic approach to Scripture, and (2) an understanding of the God of Israel as revealed in its Scriptures. We will then proceed to a discussion of God's definitive self-revelation in the history and person of Jesus of Nazareth.

Section I:
The God of Israel

Chapter IV

YAHWEH—TRIBAL GOD
OR LORD OF HISTORY?
THE PROBLEM OF THE
EXTENT OF SALVATION

THE QUESTION OF THE "EXTENT OF SALVATION"

In today's pluralistic world, where we encounter, are friends with, even marry, people of different religious persuasions than our own, the question of how one's God regards those outside one's faith community is of more than speculative interest. One might expect that such a question would receive different treatment depending on changing historical circumstances. In fact, this is the case. Religious communities that are mortal enemies will find it hard to acknowledge God's effective presence in one another. On the other hand, amiable interaction leads to mutual respect and the acknowledgment of the genuine presence of God in the other. It is this latter tendency that marks post-Vatican II Catholicism and signifies an important development in Catholic theology.

THE OLDER FORMULATION—THE OLDER SOLUTION

From the earliest days of Christianity theologians have struggled with this question in one form or another. In the New Testament itself, there is a tension between two principles, which we will call the particular and the universal. The former stresses the precise and concrete character of God's interaction with humans—that specifically in Israel and in Jesus God's self-revelation is to be found. A good example of

57

this tendency would be Mark 16:16, the risen Christ's command to "Go into the whole world; proclaim the good news to all creation. He who believes and is baptized will be saved; he who does not believe will be condemned." On the other hand, the latter principle is evident in the New Testament teaching on the universality of God's desire to save (as in 1 Timothy 2:4) and in the recognition, as in Matthew 25:31–46, that salvation depends less on verbal recognition of Christ as on concrete love of him through love of neighbor. The same tension existed in the patristic period (the period of the "Fathers," second to eighth centuries). While on the one hand it was stressed that "apart from Christ, baptism, and the Church (*extra Christum, extra baptisma, extra ecclesiam nulla salus*) there is no salvation," it was also acknowledged that *movement toward* baptism (the catechumen or would-be Christian martyred before baptism) or even an implicit desire to be baptized (baptism by desire), sometimes hidden in the simple search for truth would suffice. Despite Augustine's (354–430 A.D.) extraordinary influence, the Church never adopted his view that water baptism was so crucial that unbaptized babies would be separated from God forever. The medieval theologians postulated an intermediate state of natural happiness ("limbo"), undoubtedly because they felt a fundamental conflict between a too strict interpretation of the particular principle and the universal principle, which, after all expressed the unconditional nature of God's love. At the time of the Reformation this view of God resulted in Catholicism's rejection of John Calvin's doctrine of double predestination, which stated that before one even had an opportunity to act, God decreed who would be saved and who would be damned. According to the Council of Trent, the teaching contradicted the "universal salvific will" of God.

It is important to note that the question of who was saved and who was damned was framed in a very abstract, non-historical manner. When the "good pagan" (or for that matter the "good Protestant") was conceded the possibility of salvation, it was assumed that he or she had somehow neutralized the deleterious effects of his or her religion. God did not work through the religion but in spite of it.

THE NEW QUESTION—THE NEW ANSWER

When one accepts the "essential historicity" of human persons, one cannot set aside the question of the role of a person's culture, language or religion in his or her actions. Thus, in contemporary Catholic theology, the issue of who can be saved has moved from its former individualistic, abstract formulation to one which acknowledges the concrete context in which each person lives. The question began to be asked about "The Salvific Value of the Non-Christian Religions." If one must necessarily respond to God in a particular place and time, in a particular culture and language, the question must be rephrased. One asks, for example, whether the Hinduism of a Hindu is an obstacle to that person's union with God or the very means to union. Today it is not uncommon for Catholic theologians to see in the non-Christian religions the very means by which people respond to God. This does not constitute a wholesale endorsement of the non-Christian religions, nor does it ignore what is dehumanizing and reprehensible in some practices. It merely acknowledges that if the phrase "God desires the salvation of all" is valid, then God will be active in human hearts, and human hearts respond from where they are, through given cultural forms, thought patterns, and worldviews. A person's religion would mediate the response as God approached the person in the depths of his or her existence. After all, nothing less happened in biblical religion itself. Israel's response to God evolved. Thus, some theologians speak of the great world religions not as "false" but as "pre-biblical."

THE POSITIVE EVALUATION OF THE NON-CHRISTIAN RELIGIONS IN CATHOLIC TEACHING

Is the positive attitude of many Catholic theologians concerning the salvific value of non-Christian religions officially endorsed by Catholic teaching? Not in so many words, but neither is it rejected. It is one of the myriad "theological opinions" in Catholicism which is neither officially endorsed nor officially rejected. The so-called "Dutch Catechism" (*A New Catechism*, Seabury, 1966) elaborated such a position, and it was not criticized by the commission of cardinals appointed by Pope Paul VI to judge the orthodoxy of the book.

The reason is that Catholic teaching is *open to* such a view. Vatican II approached this question taking a different tack. In its key document, *Lumen Gentium*, it asked it in the following form: "Who are the people of God?" (13–16). Some pertinent excerpts show that Catholicism is far more "universalist" than is normally recognized:

(13) All men are called to be part of this catholic unity of the people of God. . . . And there belong to it or are related to it, in various ways, the Catholic faithful as well as all who believe

in Christ, and indeed the whole of mankind. For all men are called to salvation by the grace of God.

(14) This sacred synod turns its attention first to the Catholic faithful. Basing itself upon sacred Scripture and tradition, it teaches that the Church . . . is necessary for salvation. For Christ, made present to us in his body, which is the Church, is the one Mediator and the unique Way of salvation. In explicit terms he himself affirmed the necessity of faith and baptism and thereby affirmed also the necessity of the Church, for through baptism as through a door men enter the Church. Whosoever, therefore, knowing that the Catholic Church was made necessary by God through Jesus Christ, would refuse to enter her or to remain in her, could not be saved.

(15) The Church recognizes that in many ways she is linked with those who, being baptized, are honored with the name of Christian, though they do not profess the faith in its entirety or do not preserve unity of communion with the successor of Peter. . . . We can say that in some real way they are joined with us in the Holy Spirit.

(16) Finally, those who have not yet received the Gospel are related in various ways to the people of God. In the first place there is the people to whom the covenants and the promises were given and from whom Christ was born according to the flesh. On account of their fathers, this people remains most dear to God, for God does not repent of the gifts he makes nor of the calls he issues.

But the plan of salvation also includes those who acknowledge the Creator. In the first place among these there are the Moslems, who, professing to hold the faith of Abraham, along with us adore the one and merciful God. . . . Nor is God himself far distant from those who in shadows and images seek the unknown God, for it is he who gives to all men life and breath and every other gift, and who as Savior wills that all men be saved.

Those also can attain to everlasting salvation who through no fault of their own do not know the Gospel of Christ or his Church, yet sincerely seek God and, moved by grace, strive by their deeds to do his will as it is known to them through the dictates of conscience. Nor does Divine Providence deny the help necessary for salvation to those who, without blame on their part, have not yet arrived at an explicit knowledge of God, but who strive to live a good life, thanks to his grace.

What has happened here? One finds a (perhaps unfortunate) *redefinition of "Church."* The statements hold on to the principle, *extra ecclesiam nulla salus* (outside the Church there is no salvation), but redraw the boundaries of the Church or at least abandon a strict "insiders-outsiders" approach. The document recognizes that while someone who officially belongs to the Church can be a nominal member, so someone who does not officially belong to the Church can be a live (if unknowing) member.

IS THIS DEVELOPMENT CONSISTENT WITH SCRIPTURE?

There is no doubt that the initial reaction of many Christians (especially "evangelical" Christians) would be to say that not only is this emergent view not scriptural, but it is simply another example of Catholicism being lured from authentic biblical Christianity by non-biblical factors. And, in fact, one must admit the crucial role played by the notion of the "essential historicity" of man and woman, a notion, after all, which has its origin in philosophy. The classic text cited in support of a *narrow* view of God's salvific activity is Romans, chapters 9–11. It should be pointed out, however, that the thirty-eight Protestant and Catholic theologians who wrote *The Common Catechism,* an ecumenical statement of Christian faith (Seabury, 1975), agreed that Romans 9–11 and indeed the Bible as a whole does not really address the question explicitly. We have arrived at another instance of the fact mentioned in Chapter III that the Bible addresses questions that were crucial in its own time and that it can be used to answer our questions only by bringing its *central content* to bear on those questions. So whether one wishes to attack or support the view, one cannot simply cite isolated verses of Scripture; one must bring its central content to bear on the question. And against a view that limits God's saving activity to a narrow band of human history is evidence in a number of places in Scripture that God is active across the length and breadth of human history. We will pursue this question in the Old Testament to understand better the God of Israel. One of the places that supports the more "universalist" view is found in the Old Testament's most interesting and difficult-to-handle parts, the famous first eleven chapters of Genesis. A by-product of our search will be a first encounter with the "histori-cal-critical" approach to the Bible. (For an account of "Catholicism and Modern Scripture Studies" see Appendix 2.)

THE BOOK OF GENESIS

Genesis is part of the Pentateuch—the first five books of the Bible. Christian tradition attributed the writing of the Pentateuch to Moses, something both Jewish tradition and the Pentateuch itself maintain. Thus, until recent times, the accepted view was that the Pentateuch had one author and he was Moses. The implications of this view are important. If one person was responsible for these foundational doc-uments, the notion of a direct revelation to that person as the founding act of biblical religion gains credibility. Everything written there would be considered a revelation and, as such, to have divine warrant. The role of human beings in the writing would be limited to that of a sten-ographer taking dictation. A theory of verbal inspiration (or dictation) would stand at the basis of Judeo-Christian religion much as it stands as the basis of Islam.

OLD TESTAMENT CRITICISM

In the eighteenth century scholars grew uncomfortable with the traditional view of Mosaic authorship because of the seeming incon-sistencies in Genesis. For instance, in the description of the flood does God tell Noah to take seven pairs of clean animals, and only one pair of unclean into the ark (Gen 7:2), or does God tell him to take one pair of each (Gen 6:19; 7:9)? What is one to make of the fact that in one place man was created after the creation of vegetation (Gen 1) but in another *before* (Gen 2)? What is one to make of the genealogies? In Genesis 4 Enoch is the son of Cain; in 5, Enoch is a descendant (sixth generation) of Seth, the third son of Adam and Eve. Again, why does the name for God change (Genesis 1: Elohim, Genesis 2:4b on, Yah-weh)?

Furthermore, scholars began to notice *similarities* between what Genesis said and the ancient Near Eastern myths being discovered by archaeologists, particularly the so-called Gilgamesh Epic uncovered in 1853 in an Assyrian form during the excavation at Nineveh. At times the account of a *flood* in that myth and that in Genesis 6 are nearly identical (cf. *Religions of the Ancient Near East: Sumero-Akkadian Religious Texts and Ugaritic Epics*, ed. Isaac Mendelsohn, The Library of Liberal Arts, 1955, p. 104).

The *internal* inconsistencies and the *literary parallels* raised the possibility that Genesis 1–11 was not a completely original work of Moses and that it did not have just one author. In the nineteenth century the question of the "literary genre" of Genesis became a fundamental issue, especially in Protestantism. In German Lutheranism and in liberal Protestantism the purely historical approach or "historical/critical method" began to be applied to Scripture in order to deal with these questions. What does this approach entail?

Ever since the Renaissance, scholars had been asking questions about the ancient classical texts. This is called "criticism," "literary criticism." The word "criticism" misleads the contemporary ear. The method, in itself, is not as negative as the word makes it sound. Rather it consists in "questioning" a text. The historical-critical method is really a *set of questions*, which are asked of a text:

(1) What was the original text?—"textual criticism"
(2) Does the work have a predecessor(s)?—"source criticism"
(3) What does the author add to the text, and what is his theology?—"redaction criticism" (redactor = editor) and "theological criticism"
(4) What really happened?—"historical criticism"

These questions were crucial ones, especially for Protestantism, for the Reformation had adopted the principle *sola scriptura,* that is, that the Bible itself, as a self-interpreting document, is the sole norm of belief. When non-believing scholars began to draw conclusions from their research that were hostile to Christianity, some Protestant scholars began to acknowledge that the human agents involved in the writing of Scripture had to be taken more account of and that the meaning these *human* authors wished to convey had to be the focus of study. They held that God's meaning was contained in the human author's meaning and to arrive at this meaning (unfortunately often called the "literal" meaning) one had to analyze the text from its "situation-in-life" (*Sitz-im-Leben*), the concrete historical circumstances in which the text had its origin. Scholarship became the *sine qua non* of understanding the true meaning of the foundational biblical documents.

By the second half of the nineteenth century many Protestant scholars believed that underlying the Pentateuch were four "*documentary*" sources. The documents were usually symbolized by the code letters J (to indicate the Yahwist [German: Jahweh], the writer who used Yahweh for God's name), E (the Elohist), D (the Deuteronomist), P (the Priestly source). Julius Wellhausen solidified the theory in the last quarter of the nineteenth century. He is a good example of how genuine insights were often obscured by philosophical presuppositions. Wellhausen's theory was soundly condemned by traditional Christians, both Protestant and Catholic, because they failed to distinguish between his literary and historical hypotheses. Today, however, most Old Testament scholars of both persuasions acknowledge their debt to Wellhausen and agree with his fundamental thesis, at least to the extent that they acknowledge that the Pentateuch is the result of the *combining of sources*. (For recent criticisms of the four source theory see J. Blenkinsopp, "The Documentary Hypothesis in Trouble," *Bible Review*, 1/4 [Winter 1985] 23–32; also *Genesis: An Authorship Study in Computer Assisted Statistical Linguistics*, by Y.T. Raddy, Rome: *Analecta Biblica*, n. 103, 1985.)

Today many variations on the four source theory are trying to tackle the complexity of the five books. Normally it is emphasized that the four sources did not exist first as separate *books*. Rather each source had a long and complicated *oral* phase and found written form only in later times. These *oral traditions* were not merely tribal folk tales; rather they were professions of the faith of Israel, the expression of a unique national consciousness. They constituted an oral *history of salvation*. This is an important point. Israel was never content with a mere record of events (what a nineteenth century German scholar would call *Historie*). Rather the traditions were *interpretations* of events, from the point of view of faith. The account of events incorporated an interpretation of their significance for Israel's salvation (what that same scholar would call *Geschichte*). Some elements of the story may have had secular origins; for example, the form of the Mosaic covenant seems to be modeled on a widely employed treaty form used in the ancient Near East, the "suzerainty treaty." Nor can borrowings from other religions be ruled out. Nevertheless, these materials were transformed to express the faith of a people who believed they had a special relationship to God. Thus their oral tradition and, later, their writings, became a *history of salvation*. Probably parts of the tradition were preserved at various cultic sanctuaries and recited periodically at the great festivals. So again and again the people would hear the deeds of "the Lord" on their behalf. Because the oral tradition was preserved in different places, different traditions grew up. A common account of the origin and combining of four components of the Pentateuch would look something like the following:

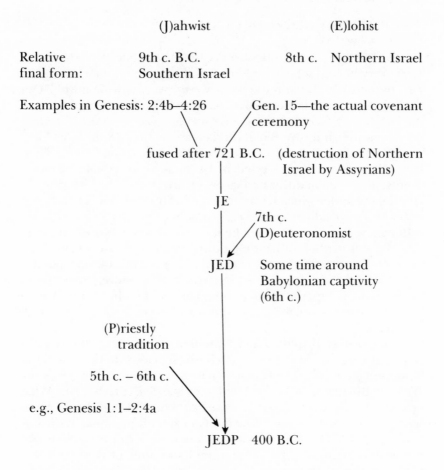

Most Old Testament scholars today, however, agree there was a core story that all traditions regarded as canonical (normative). This is given in the Pentateuch at Deuteronomy 26:5–10. The setting of this "historical creed" in Deuteronomy seems to correspond to its actual situation-in-life in the Israelite community—the annual renewal of the covenant. Recitation of the "saving deeds" of God by the people was integral to the renewal of the covenant, for those deeds, and the promises connected with them, formed the basis of the covenant. Recitation of the creed by the people was probably followed by an exhortation by the priests to fidelity to the covenant, the pronouncing of "woes" and "blessings," and to *interpretation of the present situation of Israel* in light of the covenantal relationship. The distinctive Hebrew form of recording history was in the making at these celebrations.

THE LITERARY GENRE OF GENESIS 1–11

We are now in a position to ask the crucial question which contemporary biblical scholarship insists is the key to understanding any part of the Bible: What is the literary *genre* we are dealing with? Our analysis alerts us to the distinctive character of the extraordinary opening chapters of Genesis. As we have seen, according to the historical-critical approach to the Bible, the Pentateuch is a synthesis of long-evolving traditions that existed for centuries in an *oral* form. Their core was a memory (expressed in Dt 26:5–10) of certain historical events, preserved in different places and affected by the historical circumstances under which it was preserved. This memory *grew* as interpretations were added as the years went by. The memory, as a living tradition, was expected to shed light on *present* and *future* events. *In its own way,* this method of handing down a memory to succeeding generations can preserve history even over long periods of time, but it is not concerned with just recording facts. Furthermore, according to biblical scholarship, the memory originally went no further back than the eighteenth century B.C., to the story of Israel as it begins with Abraham.

That brings us to the crucial question: What is the literary form (*genre*) of that part of the Pentateuch which deals with the time *before Abraham* (Gen 1–11)? The Pentateuch is an expansion of Deuteronomy 26:5–10. But that profession of faith only goes back to Abraham. What happened when such questions arose like "Why did God choose Abraham?" or, for that matter, "Why did God enter into human history at all?" Genesis 1–11 attempts to answer questions that the tradition did not originally answer. Two of the traditions attempted to meet this need—in the tenth century the Yahwist, in the sixth century the Priestly. Genesis 1–11, as we have it, weaves together the two traditions. But the crucial point is: What are the questions and where did the answers come from? The questions are among the most profound entertained by human thought. Some are questions raised by those times—not our questions, those raised by science, but questions raised by the religions of Israel's neighbors. Others are timeless. Is the world divine? If the world is not God, what is the relationship of God and the world? If God is good, where did evil come from? Is there another god—a god of evil? If there is evil in the world, is the world evil? What is the present relationship of God and his creation—are they alienated? Has God withdrawn from the world he created? Is there hope?

How could the Hebrews answer these questions? Their normal source of information, their tradition, had never addressed them.

That means that the answers cannot be considered the same literary form as the story of Abraham, Isaac and Jacob and their historical descendants. From Genesis 12 on, we have an account of the period that the tradition said something about, but it originally said nothing about what went on before Abraham.

Nevertheless, the Hebrews understood God to be "faithful"—let us say here, to be "consistent." God could be counted on to act consistently. On the basis of their recent or present experience of God they were willing to extrapolate—into the remote past and into the remote future, the beginning and the end. They produced a protology and eventually an eschatology. They sketched a *past* (and later a future) relationship between God and humanity on the basis of their *present* experience of God. Genesis 1–11 is sometimes called "retrospective prophecy." While prophecy is usually concerned with the question "What *will* happen?" Genesis 1–11 asks "What *did* happen?" So it is "history" not myth (because it is based on extrapolation from historical events, not events in nature), but it is history with a difference, because it changes the question from "What happened?" to "What *must have* happened?" The form of the answer is *story*, like myth, but the story does not concern what happens in the life of the gods as personifications of natural forces, but the world and men and women as actors in the world. Unlike the myths, it confines its answer to saying what happened in history and not outside it.

Genesis 1–11 answers a lot of questions in this way, very basic questions, that are answered by myth in other religions, and by philosophy once it emerges. It gives us a picture of humanity's and the cosmos' condition in a story about origins constructed on the principle that God is *emet*, faithful, consistent, and *hesed*, loving.

GENESIS 1–11 ON GOD'S ATTITUDE TOWARD NON-ISRAELITES

One of the questions asked in Genesis 1–11 is that of the extrabiblical religions, insofar as it was possible at the time. So we have returned to our original reason for discussing the Old Testament, to see whether the common impression people have, that the Bible confines God's salvific activity to a narrow band of human history, is true. I would like to make the case that in the Old Testament, specifically in the contribution of the Priestly tradition (P) to the story of Noah (Genesis 6–9), is a view of history that is open to the proposition that God's salvific activity is not confined to some one people, some narrow axis in history, but is coextensive with human history. The God of Israel is not a tribal God but the Lord of history. We find evidence of this in "The Covenant Theology of the Priestly Writer."

THE COVENANT THEOLOGY OF THE PRIESTLY WRITER

In formulating an understanding of their origins, the Hebrew people structured their view of their history around the notion of "covenants." The major covenant, the one that gave them their decisive identity as a people, is undoubtedly the one made between the people and Yahweh at Sinai through the mediation of Moses (thirteenth century B.C.). It is very difficult to account for the Hebrews as a nation without acknowledging the role of Moses and that he had some extraordinary religious experience that he then shared with the people as a whole. Their identity as a people, their consciousness of a special relationship to God, originated in that event. According to most Old Testament scholars, they were a distinctive people with a distinctive religion before that time. They may have even known their God as "Yahweh." But before the Sinai, they did not express their relationship to God in terms of a *covenant.*

According to the theology which emerged in Israel after the settling of Palestine (thirteenth to eleventh centuries B.C.), Abraham, living perhaps five hundred years earlier, had a special relationship to God. But when we separate the layers added to the tradition as it was handed down, we see that while Abraham was pictured as having encountered God in a special way, this relationship was not expressed in terms of a covenant. Scholars who feel they can recover the earliest stratum of the Abraham tradition do not think it portrayed Abraham making a covenant with God. Abraham was portrayed making alliances, but with other human beings. God enters in only as a witness. While it is true that both the Yahwist and the Priestly account have Abraham make a covenant with God, such was not the case in the earliest tradition.

In the oldest layers of the tradition the first covenant is the Mosaic covenant. In the Bible there are actually two separate traditions concerning this covenant. In one, in Chapter 24 of Exodus (the Yahwist is at work), the covenant is made by the people eating a meal in God's presence. Then, through Moses, God issues a decree regulating the life of the community like a king. In effect, God becomes their king.

In the other tradition (Exodus 20, the Elohist tradition), the covenant is presented more as a *contract,* the terms of which are the ten "words"—the ten commandments. Moses repeats these "words" to the people and they accept them. A sacrifice is made in front of twelve stelae (upright stones representing the twelve tribes) and the blood of the victims is poured on the altar and then sprinkled on the people to signify the bond.

In the remnant of the oral tradition hidden in these accounts this covenant is *bilateral*. Each side promises to do something conditional on the performance of the other party. Yahweh becomes their God with all that that implies—protection, guidance, "salvation" in a very secular sense, and from their side the people bind themselves to respect the religious and moral demands of Yahweh. He will be their God; they will be his people.

The consciousness of this covenantal relationship is the key to the Israelites' self-understanding. They saw themselves as the people of the covenant—and over the course of time they came to the belief that this God with whom they had made the covenant is the only God. Moreover, he has "created" the world and is acting in history through them. In other words, they eventually came to see themselves as the point of union between the one God and humanity, the Creator and his creation. The story of Israel in the Old Testament is a story of the struggle of God to keep Israel faithful to the covenant. When the monarchy was established (eleventh century B.C.), the covenant was institutionalized at Jerusalem in an organized worship around the temple and the royal court, and the priesthood was established. (It is probably out of this circle that the Yahwist tradition emerges.)

In the years following, during the decline of the monarchy, it was the *prophets* who kept calling Israel back to its covenant. It was at this time that a very important change in the nature of the covenant took place. Especially in Hosea, Jeremiah, and Ezekiel, there began to be hints that God was going to replace the old covenant (that was not being kept) with a new covenant based, not on Israel's response, but on God's own *hesed* (love) and *emet* (fidelity).

In effect, the prophets reoriented the theology of the covenant. It would no longer be a bilateral contract or alliance between two parties, each of which binds itself to certain duties only on condition of performance by the other party, but a covenant in which the superior party promises to be faithful to the relationship, despite what the other party does. God's relationship to Israel would be based solely on God's own *gratuitous, unconditional love* of Israel. In return, God seeks love from Israel, but his love for Israel would not depend on Israel's response. Yahweh will be faithful despite all—he will preserve Israel no matter what, even if only a *remnant* of faithful followers is left.

In the period following the prophetic reinterpretation of the covenant the Priestly tradition arose. It was heir to the covenant theology of the prophets. Thus the Priestly author never speaks of God "making" a covenant with Israel but of God "giving" it. Furthermore, as the Yahwist tradition had previously done, the Priestly tradition retells the Abraham story in such a way that Abraham's relationship with God is described in convenantal terms. However, there was no covenant before Abraham before the Priestly tradition arose. It remained for the Priestly writer to take the question further. Why this gracious act of God symbolized now by a covenant with Abraham? Is the covenant just for Israel? Why did God call Abraham? Already, even in the Yahwist tradition, the covenant with Abraham was made not for the sake of Abraham himself, nor even for Israel, but for the sake of the world (Gen 12). But what was the situation of the world and God before Abraham? To put it differently, *what is the status of men and women outside the Abrahamic covenant?* This is the Priestly author's question. His answer is embodied in genuine Israelite categories. To give expression to his view he used the central Israelite concept of covenant and described a covenantal relationship *before* Abraham, drawing on a widely known ancient Near Eastern story of a flood. In P's contribution to Genesis 1–11 a universalist covenant theology is elaborated in the story of Noah (Gen 6–9) in which the idea of a covenant given by God embraces *all* human beings because Noah is presented as a second Adam. The Priestly tradition uses the very same word, *berit*, that was used to describe Israel's relation with God, to describe *Noah* and Noah's descendants' relationship with God. The effect is to include *all men and women* in covenantal relationship with God, because "Noah," like Adam, is the father of *all* subsequent men and women. Furthermore, Noah is given the same commands as Adam. It is a fresh start, and the new start is under a covenant. In the Priestly view there is a covenant of God not merely with Israel but with creation itself.

Let us summarize. Genesis 1–11 was written after the *historical* tradition had been in existence for hundreds of years. It is inspired theological thinking on questions not explicitly answered by the historical tradition. Just as the Yahwist in an earlier age brought the tradition to bear on basic questions like the origin of woman, the relation of God and the world, and whether the world is fundamentally good, so the Priestly author asked the question of God's relationship to men and women not covered by the Mosaic covenant.

In the Priestly view, the activity of God in history is very broad. God has a covenantal relationship with *humanity,* symbolized by the covenant with "Noah." The Priestly author seems to see *history generally* as a history of salvation, in the sense that God's covenantal love extends to all men and women. But let us not overdo it; we cannot claim to have solved the question of the extra-biblical religions. We can merely say that the development in Catholic theological doctrine by which the extra-biblical religions are given a salvific value has some support in the Bible. The development is not just a seduction of Catholic doctrine by philosophy. A contrary view, that would confine God's covenantal love just to the biblical peoples, would itself not be biblical.

Furthermore, as regards the more fundamental question—what light does the Old Testament shed on God?—we have gained a valuable first glimpse.

DEVELOPING THE PROPHETIC INSIGHT

The Priestly tradition inherited from the prophets the insight that Yahweh is a God of unlimited compassion who stands always ready for Israel's conversion. It is a crass oversimplification to oppose the Old Testament as a "religion of law" to the New Testament as a "religion of grace." The God of the Old Testament is a God of love. The Priestly tradition boldly drew out the implications of the prophetic view, universalizing, "de-conditioning," God's love with respect to "the nations." What was the logic at work in his speculations? And could he have gone further?

One must not overlook the magnitude of the prophetic insight, which prefigures the message of Jesus. A relationship with God, of an individual or a people, is unlike any other. It partakes of the fundamental relationship of Being and beings, of that which is the origin of its own existence and that which is *given* existence. It is the relationship of creator and creature. It is not a relationship of equals but of that which is and that which need not be, but is by virtue of the free unmerited gift of existence.

Yet the prophets saw, without losing sight of the awesome unchallengeability of God (God's sovereignty, God's transcendence), that God is *hesed* and *emet*, that God has limitless compassion and fidelity. What God created would be what God willed it to be. What refused to respond would not be abandoned but relentlessly pursued in God's inexhaustible fidelity to that which he had brought into existence.

The genius of the Priestly tradition was to see that implied in this limitless love in the dimension of depth is a limitlessness in the dimension of extension. What the prophets saw in depth it saw in width.

What was at work here? A profound insight into the nature of love. To say God is *hesed* and *emet* is to say God is love.

THE HEBREW WORLDVIEW AND THE IMPLICATIONS OF THE LOGIC OF LOVE

It is often said that the Hebrews "were not a philosophical people." It is true if it means that they did not examine the world around them using only reason. It is not true if it means that they reached no conclusions about the ultimate nature of reality. They did not concern themselves with abstract questions like the Greeks. Nevertheless, we have seen that they were willing to draw out the implications of their historical experience to say what "must have" happened in the past and what would happen in the future. They were willing to draw startling speculative conclusions. It is significant that following the prophetic reinterpretation of the covenant there emerged in Israel not only (as we have seen) a more "universalistic" outlook but also an "eschatological" outlook. The importance of this latter notion cannot be exaggerated, for, as twentieth century New Testament scholarship insists, the preaching of Jesus of Nazareth concerning the reign of God has, as its fundamental context, the eschatological expectations of Israel.

"Eschatological" (Greek: *eschaton*, end or final point) means "definitive," "final." Unlike their contemporaries who tended to see history as an imitation of the cyclical patterns of nature (or who even failed to distinguish the two), the Hebrews saw history as moving toward a final, definitive state. This is called eschatological thinking. One cannot help but connect this line of thought with the unique and profound Hebrew understanding of reality. Better than the Greeks themselves, they understood "the infinite qualitative difference" between Being—that which is the source of its own existence—and beings—which derive their existence from Being. They saw clearly the non-identifiability of God and world. Thus they had a doctrine of *creation*. Whatever existed owed its existence to a sovereign, free act of God—and was radically distinct from God. The world was no accident; it was the work of God both in its beginning and in its continued course. They believed in the commitment of God to his creation, and in the unconditional nature of that commitment. Standing outside his creation, God was not subject to it but reigned over it. He brought it into existence and continued to influence it purposefully. It was an "open system" which could continually transcend itself through new participations in the very power which brought it into existence. Because in its own history Israel had experienced this power of God as benevolent, it began to anticipate that the world itself had direction, that God would eventually bring it to a good, final state. In other words, Yahweh God, who had created Israel in a series of contingent saving acts, would eventually act in a definitive way through Israel to bring his people and his world to a state of beatitude. What logic is at work here? Or is this sheer God-given prophetic insight? It is probably a combination of both. If logic is at work, it is not spelled out, but one suspects the mining of the central prophetic insight like a rich vein of ore by a relentless, if unreflective sense of God. Only at the end of the history of biblical revelation would an author baldly state "God is love" (1 Jn 4:8, 16), but the prophetic insight already contains that statement implicitly. The development of eschatological thinking stems at least in part from the recognition that Yahweh God's love, which is unconditional toward Israel and toward creation as a whole, in fact is *unconditional in its very nature,* and thus would seek to bestow on both Israel and creation unconditional, permanent, and unassailable beatitude. Unconditional love would do just that.

Could other manifestations of this love have been expected? If we acknowledge that the *expression of love* is not merely a consequence of love but a very constituent of its existence, one might expect that integral to God's eschatological saving act would be an expression of God's love for his people and his creation. Would there be not merely an act *on behalf of* creation but *a bestowal of God's very self?* Would the unconditional nature of God's love take an unconditional form? Would there be a union of creator and creation? Would there be incarnation?

And what about the life of God in and of itself? If one could take what God does (God loves) to be a reliable indication of what God is (God is love), could one ask about the very inner life of God? If God is love, what was God loving "before" he created? Did God need the world to escape from a self-enclosed isolation, a narcissistic love-life? Or was creation the result of an overflow of love, a superabundance of love being continually given and received *within* God, but now bestowed *outside* of God? If God is love, is God an exchange of love?

No doubt we have carried our speculations far beyond what was concretely possible for the people of Old Testament times. In a world of idolatry the notion of *incarnation* was highly suspect, especially in a religion which rightly stressed the transcendence of God. And in a world of polytheism the notion of *relations within God* could hardly find a sympathetic understanding in a religion which rightly stressed the unicity and simplicity of God. In fact, only the eschatological event could make such revelations possible.

Appendix 2:

CATHOLICISM AND MODERN SCRIPTURE STUDIES

Beginning with the condemnation of the priest Richard Simon in the seventeenth century (who agreed with the philosopher Spinoza that the traditional position that Moses had written the Pentateuch could not be true) until our own century, the application of "critical-historical method" to Scripture was resolutely resisted by Church leaders. Both the height of reaction to this approach and a surprising reversal and embrace of it have occurred in the twentieth century.

"Historical-critical method" is a catch-all phrase. It embraces a number of critical approaches to texts, all of which seek to determine the *Sitz-im-Leben,* the situation-in-life or the historical context in which a text had its origin. The goal of these procedures is to find what the originator, whether one or several individuals or a whole community, meant to say. These methods are "critical" because they do not begin from a traditional understanding of the meaning of a text but seek to determine the meaning the author(s) intended by employing such scientific tools as linguistics, archaeology and ethnology. An attempt is made to reconstruct the historical context in which the text originated, its sources (source criticism), the role of editors (redaction criticism), what really happened (historical criticism proper), the theology of the text (theological criticism), and so on. Central to the task is the identification of the literary form or *genre* of the text, for the meaning of a text is dependent on the type of literature it is.

It was only toward the end of the nineteenth century that a number of Catholic scholars began to ask the complex questions that constitute the historical-critical approach to Scripture. They had been encouraged to do so by the positive attitude toward scholarship of the learned Pope Leo XIII (1878–1903). But even Leo was worried by the direction things began to take and tried to slow it down in his encyclical *Providentissimus Deus* (1893). Under

Pius X (1903–1914), whose concerns were largely pastoral, the reaction against the method intensified, fueled by genuine excesses not warranted by the method itself. Although the decree of the Holy Office *Lamentabili* (1907) and the encyclical *Pascendi* (1907) dealt with more than the historical-critical approach to Scripture, they, together with subsequent decrees of the newly erected Pontifical Biblical Commission, established an official position with respect to Scripture that can only be called fundamentalist. Because of these decrees, an older generation of Catholics, including priests, find much in modern Catholic biblical studies suspicious. But the emergence of modern Catholic biblical studies is not the result of underground scholarship but of a change in attitude at the top.

In 1943 Pius XII issued what has been called the *Magna Carta* of Catholic biblical studies, the encyclical *Divino Afflante Spiritu.* It exhorted the biblical scholar to

try with the utmost care, and without neglecting any data provided by recent research, to establish the manner of expression and situation of life of the biblical writer, in what period he lived, what oral and written sources he used, and what literary mode he adopted. In this way (the biblical scholar) will more adequately recognize who the biblical writer was and what his intention might have been. No one should forget that the most

important rule for the exegete is to determine precisely what the writer intended to say.

Twenty years later, Vatican II, in its *Dogmatic Constitution on Divine Revelation (Dei Verbum),* adopted these recommendations, again stressing that those who try to explain Scripture must be aware of the literary genre. It accepted as self-evident that the Bible contains not only historical or prophetic texts but "poetic" writings, and that the divine truth can appear in any of the literary forms known to us.

The official recognition that the Bible contains not just one or two types of literature but a variety (including at least one, the *Gospel,* that is unique) makes Catholicism non-fundamentalist. When a community no longer is asking "Can a man really survive three days in the belly of a large fish?" but is asking "What is the literary genre of the Book of Jonah?" that community has made the switch.

The introduction of the historical-critical approach into Catholic biblical studies has influenced modern Catholicism more than any other purely intellectual factor. It played a key role in the emergence of the post-World War II continental theology that was so influential at Vatican II. It has contributed significantly to the general "turn to historical consciousness" among Catholics, that is, to sensitivity to the historical conditioning of all human expressions, including even inspired Scripture and the ecclesial expression of divine revelation that Catholics call "dogma." Perhaps its most important effect has been its contribution to a scholarly picture of the pre-Easter Jesus. Catholics tend toward the heresy called *docetism* (from the Greek *dokein*, to appear), that is, they tend to regard Jesus as merely *appearing* to be human. The richness of the picture of the "earthly" Jesus holds a treasure for a renewed spirituality that only now is being tapped.

The turn of Catholicism to a critical approach to Scripture is not without its difficulties, however. After all, would millions of people be fundamentalists if they did not think that was necessary to preserve their union with God? In Catholicism the vigorous resistance to this method was not simply because the critical approach to the Bible was initially employed by scholars hostile to traditional Christian faith. Even exegetes who are well within the mainstream of Christian belief, and who consider themselves loyal to the substance of Christian faith as it has always been known, reach conclusions with the method that startles traditional understanding of the faith. One of them, German New Testament scholar Joseph Blank, a Catholic, said recently that the official Roman

theology has gravely underestimated both the premises and the consequences of historical-critical methodology.

Perhaps the most disturbing of these conclusions so far concerns the formation of the four Gospels. Until 1964, the Catholic Church resisted the claim of some Protestant scholars, who employed a technique of the historical-critical method called "form criticism," that the Gospels show that the accounts of Jesus' actions and words were transmitted by word-of-mouth in the primitive Christian community. This was a worrisome proposal, not only because it conflicted with the traditional position that the Gospels were based on accounts of eyewitnesses or companions of eyewitnesses, but because it meant Gospel materials were transmitted by a method that seems notoriously unreliable, at least to moderns. In 1964, in a document entitled *Sancta Mater Ecclesia*, or, as it is more commonly known, "Instruction on the Historical Truth of the Gospels," the Pontifical Biblical Commission substantially adopted this view of the formation of the Gospels, and the position was incorporated a year later in the Apostolic Constitution *Dei Verbum* of Vatican II. The adoption of this position is significant because it acknowledges that in the formation of the Gospel traditions the community played not merely a preservative but a creative role. The Gospels become not merely a record of what Jesus said and did but an interpretation of the *meaning* of what he said and did. The Gospels are not just history but a fascinating combination of history and theology. Two questions which we moderns have learned to distinguish—"What happened?" and "What is the significance of what happened?"—are answered as one question in the Gospels. The biblical scholar tries to distinguish the two answers.

Where does the introduction of historical-critical method into Catholicism leave the average Catholic? Envying the fundamentalist? In some cases it means not only envying but joining, for fundamentalist Christian communities offer the same sort of authoritarian, black-and-white positions (and demand strict adherence to them) that was a principal attraction of pre-Vatican II Catholicism.

But a fundamentalist is in a very vulnerable position. Two experiences threaten a fundamentalist. (1) Talking to another fundamentalist—for to read is necessarily to interpret and to interpret is to open up the possibility of disagreement. And fundamentalists do disagree. The meaning of Scripture is not immediately obvious and unproblematic. (2) Reading the Bible with an eye to its complexity. A close

reading reveals variations in the accounts of the same events. The authors of the various books of the Bible did not submit their manuscripts to a central committee for harmonization. There are divergences in fact, theology and norms. And so, while I have no doubt that proximity to God has little to do with theological sophistication, fundamentalism seems to be a mistaken way of being a Christian, for it tends to want to replace faith with a forced certitude, making of the Bible a history book rather than a library of faith documents.

A review of the present situation in theology should shed some light on the situation of the average Catholic today, confronted by the historical-critical approach to Scripture, for theology itself is struggling with our question. Misgivings about the historical-critical method from within the theological community itself come from two directions. First, there are those who wish to employ other methods to determine the meaning of a text; second, there are those who find the historical-critical method "imperialistic," at least when it presumes to present itself as a *fully theological* method.

Maybe because of its success, the historical-critical approach to Scripture today has engendered some rivals. Oversimplifying dramatically (for combinations of methods are possible) one can speak of three types of methods in Scripture study: (1) those which regard a text as still belonging to its *author,* (2) those which regard a text as essentially *independent* of its author, and (3) those which regard the text as belonging to the *reader.* The historical-critical method is itself a prime example of the first approach. Its goal is to explore the mind of the author through the text he has produced by reconstructing the historical situation of the author.

Recently this approach has come under attack from *literary criticism,* by interpreters using *psychoanalytic* tools, by *Marxist* criticism and by the theory of interpretation known as *structuralism.* As diverse as all these approaches are, they agree in their tendency to see the meaning of a text as something independent of the author. The author is merely someone through whom structures—psychological, artistic, linguistic, even economic—have spoken. The text is seen to have a life of its own, sometimes (in the case of psychoanalytic and Marxist interpretation) even a meaning hidden from its author and determined by unconscious factors.

The most promising of the new approaches appears to be genuine *literary criticism,* which focuses on the text as we have it, rather than how it came to be. The literary critic charges that the historical critic tells us what came *before* the text and *outside* the text but neglects the one thing we are certain of—the text *itself.*

True literary criticism of the Bible is only now making its way into theology. It maintains that a text is a self-contained reality, and when the author writes, he or she creates something that has a life of its own. Literary criticism draws the contrast between the written and the spoken word. In speaking there is an immediate exchange between two or more persons present to one another. In writing there is author, text, and reader. It is possible that the text does not say what the author intended, but he or she cannot "take it back," control it or amend it, as a speaker can. It has assumed its own existence.

Yet just as literary criticism sees historical criticism's letting the author "hold onto" the text as a flaw, so the third school, the "reader response" approach, believes that literary criticism must take into greater account the subjectivity of the reader. This third approach sees a written text like a painting or a piece of music. While the "reader-response" school acknowledges that the reader cannot see just anything in the text, and that the text "permits" certain meanings and "resists" others, it maintains that the text, especially a religious one, is made truly significant by what the reader brings to it, by how the reader *lets* the text be revelatory for him or her.

Besides the challenge to the historical-critical method from other methods of interpretation, there is a challenge from within theology. Is the historical-critical method *adequate* as a fully *theological* approach? For many theologians, even many who use it, there is a major flaw in the way the method is used by some of its practitioners in that it fails to come to grips with the real issue it is trying to address—the type of literature the Bible is. The charge is: Biblical texts are the product of faith, and written from faith for faith. How, then, is it possible to comprehend these texts using a purely rational, scientific method?

The answer is, of course, that it is not possible. This has come to be widely admitted by biblical scholars who know very well that the Bible is the expression of believing individuals living in believing communities. It is precisely the historical-critical method that has established this. But by that very fact it has established its own limits. For that which is an expression of faith can only truly be understood by one who shares that faith. Or, as John H. Wright put it:

If the Bible is regarded as the faith expression of a community, it is not enough to use the tools of historical-critical research in order to use the Bible in theology; for the most basic view of theology is that it is "faith seeking understanding." Hence new

scientific methods for researching the text of Scripture will not by themselves determine how Scripture is to function in a discipline whose primary concern is to seek understanding of faith. It is clear that the historical-critical method is indispensably necessary, but it is not sufficient (*Theological Studies*, 43/4 [December 1982], p. 653).

Whenever a believer opens the Bible he or she is, willy-nilly, a theologian. His or her faith is seeking understanding of the deepest, most existential kind. It is clear, then, that whatever methods one may employ, none can finally dispense with the method used by those who have understood Scripture best through the ages. It is to read Scripture as a member of the community which produced Scripture. It is to take Scripture on its own terms, as a message of faith, written by believers for believers, written not to present mere information but to encourage, to strengthen, to move. It is to let the Bible, written out of faith experience, create faith experience in the reader. But does not Scripture communicate a record of events? The contemporary biblical scholar answers with an emphatic, "Yes, but after its own fashion." The question about events, fact, the question "What happened?", was neither the sole nor even the primary question that concerned the biblical writers. They wrote out of an experience of God acting in events, and they wanted to share that experience and make its *significance* known in a way that would move the human heart. Only by the same fundamental stance as the original community—a faith stance—can we derive the same meaning from Scripture.

If the believer, like the farmer who thinks he must know some meteorology and the business man who must know some economics, feels the need to be more sophisticated about his faith, "critical" approaches may become necessary. They can enrich but cannot replace the approach called faith.

One final point. The historical-critical approach to Scripture shows, if anything, that the Bible had its origin not merely in faith but in a faith community. It was not the work of isolated, solitary individuals. "Inspiration" in the case of the Bible must be understood as the continuing presence of the Spirit *in a community*. The writing of Scripture is a *part of* the effect of that continuing presence. The New Testament is considered definitive by Christians because it is *part of* the effect of the eschatological (definitive) gift of the Spirit. Therefore to separate the interpretation of Scripture from the historic understanding of the eschatological community that produced it is a fundamental mistake. Such an oversight ignores the essentially communitarian nature of God's action in history. For the same reason, when the eschatological community fails to nourish itself with this definitive expression of its faith, it is on its way to communal inauthenticity.

Section II:
The God of Jesus

Chapter V

THE SOURCES OF OUR KNOWLEDGE OF JESUS OF NAZARETH

INTRODUCTION

There are many ways to describe the significance of Jesus for Christians. One could say that the covenants made through Noah, Abraham, Moses and David reached their eschatological fulfilment in Jesus. Or one could take the late Old Testament specification of Israel's eschatological hopes, the hope for a definitive mediator, the *messiah*, the "anointed" one, and capture the centrality of Jesus by designating him the Christ (Greek: *christos*, anointed). Finally, one could take the formulation out of purely Old Testament possibilities and acknowledge in Jesus the definitive self-revelation of God, Jesus as God's Son, as the very expression in time of the Father's timeless self-expression.

Common to all these formulations is the point that to know Jesus is the way to know God. The fundamental Christian conviction is that God's definitive self-revelation occurred in Jesus, in his teachings, and in his history.

This raises a question that stands at the forefront of theology today. If Christianity's answer to the most fundamental question of human existence, the God question, is an historical person, then historical knowledge plays a crucial role in Christianity. Christianity is not a philosophy. It is not a purely rational analysis of the human situation. It is a religion. It claims to be *given*, to be revealed, not discovered. Moreover, Christianity claims to be an "historical religion." It is rooted in concrete events and persons. It claims that "something happened." It is not an abstract doctrine but an eminently particular statement: "This man (Jesus) is the point of union between God and creation." The conclusion must be: when Christianity dispenses with events, with history, it loses its deepest identity.

But this is precisely where the problem of modern Christian faith and theology becomes most perplexing. Given that the first Christians were Jews, they were undoubtedly attuned to the crucial importance of *events* as the *locus* of revelation. They would be concerned with *what happened*. By the same token, as Jews, they would not be content to merely pass on a bare "objective" account of what happened. They would not leave us a "documentary account," that is, an attempt to simply *describe* events. They would, as was their tradition, include in their account their *interpretation of* the events. Furthermore, their belief that these events were of utmost significance for the very salvation of the world would impel them to *proclaim* them. We must not lose sight of this. From the very beginning the Christian message was a proclamation of the "good news" (Old English: god-spel, Gospel) of salvation. It was never a neutral "objective" historical report but always a *faith proclamation* of events and their significance. When the oral *"good news"* found written form, the new literary genre called a Gospel, it retained this fundamental characteristic of being proclamation. This fact leads us to what is the most difficult problem of modern theology: If God's self-revelation, the answer to the God question, takes place in history, and specifically in the history of Jesus of Nazareth, knowledge of Jesus' history is crucial. But how are we to know that history with sources which are proclamations of *faith* in Jesus? This question bedeviled nineteenth century Protestantism and continues to be a major issue in that branch of Christianity as we approach the twenty-first century. In nineteenth century Catholicism the question was suppressed, but in the last thirty years it has become a question that refuses to be ignored. What is the difficulty? The problem is that apart from the Gospels we have no significant sources for knowledge of Jesus. But the Gospels themselves are faith proclamations, and thus they were not written with the modern question in mind. The Gospels are really preaching. They were written, but they take their most fundamental character from their origins in the oral tradition of the early Church. They are faith speaking to faith. No one would expect a preacher to merely recount bare historical detail. What happened is important, but what happened is not the most important concern of a sermon. What preoccupies the preacher is the *significance for salvation* of what happened.

Because of this distinctive character of the Gospels, to treat them as purely historical documents is a mistake. This is not to say they misrepresent the history of Jesus of Nazareth. If asked that question—"Do the Gospels misrepresent the history of Jesus?"—all but the most radical critics (who invariably begin with the presupposition that the history of Jesus *cannot* be as the Gospels present it) would reply with a firm "no." On the other hand, to assume that the Gospels are always recounting pure history is not warranted either. Whether the question being answered at any given point in the Gospels is "What happened?" or the more important one, at least for the Gospel writers, "What is the *significance* of what happened?", it must be attended to. And it is here that scholars differ. What is record of Jesus and what is witness to him? What is narration of his history, and what is testimony of the Church's faith in his significance?

THE LIMITATIONS OF HISTORICAL KNOWLEDGE

So we are about to embark on historical research. But while historical knowledge is necessary, it is not sufficient for Christian faith. It is necessary because Christianity claims to be based in historical events. It is not merely that we need to verify those events in order to "have a reason for the faith that is in us." It is that God is revealed in those events. Full, accurate knowledge of the history of Jesus puts one in contact with a privileged source of the revelation of God.

But Christian faith is not faith in events of the past, in Jesus as he was. It is faith in Jesus as he is; it is faith in the risen Christ, the one who is present because he now transcends historical limitations. Thus we seek to know the history of Jesus better, not because Jesus as he was is the object of our faith but because it enables us to know better the risen Christ who is our contemporary.

Our historical research is not an end in itself, then. Neither does it begin from a disinterested point of view. Like everyone else, believer or unbeliever, I have a pre-understanding of Jesus. Mine is guided by the faith I adhere to. In some cases this faith may conceal from me what another researcher will see, and will be called to account by that research. On the other hand, it may reveal something that other researchers will miss, contributing to historical knowledge. By a dialogue between my faith and historical research, including the opinions of other researchers, my faith is fleshed out by what I find. My experience is that historical research has deepened my understanding of Jesus and thus helped me to understand better the risen Christ in whom I believe and to face what he calls me to. From the other side I have found that my faith has not misled me in historical research but shown me where to look and what to look for.

A corollary of the method we will pursue in the next few chapters is that we will be approaching the Gospels in a way different than their authors intended. The intention of the Gospel writers was not to write a history of Jesus. They were believers writing for believers. They wished to portray the object of faith—the risen Christ. They did this by narrating what the traditions of their several communities said about his earthly life. That was a means to an end. The end was not mere factual knowledge of Jesus' history but better knowledge of the risen Christ whom they experienced in their midst through the Holy Spirit.

The Gospels, thus, are sacramental. They are means by which the risen Christ is present to the believer. They are like the eucharistic celebration (indeed they are part of it), or the person in need—for the believer they mediate the presence of the risen Christ. To treat the Gospels as we will in the next few chapters as sources for historical knowledge may be useful for the theologian, and necessary for the post-Enlightenment person, but it can only be a stage. We seek knowledge of Jesus as he was before his death so that we may better know him as the Risen One in our midst.

Perhaps relating a personal experience will help. Although a Roman Catholic, I once had an experience more associated with the Orthodox tradition. I entered the twelfth century Norman-Gothic cathedral in Monreale, Sicily. The inside of that building is covered from floor to ceiling by an extraordinary profusion of mosaic scenes from the Old and New Testaments, but my eyes were drawn irresistibly to the far end of the church, to the gigantic mosaic icon of the face of Jesus in glory. I experienced in that moment why that icon especially is considered sacred in the Orthodox tradition, for it mediated to me the presence of the risen Christ. It did for me in that moment what the eucharistic celebration normally does—not merely recall the earthly Jesus but make the risen Christ present.

The Gospels were intended to do the same thing. In the course of my visit to the cathedral I examined the icon from a closer distance and grew in appreciation of it. I looked at it from different angles, saw it in different lights, and saw its relation to other icons around it. But at the end of my visit I returned to the door by which I had entered and now, knowing more, let it again be what it was intended to be, not a piece of art but an icon, a symbol which possesses a unique power to make Christ present to the eyes of faith. While historical research on the Gospels is enriching and perhaps even necessary because of recent religious history, the Gospels also must be allowed to again become what they were intended to be— privileged mediators of the presence of Jesus as he is. (For a sketch of the long journey of scholarship to the current view of the literary *genre* called "Gospel" see Appendix 3, "The Search for the Historical Jesus—Past and Present.")

Appendix 3:

THE SEARCH FOR THE HISTORICAL JESUS—
PAST AND PRESENT
AN INTRODUCTORY SKETCH

THE BACKGROUND—
THE ENLIGHTENMENT

Historical research into the life of Jesus is one of the numerous byproducts of the epochal movement of the western spirit known as the Enlightenment. In the seventeenth century the success of the new, more critical, scientific method employed by Galileo, Copernicus, Kepler and others generated a confidence in human reason that soon pervaded all areas of scholarship. The desire for *critically generated* knowledge rather than knowledge based on *received opinion* became widespread. This critical spirit was the heart of the Enlightenment, the motto of which was Kant's famous injunction, *aude sapere*, "dare to know."

Since the Renaissance, scholars had practiced literary criticism on classical texts. Already questions were being asked about the accuracy of manuscripts (textual criticism), sources of material (source criticism), and the historical reliability of a text (historical criticism). The first scholar to examine the Bible in this way, and thus question the received opinion that had reigned in Christianity for more than a thousand years, was Richard Simon, a seventeenth century French Oratorian priest. He was disciplined for his temerity. In Protestantism, the pioneer was J.D. Michaelis (1717–1791), who sought to understand the New Testament without dogmatic presuppositions. Against the reigning Protestant orthodoxy of the time, which adhered to what we would call the theory of verbal inspiration (and its corollary, the complete inerrancy of Scripture), Michaelis was prepared to find contradictions in Scripture. But neither Catholicism nor Protestantism demonstrated a desire to challenge the fundamental Christian story as portrayed in the Gospels.

That was soon to come, however, from a quarter basically unsympathetic to traditional Christian faith. When reason is exalted as the *sole* norm of truth, that is, when the Enlightenment becomes a *rationalism,* there is little room for Christianity in the traditional sense. Already Locke and Spinoza had exhibited a desire to empty Christianity of that which reason cannot account for, the miraculous and the supernatural, and to erect a religion "within the limits of reason alone." If this was to be "Christian," it would be traditional Christian faith radically reinterpreted, desupernaturalized, or, as a later age would say, demythologized. English *Deism* attempted this. It sought a God found in the inexorable "laws" of nature so lately revealed by Newton and others. The God of Deism stands behind nature and is the designer of its immanent "watch-like" consistency. The notion of any intervention by God into such a rational, self-enclosed, and self-perpetuating system was self-contradictory. Hence there could be no "miracles," and certainly no bodily resurrection. Fundamental Christian beliefs were not only not based on fact; they were, in principle, impossible. Revelation itself, conceived as an intervention of God into history, was not only unnecessary, it was impossible, because it did not respect the inherent, self-contained rationality of the world.

God was revealed only in "nature." As Thomas Jefferson (himself a Deist) would say in the American Constitution, the ground of all else in human life is not the God of Abraham, Isaac and Jacob, but "nature and nature's God." God's possibilities were limited to what "nature" could reveal of the deity to inquiring human intelligence which was to conduct its search solely on the basis of its own inwardly generated norms.

It was not only some of the most brilliant minds in England and the colonies in the eighteenth century that were affected by the Enlightenment. In France the Revolution was an attempt to institutionalize Enlightenment values. But it was in the *German* Enlightenment that the seeds of the *biblical* revolution were being sown. With the ground prepared by Michaelis and others, and under the influence of Deism, radical criticism of the fundamental beliefs of Christianity as enshrined in the Gospel story of Jesus of Nazareth were soon to follow.

REIMARUS

Serious historical inquiry into Jesus Christ has a very definite starting point and very definite presuppositions—those of Deism. Between 1774 and 1778, the philosopher Lessing published a series of essays from a work by the recently deceased (1768) Hamburg language professor, Herman Samuel Reimarus. These were the famous *Wolfenbüttel Fragments.* The original title of the complete work—*Apology or Defense for Reasonable Worshipers of God*—is more enlightening. A knowledge of Reimarus' presuppositions is important for understanding the content of his essays. He accepted the principles of English Deism. He had already published a work entitled *On the Distinctive Truths of Natural Religion.* From his point of view the Gospels could not be fact, and so he looked for the Jesus behind the Gospels, the Jesus who could be recovered by historical method but had been obscured by traditional supernaturalistic Christian faith. In the essay entitled "On the Aim of Jesus and of the Disciples" Reimarus located the source of the disparity between "The Jesus of History" and "The Christ of Faith." He argued that traditional Christianity was grounded in deliberate fraud. The Jesus of history was, in fact, not a religious messiah, as the Gospels present him, but a messiah within the standard Jewish expectation of the time, a political liberator (a "Davidic Messiah") who sought to cast off the Roman yoke and restore the Davidic monarchy and Jewish independence. Jesus' disciples understood him on these terms. His death was the unexpected frustration of their dreams. "Unwilling to return to their former means of employment," according to Reimarus, they contrived to invent the Christ of faith, Jesus as Lord and Savior, a religious messiah. The "systema" of Jesus gave way to the "systema" of his disciples, who must be regarded as the real founders of Christianity. Their fraud was successful because they contrived to steal Jesus' corpse and invent the story of the resurrection.

Clearly, the climate in which this historical inquiry into Jesus of Nazareth began set conditions for what could be found. Within rationalist circles it was only a dozen years before the very existence of Jesus was being questioned. Apparently the first scholar to question whether Jesus actually existed was C.F. Dupuis (in 1791). The thesis was vigorously asserted in the nineteenth century by Bruno Bauer. The origin of "Jesus" in a spontaneous, myth-making process was asserted by A. Drews and in the early twentieth century in spontaneous sociologically grounded "projections" by A. Kalthoff and K. Kautsky. The general thesis of the non-existence of Jesus is not without its proponents today. For P. Alfani, "Jesus" is a "projection" originating in a social movement of slaves and poor on their way to liberation and in the process of developing a consciousness of their alienation (*Origines sociales du Christianisme,* Paris, Publ. del'Union Rationaliste, 1959).

The theory of the non-existence of Jesus, however, has never been a serious question in mainstream scholarship. The attitude of Rudolf Bultmann, himself a radical critic, would be typical: "The doubt as to whether Jesus really existed is unfounded and not worth refutation. No sane person can doubt that Jesus stands as founder behind the historical movement whose first distinct stage is represented by the oldest Palestinian community" (*Jesus and the Word,* p. 13). As Wolfgang Trilling has pointed out, if a contemporary of Napoleon (R. Whately) could attempt to prove that Napoleon himself did not exist, there will always be attempts to prove Jesus did not exist. It does not mean such attempts should be or are taken seriously.

Nevertheless, the fundamental thesis of Reimarus that there is a disparity between the Jesus of history and the Christ of faith was taken very seriously, first by liberal Protestantism and then by mainstream Protestant and Catholic scholars.

LIBERAL PROTESTANTISM

The presuppositions of any inquiry are crucial. Liberal Protestantism was, by design, an attempt to reconcile traditional Christianity with the Enlightenment. On its left edge liberal Protestantism's presuppositions were virtually indistinguishable from those of the Deists. But most liberal Protestants were genuinely concerned, unlike the Deists, to preserve the link between the Jesus of history and the Christ of faith. Nevertheless, it was clear from the beginning that the traditional Christ of faith would have to yield to the Jesus discovered by historical research. Albert Schweitzer called the search for the historical Jesus the "greatest achievement of German theology" and "one of the most significant events in the whole mental and spiritual life of humanity" (*The Quest of the Historical Jesus,* p. 399). Yet he concluded that the pursuit was flawed from the beginning and doomed to fail. From the advantage of hindsight, both judgments are valid. In the end, the picture of Jesus that liberal Protestantism elaborated was a projection of its presuppositions about what he *could* and *should* be. Nevertheless, the century of struggle with the *nature of the sources of our knowledge about Jesus* remains a monumental contribution of what is now called "The Old Quest."

The two concerns of liberal Protestant research, to elaborate a valid historical picture of Jesus and determine the nature of the sources for such a picture, are so inseparably intertwined that their stories must be told together. Interestingly, Friedrich Schleiermacher himself, universally considered the father of liberal Protestantism, anticipated the answers to both questions that liberal Protestantism would arrive at almost a century later. Even though Schleiermacher himself elaborated a sketch of Jesus' life on the basis of the Gospel of John, his Christology lectures of 1819 stated that (1) *no life* of Jesus was possible because (2) the Gospel materials circulated in the *oral* form of *memorabilia*. As we will see, the Quest would reach the same conclusions at the beginning of the twentieth century and abandon its project. As we will also see, *contemporary* biblical critics largely accept Schleiermacher's two points. However, they do not accept that these are insuperable obstacles to attaining significant historical knowledge about Jesus.

STRAUSS

In 1835–1836, David Friedrich Strauss published a two-volume *Life of Jesus* which was an important milestone for a number of reasons. Before Reimarus, theologians had taken a largely theological approach to Jesus. After Reimarus, some theologians embarked on a purely historical approach. By introducing the category of "myth," Strauss showed how (at least to some) the theological and historical approaches could be combined. He believed that there was an historical core to the Gospel accounts, but the Gospels primarily respond to the human need to *feel*. They present religious ideas in the form of story (= myth) on the basis of a minimal historical core, and that is their major role. To locate the historical core, Strauss felt a choice had to be made between the Synoptic accounts and that of John. Here he demonstrates a primitive form of a position widely held today, namely, that (1) the Gospels speak not primarily to historical concerns, but to faith, but that (2) as historical sources the Synoptics are preferable to John. Before Strauss, Schleiermacher's opinion that John was a superior historical source had had considerable support.

THE ORDER OF THE SOURCES

While Strauss' contribution concerned the *nature* of the sources, it was Karl Lachmann's question that came to occupy scholars in the mid-nineteenth century—what is the *order* of the sources? Until Lachmann, the conventional wisdom had held that Mark was an abridgement of Matthew and Luke (the Griesbach thesis). Lachmann attacked this, maintaining that Mark was a source for Matthew and Luke. Furthermore, Lachmann theorized that a collection of the sayings of Jesus (a *logia* source) played some role in the composition of the Synoptics. Just how all this fit together was most cogently proposed in 1863 in *The Synoptic Gospels* by H.J. Holtzmann. This was a primitive form of the "two source" solution to "The Synoptic Problem" (the "Synoptic Problem" is, simply, how Matthew, Mark, and Luke are related). Holtzmann theorized that there was a lost document ("A") which Mark used in constructing the *order* of his Gospel. Matthew and Luke also knew "A" plus a *logia* or sayings source (designated at this point by the Greek letter *lambda*). Twenty years later Holtzmann dispensed with "A" and attributed to Mark itself the role as the original Gospel. This is substantially the solution to the Synoptic Problem followed by most contemporary scholars, namely that Matthew and Luke are based on Mark and a collection of the sayings of Jesus. Such a view, of course, clashed radically with the traditional view that Matthew and Luke were separate accounts written by eyewitnesses or companions of eyewitnesses.

THE LIBERAL PROTESTANT "LIVES" OF JESUS

"Lives of Jesus" were written during the nineteenth century by liberal Protestants based on the priority of the Synoptics over John, especially by authors who wished to dispense with the supernatural. As Schweitzer later showed, the pictures of Jesus portrayed by these "Lives" are really mirror images of the various nineteenth century enthusiasms. There was a remarkable naiveté among these scholars about the existence and power of their own presuppositions. One should also observe that during this period the number of sources is gradually diminishing. The nineteenth century researchers quickly realized that the non-Christian sources were of little help, as were the epistles, concentrating as they did on the Resurrected Christ, the life of the primitive Christian community, and the parousia. With the establishment of the priority of the Synoptics over John and then Holtzmann's establishment of the dependence of Matthew and Luke on Mark and a sayings source (which could only be conjecturally reconstructed and was not actually possessed) the sources for a life of Jesus, in the final quarter of the nineteenth century, had dwindled to one—the Gospel of Mark. Furthermore, Strauss' view that a Gospel is minimally concerned with history and maximally concerned with theology had been forgotten.

Accordingly, on the basis of Mark, liberal Protestantism confidently asserted that it would now tell us who Jesus really was.

In 1882 Volkmar portrayed Jesus, on the basis of Mark, as someone who did not claim to be Messiah but saw himself only as a religious reformer. But the most famous and characteristic of the late liberal Protestant portraits of Jesus was that of Adolph von Harnack, found in his famous *What Is Christianity?* (1900). For Harnack, Jesus was an enlightened ethical teacher whose basic tenets were the Fatherhood of God, the Brotherhood of Man, the Love Commandment, and the Infinite Value of the Human Soul. The individualism and dehistoricization of Jesus in Harnack's picture is striking:

Anyone who wants to know what the kingdom of God and the coming of the kingdom means in Jesus' preaching, must read and meditate on the parables. There he will learn what the kingdom is all about. The kingdom of God comes by coming to *individuals,* making entrance into their *souls,* and being grasped by them. The kingdom of God is indeed God's *rule*—but it is the rule of a holy God in individual hearts. *It is God himself in his power.* Everything externally dramatic, all public historical meaning vanish here; all external hope for the future fades also. Take any parable you wish—the sower, the pearl, the treasure in the field. In each case, the word of God, God himself is the kingdom. It is not a matter of angels and devils, nor of principalities and powers but of God and the soul, of the soul and its God (*What is Christianity?* German ed., p. 43).

For Harnack, Jesus is primarily one who enlightens me about my timeless standing before God as his creature. In Harnack, as generally in liberal Protestantism, Jesus was "nothing but" a teacher and model of authentic humanity as the nineteenth century conceived it.

THE FAILURE OF THE OLD QUEST

As Harnack lectured to packed halls in Berlin, the tide was already turning. In 1892, in his book *The So-Called Historical Jesus and the Historic Biblical Christ,* Martin Kähler had already challenged the theological legitimacy of the Quest. He pointed out that even liberal Protestantism was not really concerned with Jesus as a figure of the past, certainly not in a Jesus reconstructed by historical method, but in the *present* Christ, the Christ whose cause is contemporary to us. For Kähler the real Christ was the preached Christ, not a figure out of the past. He was merely the first to acknowledge that Christianity cannot be based on historical scholarship. Typically, it was Albert Schweitzer who would express this point for a wider audience:

Jesus means something to our world because a mighty spiritual force streams forth from him and flows through our being also. This fact can neither be shaken nor confirmed by any historical discovery. It is the solid foundation of Christianity (*The Quest*, p. 399).

In that same year of 1892, Johannes Weiss published *Jesus' Proclamation of the Kingdom of God*. Against the liberal Protestant picture of Jesus as a religious teacher of a timeless ethical message, Weiss asserted that Jesus was conditioned by the late Jewish "apocalyptic" expectations and that this was the framework of his preaching of the kingdom of God. This was the beginning of the rediscovery of the *eschatological* nature of Jesus' preaching, that is, that in some sense the kingdom of God for Jesus was not a metaphor for the timeless situation of human beings as creatures before their creator, but an *event*, an irruption of God into history in a *definitive saving event*. Again, it was Schweitzer, who with Weiss, stressed the "thoroughgoing eschatology" of Jesus, who expressed the startlingly different Jesus (from that of Harnack) that this development would eventually yield:

The Jesus of Nazareth (of liberal theology) never had any existence. He is a figure designed by rationalism, endowed with life by liberalism, and clothed by modern theology in an historical garb.

Whatever the ultimate solution may be, the historical Jesus of whom the criticism of the future . . . will draw the portrait . . . will not be a Jesus Christ to whom the religion of the present can ascribe, according to its long-cherished custom, its own thoughts and ideas, as it did with the Jesus of its own making. Nor will He be a figure which can be made by a popular historical treatment so sympathetic and universally intelligible to the multitude. The historical Jesus will be to our time a stranger and an enigma (*ibid.*, pp. 398–399).

The original title of Schweitzer's *Quest* was *From Reimarus to Wrede* (1906). The title indicates that, in Schweitzer's judgment, what began with Reimarus ended with W. Wrede's *The Messianic Secret in the Gospel of Mark* (1901). The thrust of Wrede's argument was that while the liberal "Lives" were based on Mark, there was no essential difference between Mark and any other Gospel, for example John, as an historical source. Wrede stressed that Mark was not a primitive, unreflective record of Jesus' actions and sayings, but a genuinely *theological* work which centered on a primitive Christian theme concerning Jesus as Messiah and used a device to explain why he was not recognized— namely, that he hid the fact of his messiahship. Wrede's point was that a major theme in the Gospel did not derive from Jesus but from the early community, that already the materials of the Gospel were being reworked to fit a theological viewpoint. A Gospel was not fundamentally an historical record, but a *faith proclamation*.

In his book, Schweitzer assembled the entire picture: that the tortured Quest consistently yielded pictures of Jesus that mirrored the presuppositions of the researchers; that the one clear thing about Jesus—the eschatological character of his preaching—had been overlooked and that it made any modernizing of Jesus impossible in principle; that genuine Christianity looks not to a Jesus reconstructed by historical criticism but to the Risen Christ in some form; and that the Gospels were not documentary historical sources. As the twentieth century opened, there was a consensus among theologians who used a critical approach to Scripture that Christian faith, if it was to exist at all, would have to be as Schweitzer described it:

... it is not Jesus as historically known, but Jesus as spiritually risen within men, who is significant for our time and can help it. Not the historical Jesus, but the spirit which goes forth from Him and in the spirits of men strives for new influence and rule, is that which overcomes the world (*Quest*, p. 401).

It would be fifty years before a representative of critical theology would ask whether Schweitzer's Christ was not as much in danger of being tailored to people's specifications as the historical Jesus of nineteenth century liberal theology.

RUDOLF BULTMANN

During those fifty years, one figure dominated radical New Testament scholarship—Rudolf Bultmann (d. 1976). The young Bultmann was a student of Weiss and thoroughly absorbed the developments at the turn of the century. To them he added the view (as old as Strauss but learned by Bultmann from the "History of Religions" School, for example, W. Bousset's *Kyrios Christos*, 1913) that the Gospels are "myth."

Fundamental to Bultmann's scholarship and theology is the postulating of a chasm between the mentality of the first century and the contemporary mind, the difference between a "mythical" and a "scientific" worldview. In a mythical worldview, what is not of this world is represented as though it were of this world and vice versa. God's transcendence is expressed in terms of spatial remoteness, and the world is seen as interpenetrated by the divine and the supernatural. In contrast, according to Bultmann, the modern (scientifically influenced) mind adheres to the principle of immanence; the reason for phenomena are sought within the phenomena themselves, not outside them. According to Bultmann, first century Palestinian Jews had a mythical view of the universe. It was a three-tiered structure, the parts of which communicated with one another, and the middle tier, the world, was more controlled by the other two than by what happened on its own level.

According to Bultmann, corresponding to this mythical worldview is a mythical representation of the saving *event* that forms the heart of the New Testament message: the sending down to earth of the pre-existent Son of God who effects the expiation of sins by his death, thus defeating the infernal powers, rises from the dead, and is raised to heaven at the right hand of God. This is a mythical presentation of a valid and indeed saving truth, but its mythical trappings are unbelievable for moderns. For it to be what it truly can be, saving truth, it must be re-presented for moderns in a "demythologized" form. For Bultmann, demythologization is a positive task. What Jesus did for his contemporaries with the myth of the kingdom of God, what Paul did with the myth of justification, and the Johannine school did with the myth of "eternal life," modern preaching, through demythologization and the application of existentialist categories (existential interpretation), must do for its contemporaries. It must reveal to men and women the basic teaching of Jesus, namely, of their radical dependence on God, and God's offer of forgiveness.

This is why Bultmann's theology is called *kerygmatic* (*kerygma* = primitive Christian preaching). It conceives of God as speaking, and revealing in the *kerygma,* in proclamation. *This* is the event of salvation. Preaching *itself* is the event of salvation, for it is there that one encounters the offer of salvation. What is the content of this preaching? Since Jesus belongs to the pre-history of the salvation-event (he is merely "the presupposition" of Christianity and properly speaking belongs to the history of Judaism), preaching is not really about him. The centrality of Jesus for faith in the New Testament is part of the myth. This is merely the spatialization or temporalization of God's transcendent action in an historical event. Such a presentation of God's action was acceptable to the first century mind. Furthermore, it has its roots in Jesus' own preaching about the coming of the kingdom of God. There was a functional equivalence of the message *of* Jesus about the kingdom and the message *about* Jesus as the Christ in the *kerygma.* But both presentations (of a functionally common truth) are mythical. The task of contemporary Christianity is hermeneutics—the positive presentation of the message of salvation in a way appropriate to the modern mentality. In the end one must say that Bultmann's drive is to translate *the understanding of human existence* present in the Gospels in a mythological form into a contemporary form and show its vital significance. In the process Jesus himself ceases to have a truly central role.

This is not the place to evaluate Bultmann's most fundamental proposal, demythologization. Suffice it to say that virtually all theologians agree that some demythologization is necessary in dealing with the New Testament. Nevertheless, as Karl Barth said, Bultmann's "chasm" is a vast oversimplification both of first century and twentieth century worldviews. *They* were not *controlled* by mythic forms of thinking and expression and *we* are not *free* of them. As Bultmann's own disciple, Ernst Käsemann, said in 1953, if we do not locate some historical, that is, non-mythical, statements in the Gospels, we ourselves are in danger of inventing a new myth when we demythologize.

Bultmann's other great contribution to the debate was his view of how the Gospels were formed. As he gained prominence in the 1920's, the liberal Protestant search for the historical Jesus was over, its requiem sung by Schweitzer twenty years before. Within critical theology, Schweitzer's conclusion was widely shared. Bultmann not only shared it, but reinforced it with his thesis (foreshadowed a century earlier by Schleiermacher) that the Gospel writers were dependent for their materials on the memory of the early Christian communities. Bultmann claimed that between the death of Jesus and the writing of the Gospels (30–70 A.D.—the "tunnel period") Jesus' sayings and the stories about him were preserved in an oral form. During this period there was no continuous narrative, but, instead, single isolated stories and sayings were being remembered in different early Christian communities. The stories and sayings were repeated in response to the various needs of the community, whether preaching, teaching, controversy, or ethical guidelines, and in the process they were adapted and modified to meet those needs. As the sayings and stories were repeated from one community to another, or within the same community, they fell into certain patterns (*formen* in German, hence the name given to this approach: form criticism) characteristic of oral tradition. Furthermore, Bultmann went beyond the other "form critics" in stressing the activity of early Christian prophets who spoke *in the name of Jesus* who was conceived to be still present in the community through prophetic inspiration (the so-called "I" sayings). In other words, he believed that the "authentic" sayings of Jesus were not only being modified but others were being created. He wrote:

The Church drew no distinction between such utterances by Christian prophets (ascribed to the ascended Christ) and the sayings of Jesus in the tradition for the reason that even the dominical sayings in the tradition were not the pronouncement of past authority, but sayings of the risen Lord, who is always a contemporary for the Church (*History of the Synoptic Tradition*, p. 127).

For Bultmann, then, the Gospels were the written remainder of an anonymous oral tradition, in which each item was repeated many times by unknown persons and may have been profoundly modified in response to contemporary needs, and other sayings were simply created. Furthermore, he maintained that their interest was not in remembering Jesus as a figure of the past, but rather in making him present as the risen and glorified Christ.

In 1926, on the basis of this position, Bultmann published *Jesus and the Word*. His position there is often cited as an example of extreme skepticism:

I do indeed think that we can now know almost nothing concerning the life and personality of Jesus, since the early Christian sources show no interest in either, are moreover fragmentary and often legendary; and other sources about Jesus do not exist (p. 8).

However, one must point out that Bultmann distinguished between what we could know about Jesus' *life* and what we could know about Jesus' *teaching*. Concerning the latter, he felt we could know quite a bit. This is a distinction followed by most Bultmannians (cf. N. Perrin, *Introduction to the New Testament*, p. 280). In a later work, *New Testament Theology* (1953), Bultmann was willing to make some significant statements about Jesus' life (cf. Ch. 1). Nevertheless, his skepticism concerning historical knowledge of Jesus was profound and influential.

THE NEW QUEST

Bultmann's influence on German Protestantism was widespread, especially during the period between the wars, and his opinions continue to be influential and taken seriously even by his adversaries. Nevertheless, in the 1950's even the disciples of the master began to ask whether the situation was healthy, and some began to take different paths.

Even the most faithful Bultmannians began to acknowledge that his was not the only respectable point of view. In 1957, Hans Conzelmann wrote:

We (i.e., the Bultmannian School) are accustomed to begin our thinking with the *gap* which lies between the Jesus of history and the community, marked by his death along with the Easter experiences, and with the differences between Jesus' preaching of the Kingdom of God and the *kerygma* that has him as its subject, between Jesus the proclaimer and the proclaimed Christ. Yet self-evident as this viewpoint may seem to us, we must be clear that outside central Europe it convinces only a few. The majority of English theologians either do not react to form criticism at all, or they acknowledge it merely as a formal classification of literary types and contest that it leads to historical or systematic judgments. Thus they reserve for themselves the possibility of drawing a continuous line from Jesus' understanding of himself to the faith of the community. Easter is in no way ignored, but the content of the Easter faith, and with it the basic Christological terms and titles, is traced back to Jesus' own teaching. The theology of the community appears as the working out of the legacy of the Risen Christ on the basis of his appearance. . . . To the representatives of this position the form-critical reconstruction seems to be a rationalistic abstraction, foreign both to history and to reality, and from a practical point of view a reduction of Christianity to a general religious consciousness, a formal dialectic of existence (ZThK, 54 [1957], pp. 279ff).

Conzelmann then went on to make a startling admission, namely, that the other side had a better *prima facie* case:

The advantage of this approach is that an established continuity is itself historically more probable than the assertion of a discontinuity which is hardly able to explain the formation of the categories of the faith of the community.

Conzelmann's comments were a sign of unease in the Bultmannian camp which had been provoked four years earlier by a younger member of the school, Ernst Käsemann. In 1953 Käsemann had made the startling proposal that the Quest for the Historical Jesus be resumed. He made two points. First, another half-century of intensive work on the Gospels had called into question Bultmann's (actually inherited) skepticism about the Gospels. Second, the authenticity of Christian faith was at stake. If we have no normative knowledge of Jesus of Nazareth, he functions as a mere hook for whatever understanding of human existence we wish to hang on him, the result of which is the remythologization of Christianity according to contemporary conceptions.

What the precise starting point of the New Quest is has always been the subject of debate, for it claims to have not only better techniques for finding Jesus than the Old Quest, but a clearer knowledge of its own presuppositions, the ever-crucial question in Life of Jesus research. Suffice it to say that the New Quest sought as its starting point a synthesis between two extremes, neither a pure Jesus of history nor a pure Christ of faith. It recognized that the Jesus of history is the presupposition of the Christ of faith not merely in the Bultmannian sense of the *Dass* (the That—the mere fact of his existence), but also of the *Wie* (the How) and the *Was* (the What). In other words, the New Quest presumes a basic continuity between the Jesus of history and the Christ of faith, and inquiry into each is guided by inquiry into the other.

I have given a great deal of space to a school of biblical scholarship that even by the admission of one of its own members does not represent the mainstream. Why? First of all, for decades the Bultmannians contributed scholarship of the highest order to the debate. They represent, even today, an important influence. But more important, the solution to the problem of *the nature of the sources*, the literary genre of the Gospels, emerged (while not solely, but most clearly), among Bultmann's disciples. In 1955 another disciple of Bultmann, Günther Bornkamm, captured what the years of debate had yielded. In a full scale (two hundred pages) historical study (not a "life") of Jesus of Nazareth, he described the *nature of the sources* in the following words:

Admittedly the Synoptic Gospels themselves are not simply historical sources which the historian, enquiring after Jesus of Nazareth as a figure of the past, could use without examination and criticism. Although their relation to history is a different one from that of John, they nonetheless unite to a remarkable degree both record of Jesus Christ and witness to him, testimony of the Church's faith in him and narration of his history (*Jesus of Nazareth*, p. 14).

Such a view of the sources motivated some of Bultmann's disciples to begin "The New Quest of the Historical Jesus." What brought about his new understanding of the sources?

First of all, not every central European scholar was a Bultmannian. In Germany and elsewhere, other scholars, using new knowledge, were slowly, painstakingly, accumulating evidence of continuity between the Jesus of history and the Christ of faith. This was especially true of the "sayings tradition." In 1921, in his *History of the Synoptic Tradition,* Bultmann had said that while there may be authentic sayings of the pre-Easter Jesus in the Synoptics, the burden of proof would be on anyone who would assert authenticity of a given saying. By 1971 J. Jeremias felt he could assert the opposite (*New Testament Theology,* p. 31).

Moreover, the very technique which seemed to fragment the New Testament had a positive side. Analysis of forms, of redaction, and of tradition implies an ability to speak of earlier and later stages. Secondly, the years after

World War II were fruitful in filling in the *background* of Jesus' ministry. The Dead Sea Scrolls, rabbinical literature, greater knowledge of apocalyptic and gnostic literature and of the so-called "intertestamental period," expanded significantly our knowledge of the history and mentality of Jesus' time. During this period greater knowledge of what was probably Jesus' mother tongue, Syriac or Talmudic Aramaic, developed. Finally, and of greater fruit, was the attempt to understand Jesus under the consistent light of the eschatological nature of his mission.

CATHOLICISM AND THE CRITICAL APPROACH TO THE GOSPELS

In 1906, Albert Schweitzer could write (*Quest*, p. 295, fn 2):

In the Catholic Church the study of the Life of Jesus has remained down to the present day entirely free of skepticism. The reason for that is, that in principle it has remained at a pre-Straussian standpoint, and does not venture upon an unreserved application of historical considerations either to the miracle question or the Johannine question, and naturally therefore resigns the attempt to take account of and explain the great historical problems.

Among Catholic authors, only Alfred Loisy (*The Fourth Gospel, The Gospel and the Church*) was singled out by Schweitzer for praise for his understanding of the historical-critical approach. As Schweitzer mentions, Loisy's books were condemned by ecclesiastical authorities. The introduction of the historical-critical approach into Catholic biblical studies is part of the story of the "Modernist" controversy. Given the association of the historical-critical approach with liberal Protestantism, and its obvious misuse by rationalist authors, a reaction is perhaps understandable. But history shows that the reaction was extreme. The latent fundamentalism of traditional Christianity regarding its own Scriptures became doctrinaire in early twentieth century Catholicism (as it did in parts of Protestantism).

In a series of encyclical letters, the popes of the late nineteenth and early twentieth centuries consistently rejected the historical-critical approach to the Bible. In 1893, Leo XIII began to engage the question with his letter *Providentissimus Deus*, which insisted on the inerrancy of Scripture in all areas. In 1902, by the Apostolic Letter *Vigilantiae*, the same Pope established the Pontifical Biblical Commission to act as watchdog over Catholic biblical scholarship. The positions taken on various questions by the Commission between 1905 and 1915 (for example, on the Mosaic authorship of the Pentateuch, the historical reliability of the Fourth Gospel, and the historicity of Genesis 1–3) can only be described as "fundamentalist." In 1907, in the encyclical *Pascendi* and the decree *Lamentabili,* Pius X solidified the orientation taken by Leo XIII. As a result of all this, "a dark cloud of reactionary conservatism settled over Roman Catholic biblical scholarship during the first half of the twentieth century" (J. Fitzmyer, *A Christological Catechism,* p. 98).

The situation began to change in 1943 with the encyclical of Pius XII, *Divino Afflante Spiritu,* sometimes called the *Magna Carta* of Catholic biblical studies. The Pope stressed what had been said two centuries earlier by J.D. Michaelis, that the central task of the biblical scholar is to determine what the human author of the text intended to convey (the so-called "literal sense"). He said that the key to such a task was the determination of the circumstances under which the author wrote and, especially, what literary *genre* he used to convey his meaning. The Pope urged the study of Ancient Near Eastern languages, history, archaeology and literature as essential to this task. But most significant was the recognition of a variety of types of literature in the Bible. It was not all "history."

In 1964 the Biblical Commission itself issued *Sancta Mater Ec-*

clesia (more commonly known as "On the Historical Truth of the Gospels"). Here Catholicism finally began to examine the literary *genre* called "Gospel." Besides endorsing the teaching of *Divino Afflante Spiritu,* the *Instruction* made a fundamental distinction, important to the study of the Gospels, concerning the "reasonable elements" in *form criticism* and its questionable "philosophical and theological principles." On the basis of this distinction, the *Instruction* went on to accept (what form criticism proposed) that there are *stages* in the Gospel tradition. (The unexpected character of this development can be illustrated by the fact that the otherwise venturesome "Dutch Catechism" [*De Nieuwe Katechismus,* 1966], perhaps already in preparation at this time, still clung to the older view of a more immediate connection of the Gospels with eyewitnesses [cf. pp. 206–207]). The adoption of the notion of three stages in the Gospel tradition was the acknowledgment of an intermediate stage of *oral tradition* between the tradition's origin in Jesus and its use by the Gospel writers. In calling this the stage of "apostolic preaching," the commission did depart from the radically creative character assigned to it by Bultmann. Nevertheless, it acknowledged some creativity in both the preaching period ("taking into account in their method of preaching the circumstances in which their listeners found themselves," *Instruction*, VIII) and the writing period ("selected some things, reduced others to a synthesis, (still) others they explicated as they kept in mind the situation of the churches," *Instruction*, XI).

In its constitution *Dei Verbum* (1965) Vatican II adopted the language of the *Instruction* concerning the activity of the evangelists (#19). Furthermore, it asserted that the form of *proclamation* was preserved when the preached Gospel became written.

AN ECUMENICAL STATEMENT ON THE LITERARY GENRE "GOSPEL"

It is the nature of the Gospels as *proclamation* that contemporary biblical scholarship stresses today. Perhaps the most valuable statement we have on the nature of the Gospels is neither of Catholic nor of Protestant provenance, but specifically ecumenical—that contained in *The Common Catechism* (1975). Its initial author was Rudolf Pesch, a leading Catholic scholar, and it was reviewed from the Protestant side by the eminent Ferdinand Hahn. The following are pertinent excerpts (full text: *The Common Catechism*, pp. 91–98):

The gospels are almost our only source for details about Jesus of Nazareth, his life, preaching and death, and his immediate effect on his contemporaries. The rest of the New Testament, as we have already seen, adds little of importance. The few references to Jesus in Jewish or pagan writers (Flavius Josephus, Tacitus, Suetonius) confirm that he lived, but contain no information of independent value. The four gospels are therefore our only source of information about Jesus. There are other "gospels" which came into being considerably later. These generally draw on the canonical gospels, but have a tendency to "decorate" their material with all sorts of abstruse legends or dubious imitations of Jesus' sayings. It is usually enough to read a few paragraphs to see how different they are in type from the canonical gospels.

The suggestion made earlier that even the four "genuine" gospels are not just "historically accurate documentary accounts" is justified by the facts. No one at that time wrote documentary accounts in the modern style, nor did anyone expect or demand what we expect and demand from a "historical" account. When ancient writers described the events, they always wanted to make the meaning and effects of the events clear in the description. That was the usual style of historical writing. That was why no one found it strange that a "report" about Jesus also set out to demonstrate the importance of his person and his action. The authors of the gospels wanted to proclaim their faith and arouse it in others. They wanted this as Christians who believed in a Jesus who had been raised from the dead and established in glory with God. It is clear that in this situation these two elements coloured the "reports," the intention of preaching and faith in the risen Jesus. In other words, the "reports" of the life of Jesus (cf. Lk. 1:1–4; Acts 1:1–2) are never mere reports. Even if they often read like reports (cf. Lk. 1:1–4; 2:1–2; 3:1–2, and so on), they are often really sermons. Of course, these 'sermons' on the life of Jesus include historical information as well, but the 'sermonizing' intention dominates the gospels to such an extent that it is quite difficult to discover what parts of them are historical reports of actual events, or what is genuine quotation from Jesus and what the expression of the living faith of the Church in subjection to the final authority of Jesus.

Again, the gospel-writers do not all combine reporting and preaching in the same way. You can see this immediately if you read first a chapter from the gospel of John and immediately afterwards a chapter of Mark. The writer of the fourth gospel is much more interested in clearly presenting to his readers the message of faith in Jesus, the Christ and Son of God (cf. Jn 20:31). He presents it in the form of a 'history of Jesus,' but this is much further from the historical reality of Jesus' earthly life than the other gospels.

The fact that the gospels are the expression of the faith in Jesus Christ which the early Church had reached through Jesus' resurrection does not give us any ground for supposing that the disciples deliberately 'falsified' the true picture of the history of Jesus. If they introduced the features of the risen Lord into the picture of the earthly Jesus, they did it simply because they were convinced that they now knew better who Jesus was all the time he lived on earth and what his actions on earth had meant. The gospel of John says this plainly (Jn. 2:22; 12:15; cf. 16:13).

In accordance with the findings of modern scripture scholarship we must imagine the tradition which produced the gospels as coming into being in the following way. The living faith of the Church repeated the words of Jesus in its services, its preaching, its teaching, from one community to another, but also filled these words out and made them clearer. It also reworked sayings with genuinely Christian content and gave them the literary form of a saying of Jesus, "put them into Jesus' mouth." The traditional story of the historical actions of Jesus was also given a form which would reflect the main features of the true, living image of Christ. In all this no one felt himself to be 'inventing' anything. The general attitude was that if what was taught in the Church was really the truth of faith, under what other authority ought it to be taught than the authority of Jesus, and through the teaching of the Holy Spirit? The Church therefore put what it had learnt about Jesus through faith into the form of words and actions of Jesus himself. The gospel-writers' methods may be compared with the way in which the great icon-painters painted the biblical Christ. They were painting Jesus, but they gave him the features of the exalted ruler of the universe in whom they believed.

We therefore have stories about Jesus which cannot be regarded simply as events from the life of Jesus, and sayings of Jesus which the historical Jesus never uttered. No biblical scholars of any major Church today question this. The only question is how far should we go in finding such 'inauthentic' actions and sayings. 'Inauthentic' is not really the right word here. The community and the writers who gave these sayings the literary form of words of Jesus, and 'attached' these actions to Jesus, did not act like skilled forgers. They merely took seriously in their writing, openly and directly, the implications of their conviction that all authoritative teaching in the Church should be passed on as *the teaching of Jesus*. That was the custom of the period.

Therefore it is wrong to regard the whole content of the gospels as 'historical fact.' Our eagerness to get historical statements which can be clearly proved and which are independent of faith or unbelief is a typically modern achievement. Naturally no one wants to stop people looking for historical facts in the gospels. We must merely be clear that the main intention of the gospel writers was to answer different questions. In these circumstances, if we want to know what can be ascribed with relative certainty to the pre-Easter history of Jesus, and what effect he really had on

people, we must examine the gospels in detail, saying by saying and story by story. This is the only way to discover what can count as (in this sense) 'historically' true or probably historically true, and what remains uncertain.

It will surprise no one to learn that in this work the judgments of biblical scholars differ sharply.

But the situation is not quite as hopeless as this makes it sound. The differences of opinion among scholars have to do more with the *relation* between the primitive Church's faith in Christ and the events of Jesus' life than with the question of the importance of Jesus' earthly life and activity for Christian faith. In any case, intensive examination of the biblical texts—in which the differences between denominations for the most part no longer matter—has produced a considerable unanimity about what Jesus himself taught, did, and tried to do and where the primitive Church developed his ideas in response to legitimate new questions and experience of the faith. In other words we can now say with reasonable accuracy where the boundary lies in the gospels between historical information— which is what interests us—and theological interpretation—which is what interested the primitive Church.

Appendix 4:

THE INFANCY NARRATIVES AND THE
QUESTION OF JESUS' ORIGINS

THE STATE OF
THE QUESTION

The very successful "Dutch Catechism" (*De Nieuwe Katechismus* [1966] ET, *A New Catechism* 1967, with supplement 1969, Seabury) first brought to public attention a discussion that had been going on among Catholic theologians for a few years. It concerned the traditional Catholic teaching that Jesus was "conceived virginally," that is, that he did not have a human father. *A New Catechism* did not *explicitly* teach that Jesus had no human father, nor did it say that he did—it simply did not state either explicitly. In a book intended for a popular audience (*De Nieuwe Katechismus* was commissioned and approved by the hierarchy of the Netherlands and produced by the Higher Catechetical Institute at Nijmegen in collaboration with other theologians) this was thought an intolerable omission by a commission of cardinals appointed by Paul VI to review the catechism. The commission directed that later editions explicitly teach that Jesus had no human father. As a result, a supplement was added to later editions in which the commission's concerns were responded to by two theologians appointed by the cardinals. The original text remained unchanged.

The importance of the question of Jesus' conception is threefold:

1. It touches on the uniqueness of Jesus.
2. It touches on the role and status of his mother in Christianity, especially Catholic Christianity.
3. It touches on the Church, the nature of its doctrine, and whether it can err.

Of course, the problem of belief in virginal conception is rooted in the very culture we live in. The presuppositions of our culture do not favor such a doctrine. But *theologically* the question arises from the nature of the materials contained in Luke 1–2 and Matthew 1–2, especially Matthew 1:18–25 and Luke 1:26–36.

According to common scholarly opinion, Matthew and Luke

are not dependent on each other. Both are dependent upon Mark and on the "sayings source" ("Q"), but they are not interdependent. Yet in their rendering of the birth of Jesus, each recounts his virginal conception. Two questions come to mind. (1) Do they intend to relate history, or are their narratives saying something theological? (2) If their intention is at least partly historical, how does one evaluate their testimony? What is its origin?

At this point the controversy begins. For instance, in one of the best Christology books by a Catholic author in recent years, Walter Kasper does not comment on the question beyond a general evaluation of the infancy narratives:

The infancy narratives, or stories of Jesus' childhood in Matthew and Luke, offer very little material for tracing the course of his life. They describe Jesus' early life on Old Testament models, especially by analogy with the story of Moses. Their concern is more theological than biographical; their purpose is to say: Jesus is the fulfillment of the Old Testament (*Jesus the Christ*, p. 65).

One can only conclude that Kasper does not think these parts of Scripture are basis enough for an historical judgment one way or the other. Yet it seems rash to exclude an historical intention completely. No doubt the infancy narratives embody more of a theological intention than other parts of the Gospels (which themselves are heavily theological), but they nevertheless remain "Gospel." And Gospels have a fundamental historical interest that cannot be dispensed with. Matthew in particular seems to try to make sure that the reader understands that Jesus was not the product of human conception. The story in Luke is different, but he, too, attributes the conception of Jesus to the work of the Holy Spirit and, later in his Gospel, in his genealogy of Jesus (3:23), he says "Jesus, when he began his ministry, was about thirty years of age, being the son (as was supposed) of Joseph. . . . " The "as was supposed" appears in the best manuscripts of Luke, and no biblical scholar maintains that it is an interpolation from later days under the influence of the doctrinal teaching.

Let us presume for a moment that the authors of Matthew and Luke have an historical intention here. What would be the source of their knowledge? According to contemporary analysis, the evangelists are dependent on traditions existing in the early Church for their materials. So the fact that Mark and John do not contain a virginal conception of Jesus can simply mean that this tradition was not available to them. Moreover, this event is not the type dealt with in the Gospels as a whole; it is not a public event that would form part of the core of the tradition about Jesus. On the other hand, two of the evangelists, independently, incorporate this tradition in their Gospels. So what may have been unknown to the communities that stand behind Mark and John may have been known in the communities behind Matthew and Luke.

Still presuming that the authors of Matthew and Luke have historical intentions and are dependent on a tradition, what would be the historical value of such a tradition? There are several objections to the historical reliability of a tradition of a virginal conception.

1. One objection is that if the tradition is reliable, it would have existed in some form in the earliest days of the Church. But there is a commonly held opinion today that while the Church believed in the divinity of Christ from the earliest days after his resurrection—and expressed it in such phrases as "Jesus is the Lord"—it only gradually came to a *full* understanding of what it meant. The problem lies in reconciling an *explicit* knowledge of a virgin birth and a gradual understanding of who Jesus was. This objection, however, is not very persuasive. As I mentioned, this tradition, if it is such, of its nature would not have been as public as other traditions. A tradition of a virginal conception could have existed in the early Church but need not have been common knowledge.

2. The more serious objection stems from the nature of the infancy narratives themselves; they are clearly different from the rest of the Gospels. Moreover, they differ from each other, concurring in so few details that they can hardly be called entirely historical. For example, the lists of ancestors they give are different; characteristic Matthean and Lukan themes are present in them, as are Old Testament motifs. They have a "midrashic" tone (*midrash* is the telling of an event on an already existing model). Yet the difficulties are not insuperable; there is no reason why historical truth could not be embedded in such stories. Midrash does not exclude an historical core. And the fact remains that, while the two accounts are widely different, they do agree on the virginal conception.

3. The silence of the rest of the New Testament also raises a question. Mark calls Jesus "son of Mary" (6:3), a curious designation since Jews were not identified by relationship to their mother but to their father, but it hardly amounts to evidence of belief in a virginal conception. On the other hand, it should also be pointed out that nothing in the New Testament directly contradicts Matthew and Luke.

4. There are suspicious par-

allels in non-Christian literature of the time. While the notion of a divine conception of great men is present in mythology and ancient history, there is no precedent for it in *Jewish* thought. There are several stories in the Old Testament and that of John the Baptist in the New, in which barren women conceived—but they always do so with the help of their husbands. Furthermore, in the non-Jewish and non-Christian literature, virginal conception always occurs through a type of *hieros gamos* (sacred marriage), where a divine male, in human or other form, impregnates a woman, either through normal sexual intercourse or some other form of penetration. But it is always conception by some sort of physical intercourse. This is not the case in the infancy narratives.

5. Could not the idea of a virginal conception of Jesus have arisen from the famous prediction in the Book of Isaiah (7:14), where the Hebrew text says a young woman shall conceive, but the Greek translation says "a virgin shall conceive"? In fact, Matthew cites that Greek text right in its account (1:23). Is the author moving from his belief that Jesus is the Messiah to seeing in Jesus the fulfillment of Isaiah's prophecy as he knew it? We have no evidence that that verse was understood to mean that she

would still be a virgin when she did conceive or that it was interpreted to refer *to the Messiah* before Matthew uses it that way. Furthermore, Luke shows no influence of this verse.

6. Some authorities think that Matthew's account is an attempt to counter a charge that Jesus was illegitimate, a charge made in the Talmud, the collection of rabbinic sayings from the centuries around Jesus' time made in the third century A.D. If Matthew is attempting to counter an early form of this tradition, he is not merely being theological. His intention would correspond to the intention of the charge—it would be historical. This would reinforce interpreting his statements historically rather than theologically.

SUMMARY

What would be a *general* solution to these difficulties for a scholar who thought a reliable tradition stands behind the accounts? Most likely a *family* tradition about the virginal conception circulated among a few Christians in the period between 30 and 60 A.D., before it spread and became known by those communities Matthew and Luke wrote for and whose traditions they borrowed. My own judgment is that the weight of the evidence of an analysis of the infancy narrative points in the direction of an historical intention on the part of Matthew and Luke. What one thinks is possible is a crucial factor.

CHURCH TRADITION

What does the tradition of the later Church have to say on this question? We find a mention of the virginal conception from the end of the second century on. The appellation "born of the Virgin Mary" appears consistently in the creeds down through the centuries. However, in all these creeds it is a legitimate question to ask what the article of the creed is mainly concerned with. Do these early Christian creeds intend to emphasize that Jesus was conceived without a human father or do they simply wish to say that he really was *a man* by emphasizing that he was *born of a woman*? Is the issue Jesus' conception or his humanity, that is, are the opponents that the creeds are directed at groups denying in some way the virginal conception or those who deny that Jesus is truly human? We know of no group in the early centuries of the Church which centered its heresy on denying a virginal conception. However, *docetism* and *monophysitism*, which deny a genuine humanity to Jesus, were (and probably continue

to be) major problems in the Church. It is at least *open to discussion* whether the Church has ever intended to infallibly *define*—that is, throw its whole weight behind a statement of belief in an explicit way—that Jesus was conceived without a human father. The question would be answered if the creeds were actually saying that, but is that their precise concern?

On the other hand, even if it were proven that the Church has never explicitly *defined* the virginal conception as a dogma, it does not mean that it is not Church doctrine, the adherence to which is a matter of indifference. It would be dangerously minimalistic to believe only what is *explicitly defined*. If we take seriously the belief that the Holy Spirit is definitively present in the Church, then the continuous belief of the Church is a standard of belief. On the other hand, the Church's teaching authority (magisterium) itself has endorsed the idea that the individual Catholic should affirm Church teaching with the same *degree* of adherence that the Church itself does. There is infallible teaching and there is non-infallible teaching. Given the proper competence, one can disagree with non-infallible teaching. On the other hand, only some infallible teaching has been explicitly defined. Most Catholic scholars would say that the virginal conception is infallible by reason of its being continually taught in the Church but that it is not a *defined* doctrine.

A FINAL NOTE

Does a denial of the virginal conception of Jesus amount to a denial of his divinity? That is often assumed, and it is sometimes the reason why the doctrine is vehemently defended. The assumption is unwarranted. Obviously, if Jesus was conceived of a virgin, it says something about him, but admitting that he had a human father does not amount to a negation of his divinity. He had a human mother and he is divine; it is not as though his mother supplied his humanity and God fathered his divinity, so that he is half human and half God. He does not have a combination of human and divine chromosomes. If he is divine, it is because he was always divine and became a man. Whether he became a man in a miraculous way or the way we all do does not affect his divinity, what he "always" was. It would signal his uniqueness as a human being and, with other evidence, *point to* his divinity. It would not be the cause of it.

Chapter VI

THE REIGN OF GOD IN THE PREACHING AND ACTS OF JESUS OF NAZARETH

THE CENTRAL THEME OF THE PREACHING OF JESUS OF NAZARETH

Is there one point concerning the history of Jesus that all scholars agree on? Indeed, there is. It is virtually unanimous that the *central theme of the preaching* of Jesus of Nazareth is accurately captured by the Gospel of Mark (1:15): "The time is fulfilled, and the kingdom of God is at hand." Accordingly, the heart of contemporary discussion of the "historical Jesus" in theology is Jesus' message about the coming of the kingdom of God. All other questions (his claims about himself, the fulfillment of his expectations, the importance and meaning of his death and resurrection) are answered by reference to his proclamation (For a discussion of Jesus' origins see Appendix 4, "The Infancy Narratives and the Question of Jesus' Origins"). What did Jesus mean when he said the kingdom of God was at hand?

THE WORDS

Let us begin by examining the words themselves. The first thing to be pointed out is that using the word "kingdom" can be misleading for English-speaking people. There are three languages involved here, Aramaic, Greek, and English. The word Jesus would have used would be some form of the Aramaic word *malkut*. When the sayings of Jesus were translated into Greek, *malkut* was translated by the word *basileia*. In turn, *basileia* has been translated into English as "kingdom."

"Kingdom" is a permissible translation of *basileia*. That is, *basileia* can be used for a realm, a state ruled by a king. One could say "the *basileia* of England." But *basileia* has more than one sense. It can mean

(1) "royal dominion"—the *authority* to rule, the actual power to rule; (2) "reign"—the *exercise* of royal dominion; (3) *all that is subject to* royal dominion, namely, land and people, the "kingdom." In the preaching of Jesus, *basileia* usually means not "realm" or "kingdom," not what is ruled by a king, but the act of ruling itself, the *reign* of a king. It refers not to *what* is ruled, but to the personal *act* of ruling by the monarch, the *exercise* of sovereignty. This is why in a recent translation of the Bible (*The New American Bible*) Mark 1:15 is translated not as "The time is fulfilled, and the kingdom of God is at hand" but "The reign of God is at hand." At other times *The New American Bible* translates *basileia* as "kingdom" because there are places where that is the obvious meaning. But in those sayings that most probably come from the pre-Easter Jesus himself, *basileia* is usually best translated "reign." Thus, in announcing that "the reign of God is at hand," Jesus is proclaiming that God is beginning to exercise dominion in a definitive ("the time is fulfilled") way.

There is a *second* clarification about Jesus' words which must be made. In the Gospel of Matthew, Jesus is represented as proclaiming the imminence not of the "kingdom of God" but the "kingdom of heaven." For a modern reader this formulation suggests that the main work of Jesus of Nazareth was to direct people's attention to heaven, the state of the blessed after death. When we are told to "seek first the kingdom of heaven" and everything else will follow, we tend to understand that Jesus is focusing his hearers' attention on an after-life rather than what God is doing in this life. Such is not the case, however. When Matthew has Jesus say kingdom of *heaven*, he is merely following the Jewish practice of not saying the name of God. "Heaven" is a reverent circumlocution of the name of God. It is disputed what form Jesus himself used. However, since there is no precedent in rabbinic usage for the Matthean form before 80 A.D., Jesus probably used the Markan form.

Still a third comment about Jesus' language is necessary. The connotations of "kingdom," "reign," and "rule" are somewhat distasteful to us. As emancipated people, we do not think of ourselves as being ruled. We do not have *rulers*. We elect *leaders* who, if they fancy themselves rulers, are called to account. The words "kingdom," "reign," and "rule" connote for us servitude, suppression and subjection.

In the ancient world, such connotations did not exist. Most people hoped for benevolent rule, not for emancipation. The hopes of the poor and oppressed were summed up in the notion of "just" rule. To the biblical mind, justice meant not impartial judgment, getting what was due, or getting one's rights, but a *beneficent exercise of power on behalf of those who had no power* (and no claim to rights). Accordingly, people hoped for "just judgment," or benevolent, indeed almost "gracious" rule. The focus was on the goodness of the ruler rather than on the rights of the ruled.

THE EXPECTATIONS IN JESUS' TIME

The meaning of Jesus' words was not as mysterious for his contemporaries as it is for us. In announcing that the reign of God was at hand, he was merely saying to people that an event which many were expecting was at hand.

But expectations differed. Common among many of Jesus' contemporaries was a belief in the doctrine of the two ages of the world. This is a doctrine associated with the development of "apocalyptic" thinking which emerged in Israel in the centuries just preceding Jesus. There is apocalyptic literature in both the Old (Daniel) and the New Testaments (Revelation).

Apocalyptic literature presents itself as a revelation of the future coming from a well-known figure of the past. The medium of the revelation is a vision that reveals "the future" using complicated symbols, especially numbers. The purpose of apocalyptic is to sustain hope (on the basis of God's fidelity) in the face of persecution. The religious value of an apocalypse is not that it predicts the future in detail, but that it draws a trajectory of God's faithfulness from the past into the present and the future in order to give hope to people in desperate situations. What is especially characteristic of apocalyptic literature, however, is that it puts its hope in the ending of world history. In this literature we see the emergence of "absolute eschatology," a transhistorical eschatology. That is, in apocalyptic literature, eschatological thinking has projected not a definitive stage *of* history, but the *termination* of history and the advent of "the new heaven and the new earth." It asks: How can God tolerate the continued rebelliousness of his creation, its domination by the powers of darkness ("the principalities and powers")? The answer is that the clash of God's holiness and the power of evil will result in a catastrophe, but a catastrophe followed by God's reign, a reign of peace and justice. The "apocalyptic scenario" runs: There will be a crisis, a time of tribulation, then a resolution of the crisis in a complex set of events. The forces of evil will make a last-ditch struggle against God but will finally be routed, through the powers of angels, most notably the archangel Michael. In apocalyptic literature, the period in which the author is writing is always the last period before the end, the "last days." Often the pagans—for example, the Romans—are the powers through which the kingdom of evil struggles against God, and the Jewish nation, often led by a messianic leader, is the instrument God uses to establish his definitive reign over his (transformed) creation.

Apocalyptic thinking appears to be a product of Israel's political situation. It had its beginnings just about the time of the loss of national independence in 587 B.C. (Ezekiel), and became especially influential during the period of the domination of Israel by a series of foreign powers between 200 B.C. and 200 A.D.

What is especially important for understanding the preaching of Jesus is that apocalyptic thinking consistently distinguishes between "this world" and "the world to come," or "this age" and "the age to come." The belief that this world, this age, was coming to an end soon and would be superseded by a new age, a new world, was an expectation among many of the people Jesus addressed. Indeed, it had become an unchallenged assumption.

Thus, apocalyptic thinking intensified and gave a distinctive turn to Israel's eschatological orientation. Different groups—all of which thought eschatologically—were influenced by apocalyptic thinking in different degrees. Not all agreed that the-world-to-come would involve the transformation of the cosmos. *The ordinary people* whom Jesus would have encountered, insofar as they entertained hopes at all, believed that the age-to-come would be initiated by the arrival of God's anointed one, his messiah, more precisely his messiah-king, who would reestablish the political independence of Israel in a sovereign state just as it had been under David. This desire for a restoration of the Davidic monarchy is called the "nationalistic eschatology." It seems to have been the expectation even of some of Jesus' own disciples. It is influenced by apocalyptic thought, but it really is more closely linked to the older *prophetic* teaching of an end (Greek: *eschaton*) *within* history (an "*infra*historical" *eschaton*).

The full-fledged apocalypticists had more grandiose expectations. They looked forward to an age when the very cosmos itself, and not just historical circumstances, would be transformed (a "*trans*historical" *eschaton*). According to this view, the current age is under the domination of Satan, the prince of "this world," whose reign is manifested in injustice, suffering, sickness and sin. When the age-to-come arrives, Satan will be overthrown by God, and the world will be transformed. This is the so-called "cosmic eschatology."

Although many of Jesus' fellow Jews, then, expected the coming of the reign of God in the near future, they differed in their understandings of what it would be. This introduced deep divisions and animosities into Israel. People took sides and elitist groups emerged which claimed to be the only true Israelites, the "remnant" spoken of by the prophets. We know much more about these groups now than we did even thirty years ago.

The most significant new information comes from the "Dead Sea Scrolls" found in 1947 near the wadi of Qumran. Excavations have revealed the existence there of a pre-Christian monastic community living in isolation from the rest of the nation of Israel. Its members regarded themselves as "the sons of light" and the rest of Israel as "the sons of darkness." The group seems to have been an offshoot of a group called the Essenes known to us from the Jewish historian, Josephus. They were probably related to the Pharisees who, of course, are familiar to us from the Gospels. While the monks of Qumran lived in separation from ordinary life, the Pharisees lived in society but without really mixing into it. The Pharisees do not appear to have been as apocalyptic as the Qumran sect, but there are similarities. If the Gospel accounts are accurate (some scholars feel that the picture of the Pharisees in the Gospels is exaggerated by the later conflict between Christians and the Pharisees), they had the same negative attitude as the Qumran monks toward people who did not follow their own rigid observance of "the law"—that complex of Old Testament and rabbinic teaching that had come to regulate every phase of Jewish life at the time of Jesus. Apparently the Pharisees believed that the coming of the kingdom was being delayed by those people who were not observing "the law." On the other hand, the Pharisees thought they were hastening its coming by their observance. The kingdom would come when Israel finally lived in full observance of the Torah. Accordingly, the Pharisees tended to regard the ordinary people as "God's enemies." Although there is no evidence that they were ordered to curse those who did not follow their strict code (as we find in Qumran), they did regard such people as under judgment and enemies of the reign of God.

The vast majority of the people, and especially "the people of the land," peasants, day laborers, shepherds, could not follow the Pharisaic code. Nor did they seem inclined to follow the political revolutionaries, the Zealots, who were committed to the violent expulsion of the Romans. And, of course, there were "public sinners," such as tax collectors, prostitutes, and swineherds. According to the Pharisees, these were beyond God's mercy. Apparently the Pharisees expected that the reign of God would manifest itself primarily as *judgment* on these people—that is, that it would come as the destruction of those people who were not following the law and as a vindication of those who were.

Was there a *normative* view at this time of what the kingdom would be? Apparently not. What was common to the varying views was the belief that humanity's hopes for a kingdom of peace, justice, freedom, and life could not be satisfied by men and women alone and unaided. The biblical view is that humanity cannot generate by itself the freedom and power necessary to fulfill its hope. This view was sometimes expressed as slavery to "principalities and powers," the demonic. But its fundamental point is that a fresh start is needed, that something radically new in the sense of something underivable from the world as it is, is necessary, and this can only come from outside the situation of humanity. The fundamental biblical view is that only God as Lord of history can provide the breakthrough. In the most basic sense, this *act* that only God can do is what is meant by the reign of God. Humanity cannot effect it; it can only pray for it. Thus, the kingdom of God in Scripture involves God's absolute sovereignty and transcendence. Any understanding of it which eliminates those characteristics is a misunderstanding, for the reign of God is precisely that, the reign of *God*, and partakes of God's mystery.

THE KINGDOM OF GOD IN THE PREACHING OF JESUS

It is disputed just how apocalyptic Jesus himself was. However, even if we concede that he used apocalyptic language when he talked about the end (for example, a time of tribulation, and the reign of God as the casting out of Satan), nevertheless Jesus' distinctive medium for talking about the reign of God is the parable, and the parables are not apocalyptic. Although he obviously was a man of his time, Jesus' understanding of the reign of God does not match the expectations of any of the groups of his time. What he shares with them is an expectation of the imminence of the kingdom—in fact, to some extent he thinks it has *already arrived*. Like his contemporaries, he uses apocalyptic imagery to talk about it in its final consummation, but for the most part he uses very ordinary language when he talks about it as already present. The very fact that he used parables points to the nature of the kingdom (even as apocalyptic does): this is an act of God, and it partakes of God's freedom and transcendence. The reign of God is something that God is doing—it is the reign *of God*—and therefore it can only be approached through symbols.

This deserves further discussion. Jesus' parables must be understood against the background of the preaching of the Old Testament prophets. He saw himself in that tradition. Indeed, he saw himself as the definitive (eschatological) prophet, for he understood his mission to be the proclamation of the reign of God, the definitive (eschatological) saving act of God on Israel's behalf.

To say that Jesus is in the prophetic tradition, however, involves us immediately in a common misunderstanding about the nature of prophetic language which in turn affects our understanding of Jesus' proclamation. "Prophecy" has come to mean "prediction of the future." But we must recognize that Old Testament prophecy, while it looks to the future, cannot be an exact description of the future. The reason is that in the prophetic mind the future is not fixed. Prophecy is not a description of what God has determined must happen but the announcement to Israel of God's *initiatives*. The initiatives look for *a response from Israel*. The future is the result of both factors and so is open-ended. Israel's history is the result of what happens when God's initiatives and Israel's responses meet. The words "God's plan," "Divine Providence," and "God's will" do not indicate that history runs according to a pre-determined scenario (a "fatalistic" view of history however benevolent the end result may be). Rather they speak of God's role. Men and women are not actors in a divinely written scenario who can only say their lines well or poorly but cannot change them or change the plot of the drama. We are not puppets on a string controlled by a divine puppeteer. God's role is not the exercise of the sovereignty of a despot but the sovereignty of a loving freedom which, when rejected, continues to love. "God's plan," "God's Providence," "God's will" are expressions of the belief that human history is embraced by God's active *love*. The prophetic view is that God acts to save Israel but that history itself is also determined by Israel's response, which response is incorporated in a new divine initiative.

In this light prophecy is not so much prediction as challenge. It does not tell Israel what the future will be *despite* what Israel does but precisely what it will be *depending on* Israel's response. It challenges Israel to respond to God's initiative. It asks of Israel that it "turn and be converted," that it open itself up to God's saving activity. In the same way, Jesus' parables of the reign of God are prophetic language. They challenge the hearer to open up to God's definitive saving act now breaking in. But the concrete shape of that saving act remains open because the hearer's response is awaited.

What picture finally emerges of Jesus' understanding of the reign of God?

(1) It is not what the popular notion, the nationalistic eschatology, thought it would be—the reestablishment of the Davidic monarchy. Jesus refuses to be understood as the mediator of such a kingdom. Nevertheless the kingdom would result in the "restoration" of Israel (see Appendix 6, "The Aim of Jesus").

(2) It is not what the Pharisees thought either, that is, the destruction of those who were not keeping the law and the vindication of those who were. Jesus does not accept that the reign of God is primarily an act of judgment. For Jesus judgment is delayed; the reign of God is manifested first as an offer of *mercy*. There is a difference of emphasis when we compare Jesus' preaching with that of John the Baptist. John's imagery (the winnowing fork, wheat and chaff, purifying fire) emphasizes that judgment is at hand. Yet John is also announcing a time of mercy before judgment. Without denying judgment, Jesus emphasizes mercy.

(3) It is not what the "cosmic" (apocalyptic) eschatology believed it would be. Jesus does not locate the coming of the reign of God solely in a cosmic transformation occurring in the near future. Rather Jesus says that the reign of God is already present. This can be seen in such sayings as: (1) "The time is fulfilled, and the kingdom of God is at hand" (Mk 1:15a); (2) "But if it is by the finger of God that I cast out demons, then the kingdom of God has come upon you" (Lk 11:20); (3) "The kingdom of God is not coming with signs to be observed, nor will they say, 'Lo, here it is!' or 'There,' for behold, the kingdom of God is in the midst of you" (Lk 17:20–21). Jesus' preaching that the reign of God is already present is a distinctive note. But he is not merely pointing to a reality that has been there all along and merely needs to be awakened to. The King James Bible misled many here when it translated what is generally held to be an authentic saying of Jesus—Luke 17:21—as "the kingdom of God is *within* you," thus individualizing and deeschatologizing Jesus' message. The proper translation is "in your midst." Jesus is saying that the time of waiting is over— God is acting on behalf of men and women in a definite way *now*. The reign of God is breaking into human history.

(4) On the other hand, in the preaching of Jesus the reign of God is *still coming*. For example, he teaches his disciples to pray for its coming in the Our Father. Thus it is both *present* and still *coming*. Various attempts have been made to reconcile the present and future aspects of the kingdom in the preaching of Jesus, sometimes involving suppression of one or the other aspect. To eliminate either aspect does not do justice to the data. The tension must be

maintained. The reign of God is "already but not yet" in the preaching of Jesus.

(5) Although the reign of God is the reign *of God*, it does not take effect automatically, that is, without incorporating the response of the hearers. They must "repent and believe the good news." Repent here does not primarily mean moral conversion, although that is certainly involved. The sentence is a parallelism. Repentance is *religious* conversion, *metanoia*, changing of one's mind, belief, acceptance of God as Savior, renunciation of self-sufficiency, acceptance of creaturehood. The people who heard Jesus' preaching were called to act. Because the reign of God was present—because salvation history had entered its crucial time—the people had to respond. They are not to wait for a catastrophe. What they were expecting was indeed already present, had to be discerned and seized. The proper response was faith—accepting the offer of forgiveness that Jesus proclaimed, turning to God and to the neighbor in response to God's love in one integral response.

(6) Finally we must recall again that the kingdom in Jesus' preaching is open-ended, that is, he is not preaching something which is already a fixed reality. There are two reasons for this: (1) It is God's reign, so the concrete shape of the kingdom partakes of God's sovereign freedom; its final shape is determined by God, not men and women. (2) Yet since the kingdom expects a response, its concrete shape is affected by the reaction of men and women to it. The result is that, in the preaching of Jesus, while we can say what the *characteristics* of the definitive saving act of God are, we cannot say what that act *itself* will be because it is not determined. Jesus left it to God to fill in the content of his preaching, and God's definitive saving event incorporated Israel's response.

THE REIGN OF GOD IN THE ACTS OF JESUS

The distinction made in some form by many authors between the message of Jesus and his life can lead to an oversight precisely when one wishes to determine his message. The reason is that it fails to take into account that Jesus did not merely speak his message but acted it out. No account of Jesus' understanding of the reign of God can limit itself to discussion of his words; it must pass on to the embodiment of those words in his actions. Here we single out four characteristic acts of Jesus. If these are taken to be Jesus acting out his message with symbolic gestures (prophetic acts), what do they tell us about his understanding of the kingdom?

"EATING WITH SINNERS"

Jesus regularly practiced "table fellowship" with the marginalized and public sinners, those considered by the Pharisees to be under God's judgment when the reign of God came. The significance of this practice can only be understood against the background of his culture. Eating a meal with someone was an expression of solidarity with that person, an identification of one's life with the guest's. The various sects in Israel at the time were very conscious of the importance of maintaining ritual purity and thus shared meals only with like-minded people. The humble human action of eating together symbolized the union of the elect before God.

In a deliberately provocative manner Jesus used this symbol-laden practice to convey that the reign of God came precisely to "sinners." The definitive act of God was "saving," an offer of mercy, not judgment. This action also helps us to see more clearly what Jesus' "aim" is: not the separating out of an elite of the pure and justified, but the "gathering of Israel" in response to God's offer of mercy now present in Jesus' ministry. Whom Jesus ate with, God forgave, and thus formed God's eschatological people. The diversity of people at Jesus' meals is striking. Jesus ate with whoever accepted the offer of mercy present in his preaching and acts. Thus, in this simple symbolic act Jesus embodied the message that the kingdom comes as a gathering of "the lost sheep of Israel" into the eschatological community forming around Jesus.

THE FORMATION OF DISCIPLES

Hearing and accepting Jesus' proclamation made one a member of Jesus' new eschatological people. In a fundamental sense the only distinction between people that Jesus recognized was between those who heard and those who did not. Nevertheless, Jesus did choose some who accepted his message to aid him in the work of preaching, no doubt for the very practical reason of giving his message greater extension. Jesus certainly had a group of disciples with whom he shared something of his authority. Sometimes the New Testament designates a group called the twelve. If Jesus himself is the origin of the designation "the twelve," is there a prophetic gesture being made?

Taken together with Jesus' other "gathering" behavior, the designation of a group of twelve is intriguing. The larger discipleship of Jesus included people from the diverse quarters of the Israel of the time: Galileans, who would have been influenced by Greek culture and were probably regarded as of mixed blood because of the Assyrian conquest of the eighth century, some Pharisees, a Zealot, and former disciples of John the Baptist (perhaps himself influenced by the Essenes and/or the members of the sect at Qumran). It is, of course, staggering for the time that Jesus of Nazareth had women disciples, a development without parallel among the rabbis. While all of these groups are not represented in the twelve, this core group of Jesus' disciples are a cameo of the larger picture—of Jesus' desire to gather a fragmented Israel into one people. Against the background of the history of Israel, which saw itself as the *twelve* tribes formed on the *twelve* sons of Jacob (Israel), the number of the members is too symbolic to be ignored. This group would represent for Jesus the eschatological Israel, the true sons of Jacob. As such it would symbolize the nature of the reign of God and the norms of entrance into the kingdom. The reign of God comes as an unconditional offer of mercy to whoever will accept it. It seeks to unify the disintegrated and divided Israel into an eschatological people transformed by the acceptance of God's mercy. The reign of God is God's eschatological gift of mercy. It constitutes a people which does not make a claim to righteousness but is given it. As gifted with mercy, it seeks reconcilation not division among its members.

THE CLEANSING OF THE TEMPLE

Some authors have suggested that Jesus' "cleansing of the temple" is also to be understood as a prophetic act symbolizing the nature of the reign of God. According to the Synoptics (in the final week of Jesus' life) and John (nearer the beginning of his public ministry), Jesus drove the dealers in sacrificial animals and the money changers out of the temple compound in Jerusalem. Rudolf Pesch suggests that the place Jesus would have encountered this commerce on sacred ground was in the "Court of the Gentiles." No doubt Jesus could not have hoped that his one effort would restore purity to the temple precincts. Pesch's theory makes what many see as a symbolic, provocative, prophetic act even more pointed in its symbolism. By cleansing the Court of the Gentiles Jesus would be announcing that the reign of God comes also to the Gentiles. The temple stood for Israel. Its purification would symbolize the purification of Israel through the coming of the reign of God. In turn the preparation of the Court of the Gentiles would symbolize that the reign of God in Israel begins the incorporation of the Gentiles into God's eschatological people. According to the prophets, especially Zechariah, the coming of the reign of God would make the temple on Mount Zion a place of prayer for *all* peoples. In the final days the prayers of the "nations"—the Gentiles—would be acceptable in the temple. The reign of God would transform Israel into the city on the mountaintop, the "light to the nations." All peoples would make the pilgrimage to the eschatological Israel as the place of God's dwelling. The prophetic gesture of cleansing the temple says: the reign of God comes as the merciful transformation of Israel and envisions even the inclusion of the "nations" in that mercy. God's entire *creation* will be restored in the reunification of *all* God's people.

THE KINGDOM OF GOD IN THE "DEEDS OF POWER" OF JESUS

Even the most skeptical biblical critics admit that in the oldest stratum of the oral tradition incorporated in the Gospels, Jesus was presented as a "wonder worker." They do not normally say he performed "miracles" because an entire worldview at odds with the biblical worldview is associated with that word. For the modern mind the word "miracle" connotes an intervention of God in a closed system. God thus is seen as intervening to suspend or break "laws of nature." As we said in Chapter III, for the biblical mind the world was not a closed system—it is God's continuing creation. Anytime anything truly new is present in it, either in nature or history, the biblical mind recognizes a "miracle." Furthermore, because it drew no distinction between nature and history—it is all God's continuing creation—it did not single out a special category which would correspond to what the Enlightenment meant by miracle. (The fundamental question, of course, is, whether the Enlightenment's closed system worldview is truly preferable to the Bible's open-system view.)

Thus it seems better to stay with the biblical terms. The New Testament speaks of Jesus' acts as *dunameis*—"mighty deeds"—(in the Synoptics) or as *semeia*—"signs"—(in John). The deeds are always "saving," that is, they are not just demonstrations of supernatural power but always *help people* who cannot do for themselves what Jesus can. What did he do? Even the most skeptical critics acknowledge that Jesus had the power to *heal* people and to free them from "possession of evil spirits." These same critics say that Jesus released people not merely from psychological infirmities but from physical infirmities, too. If we interpret Jesus' "mighty deeds" as deliberate prophetic gestures, what do they say about Jesus' understanding of the kingdom? The question of Jesus' "mighty deeds," since it raises peculiar problems for post-Enlightenment people, requires fuller treatment than Jesus' other prophetic gestures.

THE NEW TESTAMENT PRESENTATION OF THE MIGHTY DEEDS OF JESUS

These *dunameis* or *semeia* of Jesus in both Synoptic and Johannine traditions are essential to the Gospel picture of Jesus. In Mark over half of the text before the passion narrative is devoted to recounting the deeds of power of Jesus. The *semeia* of Jesus are so prominent in the equivalent part of John that Rudolf Bultmann called it The Book of Signs (chapters 1–12).

These "deeds" fall into four types: (1) exorcisms (five, all in the Synoptics), (2) healings (fifteen in the Synoptics, three in John), (3) resuscitations (two in the Synoptics, 1 in John), (4) "nature" *dunameis* (six in the Synoptics, four in John). Three dunameis of Jesus are common to both traditions: the cure of the son of the Capernaum official (Jn 4:46–53), the multiplication of the loaves (Jn 6:5–13), and the walking on the water (Jn 6:16–21).

1. There is a correlation in the Gospels between the "mighty deeds" of Jesus and *faith*. The mighty deeds are religious signs and therefore appeal to faith. They do not overwhelm the observer, but address his or her faith. They seek a response of faith from the person who is the object of the deed or they appeal to the faith of other witnesses.

2. *In the Gospels these signs are not separate from Jesus' main task, the proclamation of the kingdom.* In Acts a presentation of Jesus' mighty deeds as "authenticating signs" is developing. But in the Gospels themselves they are internal to Jesus' message, *the proclamation of the kingdom.* Mark especially presents them in strict correlation with what Jesus is announcing. They are part of both the announcement *and* its fulfillment. Just as Jesus' proclamation was an appeal to faith, so are his mighty deeds. In the Gospels, then, the "mighty deeds" are part of the proclamation of the reign of God and signs of its arrival. They are not

"interventions of God in the laws of nature" but religious events announcing, symbolizing, making present God's reign. In the Gospels this reign supplants the reign of Satan. Since according to the biblical view, what we call the "natural" world is under the rule of Satan because of creation's participation in the effects of sin and evil, the reign of God comes as a dominion over nature. The "nature *dunameis*" (walking on water, calming of the storm) illustrate the comprehensive defeat of Satan taking place in Jesus' ministry. As the alienation of men and women from God is reflected in the creation, so the reconciliation of men and women with God offered in the coming of the kingdom manifests itself in the reconciliation among humanity and with the "natural" world. The "nature deeds" are signs that the whole of creation has been taken under the reign of God, and they point to the new heaven and the new earth.

3. Besides their purpose of exhibiting the presence of the kingdom, the *dunameis* are presented in the Gospels as exhibiting Jesus' *exousia*, his power, and thus his role in the coming of the kingdom. Any temptation to see the Gospels as confining Jesus' role to that of one (like John the Baptist) who merely points to an approaching event but does not mediate the coming of that event must be rejected. (Interestingly, there is no tradition of John the Baptist performing signs like Jesus.) The "deeds" illustrate more dramatically something that is already present in the preaching and other activities of Jesus: for the Gospel writers the kingdom comes *through* Jesus. The mighty deeds of Jesus are thus presented in the Gospels as a revelation of who Jesus is. The Gospels do not present them as overwhelming *proof* of Jesus' identity as Messiah. Rather, they are *part* of the revelation (which can only be understood by faith) of who Jesus is. They appeal to faith, but they do not compel it.

4. If the *dunameis* are part of the coming of the reign of God, what do they reveal about that coming? They reveal that the salvation brought by the kingdom of God is the well-being of the whole person and of society. They affect the person physically and mentally, and restore the person to his or her place in society and with God. Society itself is restored to health. The reign of God in Jesus' mighty deeds is revealed to be "integral salvation," the healing of all that is broken.

THE HISTORICAL-CRITICAL EXAMINATION

What does contemporary scholarship say about the Gospel picture? Did Jesus do "mighty deeds"? We cannot arrive at a truly religious response by a purely historical examination, but critical scholarship's views of the Gospel picture sheds light on the peculiarly modern question of whether the Gospel accounts at this point are history or theology. That is not always a crucial question. But it is important here. Whether Jesus' proclamation of the coming of the reign of God is accompanied by deeds of power helps us identify the nature of the reign of God. Is Jesus merely enlightening us about God's transcendental presence to us as creatures or is he revealing that there is a new situation in human history? In saying that Jesus did mighty deeds, are the Gospel writers presenting as an external event something which happened only internally in the form of an "awakening" to creaturehood?

The Gospel writers, of course, did not ask our question, at least with the precision we ask it. They did not distinguish the historical and theological questions as we do. Nevertheless, when we ask our questions of them, the picture that emerges from historical criticism is that, on the one hand, from more conservative biblical scholars there is the acknowledgment of *accretions* to the tradition. We can see, for instance, a tendency in Matthew to intensify the power of Jesus when he retells the mighty deeds he learned from Mark. Scholars generally acknowledge that the evangelists' lack of interest in distinguishing historical and theological elements leads to intensification, embellishment, and multiplication since retelling historical fact is not their sole concern. In particular, the "form critics" see in a number of the *dunameis* a retrojection back into Jesus' pre-Easter existence of the effect of the Easter experience. Furthermore, while there are significant differences between the Gospel *dunameis* and the mighty deeds of others appearing in rabbinic and Hellenistic literature, there are suspicious parallels, too. This compels even a mainstream Catholic theologian like Walter Kasper to conclude: "The result of all this is that we must describe many of the gospel miracle stories as legendary" (*Jesus the Christ*, p. 90), meaning that some of the Gospel *dunameis* are the final product of an "intensification" process that added to a legitimate historical core stories similar to the historical core.

On the other hand, the more skeptical scholars assert that the core of the *dunameis* tradition is historical. Thus Rudolf Bultmann states: "Undoubtedly (Jesus) healed the sick and cast out demons" (*Jesus and the Word*, p. 173). What Bultmann understands by "cast out demons" is expressed well and endorsed by Norman Perrin: "In a world that believed in gods, in the powers of good and evil, and in demons, he was able, in the name of God and his Kingdom, to help those who believed themselves to be possessed by demons" (*Introduction to the New Testament*, p. 288).

So the question is not whether Jesus did *dunameis*. Rather the question for the historian is *which dunameis* portrayed in the Gospels are history and which embody the theologizing intention of the writers concerning the coming of the kingdom. As Kasper says, "There can scarcely be a single serious exegete who does not believe in a basic stock of historically certain miracles. These would include *dunameis* of physical healing, curing disease and illnesses whose symptoms were associated at that time with possession" (p. 90).

What is not historical, then? It is common among New Testament scholars to see the "nature *dunameis*" are part of the message about the ultimate *significance* of the coming of the reign. They are not an attempt to fabricate history. They may be the result of the normal process of legend-creation but *in the Gospels* their purpose is theological, although of course a pure theological intention cannot be located here any more than a pure historical one can. The trouble is, however, that "nature *dunameis*" is not really a useful category. It prejudices the question, and seems to come from the Enlightenment worldview of a closed system.

A more important historical question is: Are the Gospels recording history when they present Jesus as regarding his "mighty deeds" as the coming of the kingdom? The answer is a universal "yes." This is bedrock tradition, for it is found in sayings of Jesus that are commonly considered to come from the pre-Easter Jesus, for example, "If by the finger of God I cast out demons, then the kingdom of God has come upon you" (Lk 11:20). For Jesus the kingdom is already present in his mighty deeds. On the one hand, like his preaching, they appeal to faith. On the other, just as he saw the kingdom as already present in his preaching, so did he claim that the kingdom was already present in his deeds.

THE CONTEMPORARY PROBLEMATIC

When the Greek *dunameis* was translated into Latin, it became *miraculum*, miracle. In turn, with the growth of science in the seventeenth and eighteenth centuries and the emergence of the Enlightenment worldview, "miracle" came to have a new connotation. No longer did it designate a saving action of God, essentially connected with faith, in which God enabled an open cosmos to transcend itself. A miracle came to be seen as an "intervention by God in the laws of nature," an event in an objective world of determined nature. Such a definition of miracles has taken them out of their proper context, the religious context.

The discussion of miracles became a discussion of events in a world of metaphysical and scientific objectivity, of events supposedly taking place within a closed mechanistic system and "interrupting" deterministic causality.

The switch from a worldview that absorbs nature in history to one where even history is absorbed into nature is due to the fact that science found the notion of a determined, mechanistic "closed-system" universe a useful presupposition of its observations. Then historiography, imitating the objectivity of science, also assumed uniformity in the phenomena it studied. It understood events by their similarity with other events. Methodologically neither science nor history had much room for that which was truly new, in the sense of not being derivable from what already exists.

Thus the question of miracles brings one into the heart of present questions: the methods of science and history, the nature of the universe, whether existence is ultimately to be understood as nature or history, whether reality is open-ended, whether the truly "new" is possible, and what would be its source.

Theologically the world is history, not nature, because, taken as a whole, it is continuing creation. The Hebrew doctrine of creation saw the physical world *and* human history as *one* continuing divine project. To discuss miracles as interventions of God in nature removes them from their proper context. A miracle in the theological sense is not a "natural" or "physical" phenomenon, happening in a sphere completely governed by physical laws, to which significance is subsequently added. It is *of its essence* a sign and is primordially interpersonal. It reveals God's presence in his creation, in which "nature" is subsumed in history. Furthermore, a "miracle" in the biblical sense occurs every time creation transcends itself. No doubt the biblical peoples saw miracles where there were none, even in this sense, for example, in the growth of crops. But *we* suffer from a reaction. We do not see the miracle every time a new person comes into existence, every time grace enables love to triumph over hatred, or even in the continuing existence of the cosmos, which after all, of itself, cannot account for itself. Furthermore as signs, the possibility of miracles correlates with the openness of people to them. Miracles are the creative power of God, which is continually acting, becoming active where it can be recognized. Such "acts" cannot be conceived as "interventions." They do not go against a closed system but enable an open one, which itself is a miracle, to transcend itself. If God's power as creator is manifest in a physical phenomenon, such a manifestation must not be understood as though God acted as a "secondary cause," that is, as a finite cause. God's causality is transcendent and would have to manifest itself *through* created secondary or categorical causes simply because God cannot be subject to the conditions of space and time the way categorical or secondary (finite) causes are. No doubt Scripture in large part ignores this constraint, attributing immediately to God's causality nearly everything that happens. But behind that view is a profound metaphysics—it is an expression of a belief in God's transcendental causality, that is, that all being which is not God derives its existence from that which is existence itself. Despite the biblical mind's mythologizing of God's activity, one must ask: Is the Enlightenment view of the cosmos as an impenetrable closed system really preferable to the biblical view of an open-ended creation?

SUMMARY

Jesus did not perform his mighty deeds to prove his words. Rather they were *extensions of his preaching.* They reveal the nature and presence of the reign of God. Since Jesus saw the miracles as *freeing* actions, then for him the kingdom of God meant the release of men and women from the reign of Satan and its effects—possession, disease, and sin. This happens not in an afterlife, but *now.* There is a *present freeing* of men and women from that which oppressed them. For Jesus, Satan and the forces of evil stand behind this oppression. The reign of God comes as the defeat of this demonic enslaving power. Since this power is primarily a source of internal oppression, it is defeated there (exorcism). But since all that oppresses has its source in that internal oppression, freeing men and women internally has its reverberations in the external sphere (healing, restoration to life in society). The *dunameis* of Jesus are directed at the whole person, on all levels, in all his or her relationships (with oneself, one's world, and with God).

Understanding Jesus' view of his "mighty deeds" is a powerful antidote to any pure spiritualization or idealization of the kingdom. A purely spiritual kingdom is totally foreign to the Hebrew mentality. The kingdom is not just the kingdom of freedom, the purely internal enlightenment, of German idealism. It is a concrete, comprehensive creative reality which has the power to embrace and heal human existence in all its dimensions and all its relationships.

Appendix 5:

THE AIM OF JESUS

INTRODUCTION

The characterization of Jesus' *goal* or *purpose* as his "aim" or "aims" can be traced to the essay which sparked the debate about the "historical Jesus," H.S. Reimarus' *The Aims of Jesus and His Apostles* (1778). Reimarus attributed to Jesus a political aim. Writing in a culture which had learned to distinguish the religious and the political, he held that Jesus' goal was to free Israel from Roman domination and that he had no religious mission. Anachronistic as the assumption of Reimarus was, namely, that the political and religious were distinguished in Israel, he did at least attribute to Jesus a clear aim bearing on the history of his people. In the nineteenth century "Search for the Historical Jesus" the idea that Jesus had a concrete infrahistorical aim was almost totally lost. He became a man without a specific goal bearing on the history of his time, a figure so religious or so spiritual that nothing smacking of a "this worldly" purpose was allowed to touch him.

But nothing gives coherence to a life as having a clear goal.

And Jesus certainly appears, both in the Gospels and in critical scholarship, as a man living a coherent existence, a life focused on a task. What was that task? It is virtually unanimous that Jesus set himself to announce the coming of definitive salvation:

The time is fulfilled, and the kingdom of God is at hand; repent, and believe in the Gospel (Mk 1:15).

But the question of Jesus' aim goes one step further. What did Jesus hope to accomplish by his proclamation? Did he have a concrete, infrahistorical goal? Did he wish to change *Israel*? Did he seek to found *a new community*? Or was he merely seeking to awaken *individuals* to their situation before God?

A start can be made by recalling Jesus' context as a Jew. As such he would be predisposed to see God's definitive saving act as bearing on Israel *as a people*. If one acknowledges this as Jesus' context, a number of his otherwise perplexing sayings fall into place. Two recent books have made especially important contributions to this question: *The Aims of Jesus* by Ben F. Meyer (SCM, 1979) and *Jesus and Community,* by Gerhard Lohfink (Fortress, Paulist, 1984).

SAYINGS OF JESUS ON JOHN THE BAPTIST

Understanding John's aims helps to understand Jesus' aims. There is no doubt how the *early Christians* saw John the Baptist— he was to *prepare* Israel for the final days, the coming of definitive salvation that had occurred in Jesus. Thus Mark situates John by combining the prophet Malachi (3:1) and Isaiah (40:3):

Behold, I send my messenger before
  your face
who shall prepare your way;
The voice of one crying in the
  wilderness:
Prepare the way of the Lord,
make his paths straight (Mk 1:3
  par).

Nor is there any reason to challenge that this is the way *John understood himself.* While there may have been aspects about the relative roles of John and Jesus which influenced the portrayal of John by Jesus' disciples, there is no reason to doubt the historicity of the scene in which John sends messengers to Jesus to ask if he is "the one who is to come" (Mt 11:2–6 par). He thus seems to have seen himself as *preparing* the way for the one to come.

But what is most enlightening for our purposes is how *Jesus* viewed the Baptist. This throws light on Jesus' understanding of his own purposes. The clearest statement that Jesus saw John as the early Christians and John himself did is Matthew 11:7–10; par, Luke 7:24–27:

What did you go out to the
  wilderness to see?
A reed being shaken by the wind?
Then, what did you go out to see?
A man clothed in soft raiment?
Behold, men wearing soft raiment
  are in the houses of kings.
Why, then, did you go out? To see a
  prophet?
Yes, I tell you, and more than a
  prophet!
This is he of whom it is written:
"Behold, I send my messenger
  before your face
who shall prepare your way before
  you."

In this statement Jesus is interpreting the Baptist's career as part of a fulfillment event, and thereby confirming John's own self-interpretation. He identifies John with Elijah:

If you are willing to accept it, he is Elijah who is to come (Mt 11:14).

We can get closer to understanding John's preparatory role by examining the meaning of Jesus' identification of him as Elijah. The prophet Malachi, picking up on a theme from Deutero-Isaiah, assigned a task to Elijah:

Behold I will send you Elijah the
prophet
before the coming of the great and
terrible day of Yahweh
And he shall turn the hearts of
fathers to their sons
and the hearts of sons to their
fathers
lest I come and smite the land with a
curse (Mal 3:23f).

Malachi had already specified
what the task of purification con-
sisted in: the purification of the
priesthood (3:13) and an end to
familial wrangling and strife in
the face of judgment (3:24). *Ben
Sira* (48:10) added, also with reference to Deutero-Isaiah (49:6),
that it would be Elijah's task to *reestablish the tribes of Jacob.*

Another text, which, in its
present form, even conservative
scholars would say reflects the
post-resurrection polemic between orthodox Jews and Jewish
Christians but which nevertheless
is probably rooted in the historical Jesus, confirms Jesus' identification of John's task with that
ascribed to Elijah by the prophets:

Why (the disciples ask) do the scribes
say: "First, Elijah must come"? And
he said to them, "Elijah does indeed
come first to restore all things. And
how is it written of the Son of Man
that he should suffer much and be
despised? But I tell you Elijah has
come, and they did to him whatever
they pleased, as it is written of him"
(Mk 9:11–13).

Can we say, then, what John's
mission was by interpreting Jesus'
identification of him as Elijah?
According to B.F. Meyer (*The
Aims of Jesus*, p. 127):

There can be no reasonable doubt
about the decisive significance of the
Baptist in the scheme of the eschaton
as Jesus understood it. The baptism
of John (Mark 11:30 par) was heaven-
sent; 'the days of John' (Matt 11:12)
epitomized the inauguration of eschatological fulfillment. But 'the days
of John' were no more than inauguration. . . . Elijah, then, is (so to speak)
demythologized. His return is not a
literal reincarnation but a role in the
eschatological scenario, and his mission of restoration is concretely accomplished by John's preaching and
baptizing. . . .

What does it mean to say
John had "a mission of restoration"? We determine this not so
much from *Jesus'* words about
John but from *John's* own words
and actions *and the entire Old Testament expectation of what would
happen at the end-time.* Two actions
of John shed light on his mission:
the *locale* of his activity, the wilderness, and that which gave him
his appellation—the *rite* of baptism.

"Wilderness" (Hebrew: *mid-
bar*) was a loaded symbol for Israel. On the one hand it connoted
the demonic, the temptations of
the people in the desert (cf. the locale of Jesus' temptations). On the
other hand, the wilderness signi-

fied a return to God, Israel returning to its origins, its beginnings as God's people during the exodus. Why did John set himself up in the desert but near Jerusalem? It would seem to be to call Israel out from its present state to new beginnings. He was summoning Israel to return to the Lord.

Was this merely another prophet asking what the prophets always asked—that Israel be faithful to the covenant? No. His context is eschatological: the end is at hand and Israel must be ready for *judgment.* The rite which John used fits with this interpretation. It was designed to express the conversion of Israel in the face of "the wrath to come" (Mt 3:7 par). It is true that individual Israelites were obliged to turn and be converted:

Do not start saying to yourselves
"We have Abraham for our father."
I tell you:
God can raise up sons to Abraham
    out of these stones (Lk 3:8; Mt
    3:9).

But John's activity was prologue to judgment, and judgment would come as separation and gathering—the separation of the chaff with the resulting emergence of the true Israel:

I baptize you with water for
    repentance
but one comes after me mightier
    than me

whose sandals I am unworthy to
    carry;
he will baptize you with the Holy
    Spirit and fire.
His winnowing fork is in his hand.
And he will clear his threshing floor
and gather his wheat into the
    granary
but the chaff he will burn with
    unquenchable fire (Mt 3:11–12).

At least two points seem clear: (1) John's mission was preparatory to the coming judge; (2) the appearance of the judge was imminent. Did John merely wish to alert individual Israelites to their danger? Again, to ask the question in that form is to indulge in an anachronism. It would never have crossed the mind of a contemporary of John. John would have *had* to conceive judgment in collective or "ecclesial" terms. To miss this is to miss the whole context of John's activity, and indeed the entire biblical understanding of salvation.

THE AIMS OF JESUS IN HIS PUBLIC PROCLAMATION

While Jesus affirmed the validity of John's career, the emphasis in his message was different. John's focused directly on "the wrath to come"—judgment. Jesus' proclamation had a different accent. Judgment was not absent from it, but it stressed rather the offer of salvation. Jesus proclaimed God's definitive, final, saving act—the *malkuta YHWH,* the reign of God. This is not in conflict with John but rather a difference in emphasis. Clearly John foresaw salvation for Israel if it turned to God; Jesus announced judgment to Israel if it did not recognize the time of its deliverance.

The difference and similarity of the two ministries is alluded to in Jesus' words:

To what shall I compare this
    generation?
It is like children sitting in the
    market place
and calling to their playmates,
"We piped to you and you did not
    dance,
we wailed and you mourned not."
For John came neither eating nor
    drinking
and they say, "He is mad."
Then along comes one who eats and
    drinks
and they say, "Behold, a glutton and
    drunkard,
a friend of tax-collectors and
    sinners" (Mt 11:16–19b; par Lk
    7:13–34).

The difference is obvious. John came as Elijah and consciously imitated him (in clothes and food and place of work). Jesus ate and drank like everyone else and circulated in the towns and cities.

And they said to him, "The disciples of John fast often and offer prayers, and so do the disciples of the Phari-

sees, but yours eat and drink" (Lk 5:33).

But the difference in style betrays a difference in self-understanding:

And Jesus said to them: "Can you make wedding guests fast while the bridegroom is with them" (Lk 5:34).

There can be no doubt that Jesus saw that what John had anticipated had come to pass:

Now when John heard in prison
    about the deeds of the Christ,
he sent word by his disciples and said
    to him,
"Are you he who is to come, or shall
    we look for another?"
And Jesus answered them,
"Go tell John what you hear and see:
The blind receive their sight and the
    lame walk,
lepers are cleansed and the deaf
    hear,
and the dead are raised up,
and the poor have the good news
    preached to them" (Mt 11:2–5
    par).

For Jesus, John was an authentic prophet, but a new age, the final age, was dawning.

No one greater has arisen among
    men than John,
and the least in the reign of God is
    greater than he (Mt 11:11).

Compared to John's message of *judgment,* the striking note of

Jesus' proclamation is *grace*. But they have a common *aim*.

THE RESTORATION OF ISRAEL

The *aim* of Jesus' proclamation fits squarely within the broad stream of biblical eschatology. Jesus' aim was the "gathering" of Israel, its restoration in anticipation of the end-time. If only a remnant responded, so be it—this would be the true Israel. We must never lose sight of what scholarship itself has so often overlooked—that Jesus would have spontaneously seen salvation as something that bore on Israel *as a people.*

Thus, we see Jesus presenting the coming of the reign of God in *standard Old Testament descriptions* which express that salvation comes to Israel as such:

• as the banquet of Israel:

I tell you, many will come from east and west
and sit at the table
with Abraham, Isaac, and Jacob
in the kingdom of heaven (Mt 8:11 par).

• as the gathering of the tribes:

Truly, I say to you, in the new world,
when the Son of Man shall sit on his glorious throne,
you who have followed me
will also sit on twelve thrones,
judging (governing) the twelve tribes of Israel (Mt 19:28).

• as the new temple (Mk 14:58 par, 15:29 par; Jn 2:19). (We will explore this key image further below (in *The Temple Riddle*).

We also see him using *new* images that expressed salvation as a communal event. These appear most frequently in the debates Jesus had with the Pharisees. His weapon in these debates was the parable, one of which—the mustard seed (Mk 4:30–32 par)—is especially relevant to the clarification of Jesus' mission:

And he said,
"With what can we compare the kingdom of God,
or what parable shall we use for it?
It is like a grain of mustard seed,
which,
when sown upon the ground
is the smallest of all the seeds on earth;
yet when it is sown it grows up and becomes the greatest of shrubs,
and puts forth large branches,
so that the birds of the air can make nests in its shade."

The parable is both a "parable of growth" and a "contrast parable."

Clues to its concrete definition lie in the image of the birds and in the word *kataskenoun* ("to nest"). The birds nesting in the great shrubs evoke Gentiles taking refuge with Israel; and *kateskenoun* is a technical term for the eschatological assimilation of the Gentiles to the people of God. The original issue must accordingly have been the unimpressiveness of Jesus' following. If he really had a divine mission, ran the objection, he would not be surrounded by this rag-tag band, but by the best and the brightest. The parable answers: "With the same compelling certainty that causes a tall shrub to grow out of a minute grain of mustard seed . . . will God's miraculous power cause my small band to swell into the mighty host of the people of God in the Messianic Age, embracing the Gentiles (J. Jeremias, *The Parables of Jesus*, p. 149)" (Meyer, p. 164).

Also worthy of closer examination is the enigmatic statement of Jesus in Matthew 15:24, "I am sent only to the lost sheep of Israel." It is enigmatic because Jesus took a positive attitude toward Samaritans (Lk 10:25–37; 17:11–19) and Gentiles (see quote above). He did not endorse the traditional theme of eschatological vengeance on the Gentiles (Lk 4:22; Mt 11:5f par), and he positively included the Gentiles among the saved in the reign of God (Mk 4:32 par; Mt 8:11 par; 12:41f par; 25:31–46). What does this saying mean in the light of this? Meyer offers a compelling explanation:

The solution is given in Jesus' view of the scheme of salvation. His own task and so that of his disciples (Mt 10:5–6: "Go nowhere among the Gentiles, and enter no town of the Samaritans, but go rather to the lost sheep of the house of Israel") exclusively re-

garded the winning over of Israel, for the Gentiles would find salvation by assimilation to saved Israel at the judgment bringing history to an end (cf. the eschatological pilgrimage of the nations to Zion, Matt 8:11 par) (Meyer, pp. 167–168).

Other parables of Jesus reinforce the picture emerging here, for example, Matthew 13:33 (the parable of the leaven), Matthew 12:38–42 (the reference to the conversion of Nineveh in the story of Jonah), Luke 15:11–32 (the prodigal son), and Luke 15:3–7 (the lost sheep).

THE TEMPLE RIDDLE

One would expect that the question of Jesus' *aim* and the fact of his execution as a messianic pretender are related. An element in the trial of Jesus common to John and the Synoptics is the "temple riddle." In the Synoptic Gospels it is cited by Jesus' enemies (Mk 14:58; 15:29; Mt 16:61; 27:40; cf. Acts 6:14). In John it is spoken by Jesus himself.

Destroy this temple and in three days I will raise it up (Jn 2:19).

The early Christians themselves could not fathom the meaning of the riddle. The author of John makes it refer to Jesus' resurrection. The Synoptics recount it as testimony against Jesus but do not explain it. It seems that Jesus deliberately intended it to be a riddle, much like the saying on the sign of Jonah (Mt 12:39 par) and the statement about the "three days" in Jesus' divinely destined course (Lk 13:32).

An understanding of apocalyptic symbolism can help us decipher the riddle. Jesus seemed to understand his mission against an apocalyptic background, an eschatology of fierce but brief trial, followed by a resolution of the crisis. The standard apocalyptic eschatology envisioned the destruction of the temple as part of the trial, and Jesus probably endorsed this (Mk 13:2ff par). According to the apocalyptic scenario, in the resolution of the crisis the temple was to be miraculously restored as part of the definitive constitution of Israel as God's people. This saying, like the other "three days," means "the imminent crisis epitomized in the destruction of the temple would swiftly yield to the salvation epitomized in the new temple to be built by Jesus" (Meyer, p. 182).

It is important to understand the connotations "temple" had for Jesus and his contemporaries. He probably envisioned the destruction of the physical temple, but "temple" meant more than the building. Israel saw itself as a cultic community and the center of its worship was the temple. The temple was Israel at its heart. A cultural anthropologist would say that the physical temple "replicated" the living temple that was Israel. In fact, the actual physical layout of the temple compound mirrored Israel's conception of its own internal social organization. Thus sayings such as

I will bring them to my holy
   mountain
and make them joyful in my house
   of prayer.
Their holocausts and sacrifices
   will be acceptable on my altar.
For my house shall be called a house
   of prayer
for all peoples (Is 56:7)

have a multilevel meaning. The holy mountain (Zion, the hill on which the temple was built) *is* Israel as is the temple ("house of prayer") itself. Accordingly Jesus' statements about the temple are examples of *synecdoche,* a figure of speech in which the part stands for the whole.

One final note: If the rediscovery of the *eschatological* nature of the preaching of Jesus is the single most significant factor in twentieth century New Testament study of Jesus, the next great contribution will come from those scholars who are able to see how thoroughly *ecclesial* the ministry of Jesus of Nazareth was.

Appendix 6:

THE ESCHATOLOGY OF JESUS

Was Jesus wrong about the coming of the reign of God? A number of important Protestant scholars have held that he was. This was the opinion of Albert Schweitzer. Reacting against the picture of Jesus elaborated by late nineteenth century liberal Protestantism (Harnack), Schweitzer emphasized the *eschatological* nature of Jesus' preaching. Jesus expected the imminent end of history. Not only was he not the preacher of a timeless message of "God and the soul, the soul and its God," but his central concern was to announce to the Israel of his time the fulfillment of apocalyptic expectations, the destruction of the old world and the creation of a new one.

Johannes Weiss also held this view ("consistent eschatology"). The word "irrupt" expresses how Weiss captured Jesus' understanding of how this event would take place. The end was near and would irrupt suddenly into history, bringing it to a close. Such a view places Jesus completely within an apocalyptic horizon and his horizon is invalidated by the continued roll of history.

Perhaps the most influential Protestant scholar, on this point as on so many others, has been Rudolph Bultmann. Weiss was Bultmann's *doktorvater*, mentor, and on this point the disciple never departed from the master. What is most interesting and difficult to understand is how little significance the attribution of error to Jesus had for Bultmann. This is because for Bultmann Christian faith does not rise or fall on the basis of a connection with the historical Jesus. Christianity's truth claims rise or fall only with the truth of the *view of human existence* present in the authentic letters of Paul and the Johannine literature. Furthermore, it is only in the *proclamation* of the message of Paul and John and in its acceptance in faith that one truly "knows" God in faith. For Bultmann faith does not pass through the historical Jesus but is the result of a direct encounter with God's summons through *the proclamation of the kerygma* in a demythologized form.

It is understandable, therefore, that for Bultmann there is no pressing concern to connect the preaching of the early Church and the preaching of Jesus. A "functional equivalence" exists and is certainly enough, if indeed it is even necessary at all. Since Jesus is merely the "presupposition" of the New Testament, we need only be concerned with the "that" (*Dass*) of his existence. The "what" (*Was*) and the "how" (*Wie*) are not crucial for faith. Jesus brought the people of his time face-to-face with their radical dependence on God; Paul and John did it for their contemporaries. The task of present day theology and preaching is, by "existential interpretation" of the New Testament, especially Paul and the Johannine literature, to do the same for our contemporaries. The role of Jesus here is clear. He is a mediator of salvation only in that he enlightens us about our situation as creatures before our creator, and only in that he inaugurated the process. Since, according to Weiss, Jesus' expectations were not fulfilled, Bultmann divested Jesus' eschatological message of its concrete temporal reference. What is valid in Jesus' preaching is what is left when it is demythologized, namely, the call for radical faith in God. As Bultmann puts it, the eschatological proclamation and the ethical demand that follows from it both "direct man to the fact that he is thereby brought before God, that God stands before him; both direct him into his Now as the

hour of decision before God" (*Theology of the New Testament*, p. 21).

There is, of course, something in what Bultmann said. In a real sense Now is always the hour of decision. But is that all we have left when the message of Jesus is made accessible to modern men and women? Could we not get as much from John the Baptist? Has not Bultmann resurrected the Jesus of Harnack with suitable adjustments for a less optimistic culture?

A position close to Bultmann's but with a significant difference is that of Wolfhart Pannenberg, a major contemporary Protestant theologian. In his book *Jesus—God and Man* (p. 26) he says:

There is no doubt that Jesus erred when he announced that God's Lordship would begin in his own generation (Mt 23:36; 16:28; Mk 13:30 par; cf. Mt 10:23). The end of the world did not begin in Jesus' generation and also not in the generation of his disciples, the witnesses of his resurrection. Here we stand before the notorious problem of the delay of the parousia, the problem of the two thousand years that have since elapsed without the arrival of the end of the world and God's universal rule.

Having admitted that Jesus erred, Pannenberg must ask: In proclaiming that the "reign of God is at hand" is not Jesus just enlightening us about something that is already here and simply needs to be recognized? Does he really announce something new? After all, as Pannenberg says, is not "the unqualified trust, the unreserved commitment to the imminent Kingdom of God that Jesus demands of his hearers nothing else than the childlike trust that man as creature should in any case bring to God?" (*Jesus— God and Man*, p. 231). Is it not that

. . . the natural essence of man is revealed in Jesus' eschatological preaching. By promising salvation without preconditions but demanding unconditional trust for this promise, he brings man into his natural relationship to God, corresponding to man's creaturely destiny. Or, expressed in a more modern way, Jesus brings man into the radical openness that constitutes the specific fundamental element of human nature (ibid).

Up to a point, then, Pannenberg agrees with Bultmann. But he has a significantly different understanding of prophecy and, as a result, a fundamentally different position on this classic question:

Jesus' imminent expectation did not, however, remain unfulfilled. It was fulfilled in the only way it is possible to speak of the fulfillment of prophetic proclamations and promises, namely in such a way that the original sense of the prophecy is revised by an event that corresponds to it but nonetheless has more or less different character than could be known from the prophecy alone. The Christian Easter message speaks of the mode of fulfillment of Jesus' imminent expectation. It was fulfilled by himself, insofar as the eschatological reality of the resurrection of the dead appeared in Jesus himself. It is not yet universally fulfilled in the way in which Jesus and his contemporaries had expected. In spite of this, Jesus' resurrection justifies the imminent expectation that had moved him and establishes anew the eschatological expectation fulfilled in him for the rest of humanity" (*Jesus—God and Man*, p. 226).

Thus Pannenberg leans toward taking Jesus as a prophet and understanding his expectations in terms of *prophetic consciousness*. This approach is similar to a number of Catholic scholars. Rudolf Schnackenburg in his important book, *God's Reign and Kingdom*, had anticipated Pannenberg. He acknowledges that one cannot dispense with certain sayings in the Gospels in which Jesus ties the coming of the reign of God to "this generation" (Mk 9:1; Mt 16:28; Mt 10:23). But he points out that to overlook important cultural differences is a mistake.

To approach these questions critically we shall have to abandon our empirical notions of time, which envisage time in our Western thinking as a continuously moving line, divisible into measurable sections ("spaces"). Biblical thought about salvation, on the other hand, asks what occurs in time and what fills it, and inquires what action of God gives every time its character and significance. Since Jesus proclaimed his eschatological gospel, *the whole of time* is near to the fulfilled *basileia,* because this has become tangible and certain in Jesus, penetrates through him into "this aeon" and works upon men, is in a certain sense already present and awaits only its manifestation in glory (p. 213).

In other words, our Western thinking approaches time quantitatively, while biblical thinking views it qualitatively. The decisive, eschatological moment, precisely because it is the culminating moment, would be the "final" moment *no matter when it happened* or how long history continued. Schnackenburg points out that the early Christians, while they expected an early parousia, did not admit any mistake on the part of Jesus. Did they understand something about Jesus' consciousness that we do not? Schnackenburg is suggesting this. Among Catholic scholars this view is taken further by Ben F. Meyer. Expanding on the idea that Jesus is in the prophetic tradition, Meyer points out in *The Man for Others* (Bruce 1970) that Jesus' sayings about the future fall into a pattern of crisis and resolution of crisis. Meyer believes that Jesus saw time in terms of the "apocalyptic scenario." He admits that the actual scheme Jesus seems to employ does not corre-

spond to history, as it occurred, especially in regard to the *immediacy* of events. But he points out that Jesus expectations "are reminiscent of the predictions of the classical prophets":

Their sayings, like those of Jesus, bear on the immediate future. And just as Israel did not repudiate the predictions of the prophets because they were not immediately fulfilled, but rather (while always hoping for a swift fulfillment) learned to expect its coming in the time of God's own choosing, so, too, it never occurred to the first Christians to repudiate the predictions of Jesus on the ground they were not immediately fulfilled. In Jesus' vision of the future, it would seem, both crisis and resolution were grasped as elements of a single whole. In actual fact, however, the fulfillment of the predictions turned out to be differentiated and expanded in time. The fulfillment began on the third day after Jesus' death, and not with a crisis-event but with a resolution event (p. 58).

Meyer suggests that we reformulate the question. The classic formulation—"Was Jesus mistaken, then, about the future?"—must give way to the question his contemporaries would have asked: Is Jesus the eschatological prophet? This question takes him on his own terms, in his own cultural milieu. It takes Jesus seriously as prophet and asks whether he was a true or false one, which is what his disciples would have asked. And (*pace*

Bultmann) that is a very important question which cannot be
sidestepped without calling into
question Christianity itself. It also
provides a better approach to an
answer about Jesus' eschatology.
Looking at Jesus this way, as his
contemporaries spontaneously
would have and as Jesus saw himself, takes into account the peculiar nature of prophetic
consciousness, for it opens up the
possibility that the scheme of
things intended by Jesus is *symbolic*. The question can be rephrased as follows: "Did Jesus
have determinate knowledge of
what would happen, which
knowledge he was commissioned
to announce?" The answer seems
to be "no," for that is not what
prophetic knowledge is. But did
Jesus have symbolic knowledge
which, in its capacity to encom-
pass both God's initiative and the
human response to God's initiative, leaves the future free for
God's renewed initiative to crea-
tively respond? The answer is yes.
Acknowledging that his language
is symbolic, and being open to the
Christian understanding of his
resurrection, one can say that Jesus' expectations were prophetic
and correct *within the context of
prophecy*. Like the other prophets,
Jesus left it to God to fill in the
content of his preaching which
envisioned the future in a symbolic manner and thus could en-
compass a range of responses
from Israel.

It might appear that W. Kas-
per's *Jesus the Christ,* an important
recent contribution to Christology, would not agree with this approach. In discussing several
possible solutions to the question
of the tension between present
and future on the sayings of Jesus
(pp. 76–77) Kasper rejects one
that sounds similar to that proposed by Meyer: "One which will
not stand is the psychological view
which believes that as a result of
inspirational ecstasy or of a specific prophetic attitude Jesus saw
present and future as inter-
woven" (p. 76). But Kasper is rejecting views with a common
characteristic: "All these interpretations eliminate the temporal
and historical character of the
tensions between the statements
about the present and those about
the future." Thus, Kasper is rejecting a collapsing of present and
future aspects. Meyer's solution
does not do that. It presents Jesus
as seeing the present of the kingdom as a time of crisis, and its future as a time of resolution.
Meyer's view does not collapse
present and future but maintains
the tension.

Meyer's solution is dependent on Joachim Jeremias whom
Kasper acknowledges takes the
tension seriously (p. 76). Kasper's
own solution is dependent on
Günther Bornkamm (*Jesus of Nazareth,* p. 93), whose solution turns
on the concept of the peculiar nature of "biblical time." In both

views, there is an acknowledgment that the problem arises from different understandings of time, the modern and the biblical. Kasper develops his own answer on pp. 77–78:

Jesus is proclaiming that the reign of God is coming.

But the concrete shape and time of the reign of God is determined by man's openness to it.

The *future* reign is thus determined by man's *present* response.

Hence the future reign (the "not yet") is already present as something to which Jesus' hearers must respond.

But one might ask: Does Kasper's solution (based after all on a disciple of Bultmann) really maintain what seems to be essential to the preaching of Jesus (and certainly has always been maintained by mainstream Christianity) that in Jesus we do not merely have a message about the *timeless* relationship of God and his creatures? Kasper seems to sense he must go beyond Bornkamm, for he says the problem really is the same problem you have in the Old Testament. Prophecy is not foreknowledge of a *scenario* for

history. History does not follow a scenario. Prophecy says what God is doing—but what God is doing is always open-ended. It is precisely the nature of God's activity that it seeks a free response. Thus history is not determined *solely* by God but is always the result of God's initiative, humanity's response, and God's incorporation of humanity's response into a new initiative. "God's promise opens up a new possibility for human beings, but the particular realization of the possibility depends on human decisions, on their faith or unbelief. God's kingdom, in other words, does not bypass human faith, but comes when God is recognized in faith as Lord" (p. 78).

Thus Jesus was not foretelling a determinate future. He was speaking prophetically in the strict biblical sense. The time was at hand in a way it had never been before. God's offer, Israel's response, God's response to Israel's response would fill in the content. Whether Jesus was a *true* prophet is the question and, as Pannenberg said, the answer depends on whether Jesus rose from the dead.

Chapter VII

JESUS' RELATION TO THE COMING OF THE REIGN OF GOD

Everything we know about Jesus has to be understood against the background of his message that "the reign of God is at hand," especially when we ask the question about Jesus' understanding of his relationship to the coming of the reign of God. Herein lies a problem.

THE PROBLEM

On the one hand, almost every book that discusses Jesus from the point of view of modern Scripture studies includes some version of the statement that "Jesus did not make himself the center of his own preaching; he was the proclaimer of the reign of God" (cf. *The Common Catechism,* pp. 137–138). What are the implications of this? Has there been a fundamental mistake? Has someone who only saw himself as a preacher, even a prophet, become the unwilling content of a corrupted message? How does one reconcile that while Jesus did not make himself the center of his own preaching, Christians have clearly made him the subject of theirs? How can *The Common Catechism* itself (to cite just one example) reconcile the statement that "The subject of his preaching was not his own person, but the Kingdom of God" (p. 138), with its insistence that

> only faith which is concerned with the person and the work of Jesus can properly be called "Christian faith." A person could find Jesus' "teaching" very illuminating, and his "principles" very edifying, but if at the same time he regarded Jesus himself as unimportant, he would not have Christian faith (p. 92).

144

Have we taken a message about God and made it a message about the messenger? This was the opinion of liberal Protestantism since its inception almost two hundred years ago. It is also the opinion of Islam which regards Jesus as a prophet but not the eschatological prophet (the "seal" of the prophets). Rudolf Bultmann gave it urgency for contemporary Christianity when he phrased the question, "Did Jesus have messianic consciousness'?" and answered "No" (*Jesus and the Word*, p. 9).

If you suspect that either the phrasing of the question or an oversight of obvious data is at work here, your instincts are good. First of all, the answer to the question "Did Jesus have messianic consciousness?" was for too long sought by trying to determine whether Jesus claimed any of the *messianic titles* in use at the time. The disciples of Bultmann themselves saw the narrowness of such an approach. Jesus would have had to be wary of such titles, for they had connotations (mainly political) which he would have wanted to avoid. The place to look for his "consciousness" was in his behavior, his preaching, his teaching. If Jesus was not the center of his own message, we can only reach his "self-understanding" indirectly.

This shift in focus results in a better phrasing of the question: "What did Jesus think his relationship was to the coming of the kingdom?" Did Jesus, to put it just one way, stand outside the coming of the reign of God and merely point to it (like John the Baptist) or did he think that in some sense it came through him? Did he think that he was not merely announcing the coming of eschatological judgment like John the Baptist, but that he was *mediating* the gift of mercy? In other words, to what extent is the coming of the definitive saving act of God present in Jesus? Or to what extent do we identify God's offer of unconditional love with the man Jesus? Is the kingdom present, not only in his preaching and prophetic acts but in his person? Is Jesus, as Origen (fl. 250 A.D.) would say, the *autobasileia*—the reign of God in person?

Some data is so obvious that a preliminary answer is possible. In Jesus' time the word "messiah" had no agreed upon content, but one can certainly say that it designated the mediator of definitive salvation, whatever form that would take, whether political, apocalyptic, or a life of perfect Torah observance. The evidence is that Jesus thought he was performing the messianic *task*. Like John the Baptist, he called Israel to conversion, but he went beyond John in that he claimed that the reign of God—the definitive saving act—was present in his preaching and "mighty deeds." If messiah means "eschatological prophet," Jesus certainly had messianic consciousness, for Jesus of Nazareth, in proclaiming and mediating the definitive salvation of God, was acting as the eschatological prophet.

Nevertheless, a fuller discussion of this question is called for. Before the adoption of historical-critical method, the question did not arise because in the Gospels, especially the Gospel of John, Jesus is clearly messiah and more. How does one approach the question today?

THE ATTEMPTS AT A SOLUTION: EXPLICIT AND IMPLICIT CHRISTOLOGIES

When liberal Protestantism moved in the direction of emphasizing a difference between "the Jesus of history" and "the Christ of faith," mainline Christians who also used the historical-critical approach developed a counterargument which we will call an "explicit Christology." A scholar holds an "explicit Christology" if he or she thinks that Jesus at any time claimed one of the *messianic titles* in use at the time or accepted such a title when someone else applied it to him. Before the adoption of the historical-critical approach to Scripture, the classic text (because it is a virtual glossary of messianic titles applied to Jesus) used to answer such an "obvious" question was John 1:19–51. There, one by one, Jesus' disciples predicate a series of messianic titles (Messiah, Son of God, King of Israel) of Jesus, and he seems to accept them. He certainly does not reject them. Few, if any, biblical scholars today would say that text is "meant" to be historical—rather it is a theological overture to the Gospel of John.

MESSIAH

When the Johannine text and others no longer appeared to be "historical" in the modern sense, the search for an explicit Christology narrowed considerably, and today scholars (and there are many) who continue to hold an explicit Christology favor *two* incidents from the Gospels to establish that Jesus accepted the premier Christological title of *Messiah*. It should be noted that while the Gospels show Jesus accepting the titles even they do not portray him as overly concerned with being so characterized. So, while the Gospels certainly intended (John explicitly in 20:31) to proclaim Jesus as the Messiah, and he is called by one of the messianic titles often in the Gospels, even the Gospels do not indicate that *Jesus* made being called Messiah of central importance. Only on one occasion (Jn 4:25–26, with the Samaritan woman at the well) does Jesus *spontaneously* claim to be the Messiah, and even there it is not a public claim. The Gospel of Mark shows Jesus *discouraging* demons and people from calling him Messiah or its equivalent. Scholars agree on two things about this data: (1) the "messianic secret," that is, the pattern in Mark of Jesus quieting those who call him Messiah, is a theme of the Gospel of Mark, but (2) in fact Jesus was not concerned about presenting himself as the Messiah.

Nevertheless, as I mentioned, according to some scholars, two instances in the Gospels indicate that Jesus may have accepted the title. The first is the scene at *Caesarea Philippi* where Peter makes his profession of faith (Mk 8:17–30; Mt 16:13–16; Lk 9:18–21; cf. Jn 6:67–71). A quick look at the texts shows the not unusual divergence in the accounts. The text is the same in each up to the statement,

"And you, who do you say I am?" (Peter) "You are the Messiah,"

but then there is divergence:

Mark and Luke:	"He gave them strict orders not to tell anyone about him."
Matthew:	Jesus welcomes Peter's statement, praises him, and in agreement with Mark warns them to keep it quiet.
John:	Peter says not Messiah, but "Holy One of God."

Among scholars who regard this as an historical reminiscence, C.H. Dodd's conclusion is typical. "Did Jesus, or did he not, intend to accept the title? If we follow Matthew, he did, though with some reservation. If we follow Mark, Luke and John, we can say that he did not refuse it" (*The Founder of Christianity*, p. 101). Like Dodd, a number of scholars are of the opinion that this is an "authentic" exchange which makes plausible that within the company of his most intimate followers, where he could have a say in the meaning the title would be given, Jesus accepted the title of Messiah. Several contemporary Catholic New Testament scholars maintain the fundamental historicity of the accounts (cf. J. Fitzmyer, *A Christological Catechism*, p. 43).

The other classic text used to support an explicit Christology is that of Jesus' *interrogation by the high priest* (Mk 14:61–62; Mt 26:63–64; Lk 22:67–70; cf. Jn 10:24). In the Synoptics the high priest asks Jesus: "Are you the Christ, the Son of God (Mk: the Son of the Blessed)?" Jesus' answer varies:

Mark: "I am" (Greek: *Egō eimi*).

Matthew: "You have said so" (Greek: *Su eipas*). (C.H. Dodd para-
           phrased this as: "You may have it so if you choose.")

Luke: "If I tell you, you will not believe; and if I ask you, you will
           not answer" (Greek: *Ean humin eipō, ou mē pisteusēte; ean de
           epōtēsō, ou mē apokrithēte.*) But from now on the Son of Man
           shall be seated at the right hand of the power of God."
           And they all said, "Are you the Son of God, then?" And
           he said to them, "You say that I am" (Greek: *humeis legete
           hoti egō eimi*).

Clearly, one cannot regard the various answers as equivalent. One constitutes a clear acceptance of messiahship, the others certainly do not
reject it. Accordingly, many scholars, although probably not a majority
today, feel that Mark's account is "historical" (cf. Fitzmyer, p. 86) and
concur with Dodd's reasoning:

> . . . from the gospels we gather that Jesus set himself to con-
> stitute the new Israel under his own leadership . . . that was
> his mission. . . . He could not deny his mission, he could not
> disavow the authority that went with it; and therefore, if the
> question was posed, he could not simply repudiate the title
> "Messiah." But it was an embarrassment to him, because his
> understanding of his mission conflicted with contemporary
> ideas of Messiahship (ibid).

Thus these scholars would hold that even though his life was on
the line, Jesus could not repudiate the title because he would be re-
pudiating his own claims about the reign of God, at least in the mind
of his interrogators.

SON OF MAN

There is a second (apparently messianic) title that many scholars
have customarily thought to have been used by Jesus, the phrase "Son
of Man." In the Gospels Jesus uses this phrase about eighty times (including John, where it appears twelve times). No one else uses it (except in John 12:34 [the crowd] and possibly in Mark 2:10 and parallels)
and only twice outside the Gospels (Acts 7:56; Rev 1:13). The virtually
exclusive use of it by Jesus in the Gospels and omission by the New
Testament community has led some scholars to believe that Jesus

adopted the term as a title to claim messiahship. According to this theory, the early Christians avoided it out of reverence, because it was Jesus' own chosen expression for himself.

What does it mean? In Aramaic, "son of man" (*bar e nasha*) is a quite ordinary way of saying "a man" or "the man," in the sense of an individual of the human species; it designates a "human being," "someone," or is used as a substitute for "I" or "he." But the Gospel writers must have had a particular reason for translating it with wooden literalness, for if it simply means "a man" or "the man," why not translate it so? Also, why is only Jesus allowed to use it in the Gospels if it is a common figure of speech? Although it is generally conceded that the Gospel writers have introduced it into some sayings where Jesus did not actually use it, was the reason for both its retention and its extension that it was a *characteristic* of Jesus' speech as more than a common figure of speech?

What would be Jesus' intention if he is using it as a title? The customary answer was that Jesus was evoking the figure ("one like a son of man") to whom God gives eschatological authority in Chapter 7 of the Book of Daniel. Then if Jesus identifies himself as that figure by calling himself the Son of Man, he is revealing messianic claims, for this figure is messianic, at least in that he exercises eschatological *judgment*.

But there are difficulties with this theory:

(1) The figure referred to in the Book of Daniel is not an individual but Israel itself. Jesus could have adapted the image, however, something there is some precedent for in non-canonical apocalyptic literature (Book of Enoch).

(2) In many of the sayings, Son of Man could be replaced by "I" or "me," and, as we saw above, in the Aramaic Jesus spoke it was not uncommon for a speaker to substitute "son of man" for the first person personal pronoun to avoid the appearance of egotism (as in English: "one" for "I"). Thus, it is *possible* that the *New Testament* writers made it a messianic title while Jesus used it merely as a common figure of speech.

(3) Still another difficulty is the variety of ways the phrase is used by Jesus in the Gospels. As I mentioned, few scholars hold that all of the uses originated with Jesus. It is generally agreed that there are *three* types of "Son of Man" statements:

(a) Statements describing the *present activity* of the Son of Man. Some of the most important scholars point out that sayings about the present activity of the Son of Man frequently correlate with behavior that critical-historical method affirms as distinctive of Jesus. Nevertheless, probably a majority, especially the more radical critics, would hold that the early Church introduced the words (at least as a title) into these sayings.

(b) Statements referring to the *sufferings* of the Son of Man. An overwhelming majority of exegetes hold that *in their present form* these statements come from the post-Easter period, even though they seem to have basis in authentic sayings of Jesus. In other words, the sayings are basically sayings of Jesus, in which he connected the figure of the suffering Servant of the Book of Isaiah to the eschatological prophet, but it was the early Church that used the figure of the Son of Man to present Jesus as that composite figure.

(c) Finally, there are sayings about the *future, coming* Son of Man. Formerly, even the radical critics said these are authentic sayings of Jesus. But they doubted he was talking about himself. They said he would not identify himself with this Son of Man because that would present him as a messiah of judgment rather than mercy and service— something he clearly wanted to avoid. Thus they held these are authentic sayings of Jesus, but he was not claiming to be the Son of Man. Recently the Catholic scholar, Walter Kasper, has pointed to the lack of nuance in the radical position:

> It is extremely probable . . . that Jesus spoke of the Son of Man in the third person and threatened that he would appear suddenly in the near future. . . . In this use the Son of Man saying is a vehicle of prophetic preaching; it is well suited to indicating the tension at the center of Jesus' preaching and the combination of immediate preaching and decision and the imminent coming of the Kingdom of God represented by the Son of Man. . . . [But] the Son of Man is hardly more than a symbol for the eschatological, definitive importance of the sayings and work of Jesus and of the decision of faith. . . . To claim a personal identity of Jesus with the coming Son of Man may not be justified, but there is certainly a functional identity (Kasper, *Jesus the Christ,* p. 108).

What is the present state of the debate over whether Jesus saw himself as the messianic Son of Man? There is a consensus that Jesus used the Aramaic phrase *bar e nasha.* Many scholars would continue to hold that Jesus did indeed use it as a messianic title referring to himself, but they disagree widely on which type of sayings are authentic. Catholic scholars reflect the range of the debate. For instance, Walter Kasper holds that it is probable that Jesus referred to himself as Son of Man in the first and third types of sayings, and gave grounds for introducing it into the second type, but that it was his intention to focus attention not on himself but on what he was doing (ibid). Joseph Fitzmyer is less sure of a titular use of the phrase by Jesus:

> In my opinion, the titular use of the phrase for Jesus in the New Testament is best explained as a development in the early Christian community from sayings in which he used the phrase, "Son of Man," *of himself* in a non-titular and non-substitute sense, (but) meaning nothing more than "a human being." In the pre-written Gospel tradition it then assumed a titular sense, and that is why it is preserved in its barbarous Greek form (*A Christological Catechism*, p. 89).

Kasper and Fitzmyer agree that Jesus did not identify his claims with titles but with his preaching and actions.

AN IMPLICIT CHRISTOLOGY

Even though many exegetes still maintain some form of an explicit Christology, the difficulty of reaching agreement whether and when Jesus used messianic titles stimulated another and more fruitful method of answering the question of Jesus' claims. This is the path taken by what is called an *implicit Christology*. Its presupposition is: if the center of Jesus' concern was the coming of the reign of God and not himself, his self-awareness will be revealed indirectly as a concomitant of his ministry. An implicit Christology seeks to reach knowledge of the self-understanding of Jesus on the basis of his work rather than on the basis of messianic titles. On this broader basis a revealing picture of the manner of speaking and acting of Jesus of Nazareth, and the claims implicit in this manner, emerges.

A common approach is to "try out" on Jesus the categories that his *contemporaries* would have spontaneously applied to him because of what they observed of his ministry. Despite the attempt of some present day Jewish scholars to see Jesus as a *rabbi*, it is difficult to understand him solely as such. Jesus is called "rabbi" (teacher) in the Gospels, but the dissimilarities with a first century rabbi are far greater than the similarities. Several points of behavior immediately take him out of that category. First of all, he had no formal rabbinic training. Moreover, he did not merely interpret the Mosaic law, the main rabbinic task, and indeed did little of that. Most telling is that *his main message* is "The reign of God is at hand." This is a *prophetic*, not a rabbinic function. To see Jesus as a rabbi makes as much sense as thinking of John the Baptist as a rabbi, a connection no scholars make. The similarity between Jesus and the rabbis is that he does, on occasion, address the law. But as we shall see, his attitude to the law is more radical than any rabbi. Even with regard to the law Jesus is a prophet, that is, he points to the living will of God in present events rather than in legislation of the past. But of course what takes Jesus out of the category of rabbi into that of prophet is his main work—the announcing and bringing of the reign of God.

Even as *prophet,* Jesus was more than the traditional prophet. Here we begin to come to grips with the challenge he presented to his contemporaries, and what happened to him. He made claims to *authority* that no prophet ever approached. This is the character of the historical Jesus that emerged most clearly in the "New Quest," initiated by the disciples of Rudolf Bultmann (cf. Günther Bornkamm, *Jesus of Nazareth,* pp. 58–63).

What did he do? As we have seen, Jesus claimed that the time of preparation was at an end, that in his preaching and miracles the final saving act of God had become present. Moreover, Jesus made *response to his message* the very criterion of one's salvation. He did not merely *announce* God's timeless will to save—he believed that salvation was attained by a response to *his* message that the decisive moment was at hand. That in itself reveals quite a bit about who he thought he was. A claim to be the *mediator* of the coming of definitive salvation is to claim to be the *eschatological* prophet.

Jesus' claim to be capable of mediating definitive salvation is demonstrated, among other things, in his attitude toward the *religious institutions* of his time. On the one hand he saw his role as one of bringing to fulfillment the promises of the Old Testament. He did affirm the fundamental validity of the law of Moses. As we have seen (Appendix 5, "The Aim of Jesus"), Jesus did not wish to abolish Judaism but rather to bring it to eschatological fulfillment. Yet, he interpreted the Mosaic law with a freedom and sovereignty that must have scandalized his contemporaries, and in the process he superseded it by transcending it. Not only did he challenge the myriad interpretations of the law that the rabbis and scribes had developed—the "fence around the law"—and among these the excessively rigid sabbath observances, but he claimed the authority to restore the law to its primitive form. Take, for example, the prohibition of divorce (Mk 10:1–12), a teaching usually acknowledged by scholars as having its origin in Jesus. With this teaching he abrogated what *Moses* had permitted. He claimed to have authority superior to that of Moses—who after all was *the* mediator, *the* law giver, *the* prophet. He not only claimed to be bringing to its final state what Moses initiated but to be restoring creation to its original relationship to God.

Just how far did Jesus go in his claims to mediate between God and humanity? In those phrases in the Sermon on the Mount when Jesus uses the formula "You have heard that it was said . . . but I say to you," many scholars hold that Jesus is not only going beyond Moses. The phrase "You have heard that it was said" is followed by a quote in which *God* speaks *through* Moses. In effect, the formula means "Yahweh said . . . (through Moses) but I say to you." He made *provisional* what *God* had decreed through Moses, speaking *on his own authority* on subjects that God had previously spoken about through *the* prophet Moses. Furthermore, it is striking that we have no evidence that Jesus justified his right to make such statements by saying it is God's message (as Moses and all the prophets would have). He did not say: "In the past God said this through Moses, but now God says this through me." Rather he says, in effect, "In the past God said this through Moses, but I now say to you. . . . " As proclaimer that the reign of God is at hand, Jesus' task is the prophetic task *par excellence*. But his prophetic message does not appear to derive from prophetic inspiration.

Jesus' claim to underived authority is well illustrated in the way he used the word *Amen*. Even in the Gospels Jesus rarely quotes Scripture to justify his demands or his teaching. And when he does, it is most probably the early Church supporting its claims about Jesus in disputes with the Jews. Normally a rabbi would build a case for his claims on Scripture, but Jesus, at least as a general rule, did not argue that way. Normally the rabbi's hearers would signal their agreement with his interpretation of Scripture by responding "Amen." It is always used as a response, assenting to the Scripture-based interpretation of the teacher. Jesus apparently did not wait for others to judge the truth of his message. He did not feel that what he said needed the approval of anyone else, that it had to be rooted in Scripture, that he must cite God as his authority, or that he speaks in virtue of a prophetic call. His claims to authority exceed all previous claims, but when asked the source of his authority, he appeals to knowledge of God's will, unmediated by prophetic inspiration, knowledge of Scripture or rabbinic authorities.

Did Jesus go so far as to make specific claims on his disciples to an *absolute* personal allegiance? An affirmative answer is strongly supported by Matthew 10:37 ("Whoever loves father or mother, son or daughter, more than me is not worthy of me") and Luke 12:8 ("He who does not confess me before men I will not confess before the angels of God"), two sayings which have a high claim to derive from the pre-Easter years. Both claims are extreme, the first because in it Jesus interposes allegiance to himself before the most sacred of Old Testament obligations, love of parents; the second because in it Jesus claims that his hearers will stand before God the way they relate to him.

Perhaps the most striking evidence of Jesus' sense of authority is his claim to be able to mediate God's forgiveness to people. This is a position held even by a contemporary Bultmannian (Herbert Braun). It does not depend on the establishment of a given incident in the Gospels, for it is a central part of Jesus' message and behavior, for example his practice of eating with public sinners. Even if Jesus never *said* to anyone "Your sins are forgiven" (and Mark 2:1–12, the forgiveness and cure of the paralytic, cannot be easily dismissed), this practice would reveal he thought he was capable of mediating God's forgiveness to people, something supported by the fact that the practice enraged his opponents. His message and his relationship to his message is acted out in this practice. As we saw, Jesus deliberately practiced the custom of table fellowship with anyone who would accept his message. (According to many scholars, in this there would be an implied claim to be the Messiah since the messianic age was often presented under the symbol of a banquet.) Jesus' understanding of the symbolism involved a proclamation of the forgiveness of sin. In practicing table fellowship, Jesus was saying that those who identify with him—who eat with him—have entered the kingdom, are at the eschatological banquet now anticipated in history. But because for Jesus the kingdom comes as mercy, the implication is that to accept Jesus' offer of table fellowship was to accept God's offer of mercy.

Another point must be made here. Although Jesus obviously felt that the kingdom could come only to those who are willing to receive it as a gift of forgiveness, we have no evidence, with one possible exception, that he felt himself in need of forgiveness. He mediated forgiveness but did not undergo it himself. The baptism of Jesus by John may seem like counter-evidence. Virtually all scholars hold that Jesus was baptized by John, but what the baptism meant for Jesus himself is lost in the theological use it was put to by the evangelists. In the absence of any other evidence of a sense of sin in Jesus, this one incident hardly is conclusive, for we do not know how Jesus viewed it. Probably it was Jesus' way of demonstrating his acceptance of the role of the messiah who brings salvation by becoming one with sinful humanity.

Finally, we must point out that Jesus spoke of God in a novel way for his time. The Judaism of his era stressed the transcendence of God, God's distance, even remoteness. Jesus stressed God's presence, God's intimacy with men and women. Thus it is universally conceded that Jesus addressed God as "Abba." A rough translation of it would be "Beloved Father." It is the word used by children to address their fathers, but also used by a grown son or daughter to his or her father, to express reverence and closeness. The Old Testament speaks of God as a Father, and there are occasions when it addresses God as Father. But with Jesus this became the preferred conception of God and constant form of address. Moreover, Jesus not only customarily addressed God as "Father," he used a term of extreme familiarity to do it. It is true that he taught his disciples to address God as Father, even as Abba, but he did not say "let us call upon our Father" as though they had the same relationship to God as he did. The scene (Mt 6:7–15; Lk 11:2–4) where Jesus teaches his disciples to pray preserves this distinction. Jesus does not say "let us pray to *our* Father," but rather "When you pray, say "Our Father. . . . " This distinction between Jesus' relationship to God and others' relationship to God is pervasive in the Gospels, and it seems to be founded in Jesus' own speech and behavior.

The evidence assembled by an implicit Christology shows Jesus acting with a claim to absolute authority. Yet it was a claim that Jesus left largely implicit. This is in keeping with his whole orientation which was not self-centered but God-centered, reign of God-centered. Accordingly, it is not surprising that Jesus would allow his message to speak for itself. His claims to authority, implicit as they were, would rise or fall with whether the reign of God came or not. Thus Jesus had to leave it to God to vindicate his authority because he had to leave it to God to vindicate his message.

Yet Jesus exhibits a certainty about his message (and therefore his authority) which is unshakable. If Jesus had no prophetic call, if he did not root his message in Scripture, where did this certainty derive from? How could he demand absolute personal allegiance? How could he demand a response to his message, not because he could do miracles, but simply because of his own personal authority? Granted that Jesus was God-centered, what was the necessary *self*-awareness which would be concomitant with that God-awareness? The evidence points to a distinctive human awareness in the pre-Easter Jesus. We must hold our dogmatic presuppositions in abeyance here. The discussion is about the New Testament evidence. What does it portray? It presents a truly human Jesus and (indirectly, through his behavior) a human self-awareness. Nevertheless, this is an awareness with a difference. The evidence is of an awareness of a unique relationship to God and a unique and immediate awareness of God. Jesus claimed "to speak and act in place of God and to be in a unique and untransferable communion with his "Father" (Kasper). He appeared to act out of an intuitive awareness that he was on God's side of the God/humanity relationship as well as on the human side.

We can thus understand why many of his contemporaries reacted negatively to Jesus. One can see the situation people faced who encountered him, and even what happened to him. The way he acted forced his hearers to confront an almost impossible choice. He was either a person with a unique relationship to God, or he was a false prophet and blasphemer. The middle ground, that he has been misunderstood by Christians, that he was merely an enlightened teacher of morality who was deified by misguided disciples, is inconsistent with the evidence. It does not take Jesus on his own ground the way Jesus' contemporaries had to and did. It does not explain what happened to him. His contemporaries could not ignore the extraordinary claims he was making, and he was put to death because "he made himself equal to God" (Jn 5:18). They had no convenient way out. In his own time Jesus could not be viewed as merely a teacher of morality or a challenger of the rabbinic tradition. Nor is there any evidence that Judaism sought the execution of anyone for claiming heretical opinions. Jesus' claims *were* blasphemous and false prophecy, if they were not true.

Appendix 7:

THE QUESTION OF "THE CONSCIOUSNESS OF CHRIST"

Since the 1950's, there has been a continuing discussion in Roman Catholic theology of the question of the "consciousness of Christ." There are two parts to the discussion. One part asks about the *structure* of the consciousness of Christ. Did he have a human consciousness? Did he have a divine consciousness? How could one person have two consciousnesses? How would a divine consciousness manifest itself to and through a human consciousness? It is beyond the scope of this book to address the question of structure. It will enter in only to help answer the other part of the question—the question of the *content* of Christ's consciousness. What did Jesus know? Did he know the future? Did he know about his own resurrection? Did he know he was divine?

It is not hard to see what the concern behind these specific questions is. The role of knowledge is crucial in human life. We live with uncertainty. We try to reduce that uncertainty to a minimum, but human life is characterized by lack of knowledge and the attempt to fill the void. Would a human being who knew the future really be living a human life? Or, to put it another way, would a person who knew the future, in detail and with certainty, have a truly human history? Many Christians today find great consolation in their belief that, in Jesus, God took on not merely a human *nature* but a human *history*, that is, that in Christ God took on the characteristic human task of having to "work out" a personal journey. On the other hand, many other Christians feel that to attribute ignorance to Jesus is to make him "too human," to lose or obscure that which makes him important for us at all—that he is divine. They feel that to see Jesus "working it out" the way we do is to cast a cloud over that which precisely attracts us to him—his otherness.

THE NEW TESTAMENT PICTURE

One sometimes reads that it is only in our time that theologians have attributed ignorance to Jesus. In fact, the New Testament picture itself is mixed. Even before one asks the modern question—is the text at this point conveying history or theology?—one sees *three types* of data. There are indications that Jesus had what medieval theology called *experiential* knowledge—that is, that he *learned*, through question and answer, observation, review of evidence. This presupposes that he did not know already what he was asking about and that he was ignorant of the answer and looking for it. For instance, when Jesus cures the woman with the hemorrhage, Mark (5:30–33) makes a convincing case that he did not know who had touched him and is asking a real and not merely a rhetorical question (v. 33: "But he continued to look all round to see who had done it"). On the other hand, he seems to have had some extraordinary knowledge to even know that "power had gone out from him" (v. 30). The same mixed picture emerges in Luke's account of the visit of the adolescent Jesus to the temple. Jesus clearly has knowledge superior to what one would expect (2:47: "All those who heard him were astounded at his intelligence and his replies"), yet when he returns to Nazareth he "increased in wisdom" (2:52). In other places Jesus apparently makes mistakes. In John 7:38 he cites a non-existent Old Testament text. In Mark 2:26 he says that Abiathar was high priest when David ate the loaves of offering, but the account of the incident in 1 Samuel 21:2–7 says the high priest was Ahimelech. Jesus also seems to have erred about the identity of the Zechariah killed in the temple. 2 Chronicles 24:20–22 says he was the son of Jehoidah; Jesus called him (Mt 23:35) the son of Barachiah.

No doubt too much can be made of this data if one adopts an historical-critical approach to the Gospels. But two texts, one from the Gospels and one from Hebrews, have always stood in the way of a complete denial of ignorance in Jesus. Hebrews 4:15 says that he was "like us in all things but sin." In Mark 13:32 (= Mt 24:36) Jesus appears to claim not to know when the day of judgment will come, although in accordance with the pattern we saw above, the very pericope which contains evidence of ignorance also contains evidence of supernatural knowledge, for Jesus says (Mk 13:20 = Mt 24:35) that "this generation will not pass away before all these things happen."

Luke's account of the above incident contains Jesus' statement of knowledge (Lk 21:32) but not of ignorance. This brings us to a *second set of data.* There is a *tendency* in the Gospels *to eliminate* the appearance of ignorance in Jesus. Thus, in Matthew's account of the cure of the woman with the hemmorhage (9:22) Jesus has no difficulty identifying who touched him. In John's report of the miracle of the loaves (6:4–15; = Mk 14:13–21, Mt 6:32–44, Lk 9:10–

17) Jesus' question (to the disciples in the Synoptics, to Philip in John) concerning what they have to feed the crowds is made rhetorical by John's addition of "He only said this to test Philip; he knew exactly what he was going to do" (v. 6). It is John also who makes sure Jesus knew Judas would betray him (13:11).

Finally, there are texts that indicate Jesus had *supernatural knowledge.* The Gospels attribute to Jesus (1) the ability to know what others are thinking (Mk 2:6–8, the scribes; Mk 9:33–34, his disciples; Lk 9:46–47, his disciples; Jn 2:24–25, men's hearts; 16:19, 30, his disciples; (2) the ability to know what is taking place elsewhere (Jn 1:48–49, Nathaniel under the fig tree; Mk 11:2, the colt tied to a tree; Mk 14:13–14 (= Lk 22:10), the man carrying the water jar; and most importantly, (3) knowledge of his *own* future: the three predictions of his rejection, suffering, death and resurrection (Mk 8:31–33 = Mt 16:21–23, Lk 9:22; Mk 9:30–32 = Mt 17:22–23, Lk 9:43–45; Mk 10:32–34 = Mt 20:17–19, Lk 18:31–33).

THE TRADITIONAL TREATMENT OF THE QUESTION: PATRISTIC PERIOD

Whether Jesus could have been ignorant was a question that

the Fathers of the Church debated. In particular they debated how to understand Mark 13:32, "But as for that day or hour, nobody knows it, neither the angels of heaven nor the Son, no one but the Father." Before the great Christological controversies of the fourth and fifth centuries, there appears to have been no difficulty in admitting that Jesus was ignorant (Irenaeus, Origen). At the time of the great Christological councils (Nicaea, 325 A.D., affirming the divinity of Jesus against the Arians; Ephesus 431 A.D., affirming the unity of the person of Jesus against the Nestorians; Chalcedon, 451 A.D., affirming the humanity of Jesus against the Monophysites) the position emerged that refused to acknowledge that Jesus could have been ignorant of the day of judgment. Mark 13:32 began to get some subtle interpretations. The most popular was that in the statement Jesus is admitting that the day of judgment is not known to him as *prophet*, that is, that the date of the day of judgment is not part of his prophetic knowledge. Nevertheless there was a universal reluctance to attribute complete ignorance to Jesus concerning this matter. One can only conjecture why, but it seems reasonable to assume that, because the whole thrust of the orthodox position was to establish that in Jesus there is one divine person who has become man, the attribution of ignorance to Jesus would have appeared to be attribution of ignorance to God. This certainly was what worried Athanasius. Nevertheless, against the trend of the time he admitted that Christ would be ignorant as man (J. Lebreton, *Histoire du dogme de la Trinité au concile de Niceé*, Vol. I, 563).

In Christological questions, including this one, the Council of Chalcedon is crucial. Chalcedon reaffirmed what Nicaea (the divinity) and Ephesus (the unity of the person of Christ) taught and, against those who would have let the divine nature absorb the human nature of Christ (the Monophysites), affirmed the true humanity of Christ by saying there was one person who had two unmixed and unconfused natures. Logically Chalcedon had to begin to address the question of what it meant to say Christ had a true human nature. It affirmed that he was

true man, consisting of a rational soul and a body, consubstantial with the Father in divinity and consubstantial with us in humanity, "in all things like as we are, without sin" (Heb 4:15) . . . one and the same Christ, the Son, the Lord, the Only-Begotten, in two natures unconfused, unchangeable, undivided and inseparable. The difference of natures will never be abolished by their being united, but rather the properties of each remain unimpaired . . . (DS 301–302).

In the question of Christ's knowledge two non-infallible teachings of Popes of the post-Chalcedonian period have become influential. At the time of Second Council of Constantinople (553 A.D.), but not as part of its proceedings (which had as their purpose to deal with the continued presence of Monophysitism), Pope Vigilius, at the request of the emperor Justinian, issued a letter called the *Constitutum* which said: "If anyone says that the one Jesus Christ who is both true Son of God and true Son of Man did not know the future or the day of the Last Judgment and that He could know only as much as the divinity dwelling in Him as in another revealed to Him, *anathema sit*" (DS 419). Not all handbooks of doctrine which include in their summaries of Christological doctrine the "lack of any ignorance" in Christ (cf. *The Teaching of the Catholic Church*, ed. by J. Neuner, H. Roos, K. Rahner, 1967, p. 144) cite the *Constitutum* as evidence for that position. They cite the condemnations of Modernism (1907), and decrees of the Holy Office of 1918. Furthermore, the statement, while affirming Christ's knowledge of the future and specifically the last judgment, clearly is anti-Monophysite in that it is rejecting the position that in Christ the only knowledge is what comes to him from his divine nature. In other words it is teaching he has human knowledge.

A second non-infallible teaching from a few years later has also had considerable influence. Like the *Constitutum* it is not cited by Neuner-Roos-Rahner as evidence that there was no ignorance in Christ. This is the letter of Gregory the Great to Eulogius (d. 607 A.D.) in which the Pope commends Eulogius for his treatises against the *Agnoetes*. The *Agnoetes* taught that the divine nature of Christ was absorbed in his human nature (so they are Monophysites from the other side). Gregory affirmed that the "Son" in Mark 13:32 is the Church, the body of Christ, not the head, Christ himself. Jesus himself was not ignorant. He knew the day of judgment *in* his human nature, but not *from* his human nature. Gregory is affirming human knowledge in Jesus which has its origin in divine knowledge. The Fathers of the time of the Agnoetes controversy (540–640 A.D.) also held that there was no ignorance in Jesus. Also early in this period we have the first phrasing of a question that would later become *the* question concerning Jesus' knowledge. The North African bishop-theologian Fulgentius of Ruspe was asked by one Ferrando, a deacon of Carthage, if "Christ in his humanity knew his own divinity fully." Fulgentius answered yes, but in a human manner.

What was the picture as the patristic era closed? There had been a broad-based move from the early position that admitted Jesus could be and was ignorant to a virtually unanimous position that he could not be and was not. Nevertheless this position was never formally taught by what we would call the extraordinary magisterium. Furthermore, it emerged closely connected with more important questions and may have been a way of protecting more important doctrines, the humanity, the divinity, the oneness of Christ, or even the omnipotence of God. Also, there is a definite movement toward acknowledging the implication of the constant insistence on the genuineness of Christ's humanity. Thus, in 649, a regional synod at the Lateran in Rome under Pope Martin I, against the pressure of the emperor Heraclius (who wished to unite Christian factions against an external threat) to recognize only "one active principle" in Christ despite his two natures, affirmed the genuineness and autonomy of the human will in Christ. This position became dogma at the Third Council of Constantinople (680–681 A.D.). One can see that implicit in this position (which follows from the affirmation that Jesus had a rational human soul) is the position that he had an authentic human consciousness. What the tradition was affirming against the Monophysites was well summarized at the end of the patristic period by Maximus the Confessor. He saw that the assumption of a human nature by a divine person would not result in the absorption of the human by the divine but would have just the opposite effect. Rather than the divine overwhelming the human, it would render it more human. The presence of divinity, especially in such an intimate manner, would result in a person not less human but fully human. Nevertheless, Maximus did not draw specific conclusions regarding the knowledge of Christ from this position.

MEDIEVAL THEOLOGY

In this story the contribution of Thomas Aquinas is pivotal. Even before Aquinas, to account for the biblical data and to respect the patristic tradition, medieval theologians customarily distinguished three types of knowledge in Christ. They said he had experiential knowledge, infused knowledge, and the beatific vision—he saw God "face-to-face." It seems to me that in this formulation there is an acknowledged admission of ignorance in Christ. In attributing experimental knowledge to Jesus the medievals were saying he *learned*. To say that is to say he did not previously know what he learned.

Aquinas, with his customary acuity, pushed this a step further. He held that Christ had to have human knowledge, otherwise he would not have had divine knowledge. He would not know himself as divine, as a human being, were it not indicated to him by human knowledge. How did he know his own divinity? By the possession of the beatific vision *in his human consciousness.* He knew his own divinity in a human way by a "face-to-face" vision in his human consciousness of the Father. Far from denying the humanity of Jesus, Aquinas saw the pre-Easter Jesus as having already arrived at the fullness of humanity through the hypostatic union (the union of divine and human natures in the one substance/person of the Word). In other words, the union of the divine with the human, *even in the earthly life of Jesus,* had brought the humanity of Jesus to fullness precisely as humanity. Far from being a Docetist, Aquinas had drawn out the implications of Maximus' insight. But without a critical understanding of the Gospels, he reached the conclusion that this had occurred in Jesus by virtue of the incarnation itself rather than the resurrection. Aquinas clearly thought Jesus had not only a human nature but (as we would say today) a human consciousness. But the union of the divine and the human in Jesus took its full effect immediately. According to Aqui-

nas, because the hypostatic union began at Jesus' conception, from the very moment of that conception Jesus had the "beatific vision." That is, as soon as he existed, Jesus' human consciousness enjoyed the immediate ("face-to-face") "vision" that the blessed have of God. An uncritical approach to the Gospels would not challenge such a view. Indeed, the Gospel of John could be and was used to support it. Furthermore, Jesus had infused knowledge—how else could one account for the detailed knowledge of his own death and resurrection? From such a view the questions Jesus asks in the Gospels are mainly rhetorical. His life stretches before him known in at least its major details. He especially knows the details of his death, but the struggle is substantially mitigated by his possession of the beatific vision and a complete knowledge of his resurrection.

MODERN THEOLOGY

While Aquinas' position on Jesus' knowledge is nuanced, some of his commentators were extravagant. The seventeenth century Spanish Thomists at Salamanca held that Jesus' various sources of knowledge would have given him such knowledge that he would have to be considered the greatest philosopher and scientist possible. How much Aquinas would have agreed with positions called Thomistic is an unanswerable question, but his influence on this question continues into our own time. One of the very best of the books of pre-critical Catholicism (Romano Guardini's *The Lord* [1937]) held that, even as Jesus suffered crucifixion, he was the happiest of human beings because he continued to enjoy the beatifying vision of God. Clearly not only a pre-critical, but an inconsistent use of the Gospels made such statements possible. Here tradition, conceptions of what "human" means, and Scripture were beginning to clash. Moreover, only in the most formal, abstract, non-historical sense is this Jesus human, for there is no genuine human *history* here.

In the 1950's systematic theologians like Karl Rahner and Bernard Lonergan began to insist on the full human consciousness of Jesus as a consequence of the hypostatic union, and that even if one did attribute the beatific vision to Jesus, it is a beatification of a finite human consciousness and would have to respect the structure of that consciousness. Therefore, attribution of the beatific vision does not necessarily amount to saying Jesus had a fully *objectified* understanding of God or his relation to God. At the same time, the adoption of the historical-critical approach to the Gospels freed biblical scholars

from the fundamentalism, explicit or implicit, of previous generations. That a more nuanced approach to the question of Jesus' consciousness (of his own identity, of the future, of that beyond his normal experience) would be acceptable to the Vatican was signaled by the publication in 1960 in the semi-official journal, *Gregorianum*, of an article by Jean Galot which said that after all, attribution of the beatific vision to Jesus was not dogma and was open to challenge.

As good a way as any to go to the heart of the problem is to take the question so often asked when one encounters this discussion: How can we reconcile the divinity of Jesus and an attribution to him of ignorance? Specifically, how could he have been divine and not know it? A Rahnerian-Lonerganian answer would pivot on what the word "know" means in the question. If by "know" one means awareness, the initial unthematized "consciousness of" with which knowledge *begins*, one would not have difficulty making the statement: "Jesus of Nazareth was aware of a unique sonship." The critical evidence supports such a statement. If, however, the word "know" means a comprehensive understanding, *fully* corresponding to the reality to be understood, one would have to say not only that (1) Jesus never in so many words claims to be "God," but that (2) the critical evidence does not support a claim that Jesus made *explicit* claims to being a divine person, and that (3) if he was truly human, he could *not* have "known" himself to be God (in this second sense) precisely because the question concerns the *human* consciousness of Jesus, and *his human consciousness would not be adequate to the comprehensive understanding of self that we call knowledge because the self to be understood is divine.* One can draw a parallel. A small child is aware of being human but does not "know" it. At some point, conditional on the emergence of an adequate consciousness and experience, and the mastery of language, that awareness becomes thematized as knowledge. Just as the small child is *aware* of its difference from the non-human, so the critical evidence shows that Jesus was aware of a unique relationship (sonship) with the transcendent reality he addressed as Abba. But in his human consciousness, and that is what this question asks about, he would not have, could not have, a comprehensive knowledge of his identity as the unique Son because there was an infinite distance between what was to be "known" and the means he had to "know" it. When would he have that comprehensive understanding? Only when his human consciousness was transformed by the resurrection.

We conclude with a reflection on the curious fact that in the tradition the central Christian virtue of faith was not attributed to Jesus. The reason is obvious. If Jesus had the beatifying knowledge of God, he had no need or room for faith; he "saw." Thus Aquinas specifically rejected the notion that Jesus had faith (*Summa Theologicae* III, 9, 7 a. 3). Yet probably the New Testament does present Jesus as a man of faith (cf. Heb 12:2). Thus we ask: Did Jesus only pray to give example, or did he seek strength in order to be faithful to his mission through prayer? While Jesus is presented in the passion narratives as freely going to his death, that freedom is presented as being the fruit of intense struggle. Finally we must ask: When we are urged "to follow Christ," does that mean we are to leave behind a genuine existence and imitate a pattern of behavior acted out by someone who himself experienced nothing of the risk of life—or is "following Christ" accepting our existence and "working it out" because in Christ God has accepted it and given it ultimate meaning? Is Jesus a model of the existence I should live, or is Jesus the revelation of the depth of the existence I do live?

This way of looking at the question has been adopted by Hans Urs von Balthasar, a leading conservative theologian.

Jesus is an authentic human being, and the inalienable nobility of man is that of being able and being obliged even to freely project the design of his existence into an unknown future. If this man is a believer, the future into which he projects himself is God, in his liberty and immensity. To deprive Jesus of this possibility and to have him advance toward an end known in advance and distant only in time would be equivalent to stripping him of human dignity (*La Foi du Christ*, Paris, 1968, p. 8).

Chapter VIII

THE DEATH OF JESUS

INTRODUCTION

Thus far we have shown that Jesus of Nazareth manifested a belief that God was completely behind him—that he was the definitive representative of God,

- when he announced that the reign of God was at hand,
- when he acted to release people from physical and psychological infirmities,
- when he acted out the nature of the coming of the reign of God in prophetic gestures such as eating with sinners and cleansing the temple,
- when he formed a group of disciples, thus inaugurating "the gathering" of Israel.

Jesus failed to achieve his aim in his own lifetime. His ministry ended in his execution. What does an historical-critical examination show about the death of Jesus? Is the Gospel picture substantially historical? Is it possible to say what Jesus himself thought about his death? How did the early Church understand his death? How are we to understand it in relation to our salvation?

This event has always been a crucial one for Christians. Indeed, at times in the past, the significance of Jesus for humanity has been expressed almost *completely* in terms of his death. In contemporary theology his death is never discussed in isolation from his resurrection, or indeed from his life before his death. The influence of Anselm of Canterbury's "satisfaction theory of redemption," which, at least in its popularized form, saw salvation occurring almost exclusively in relation to Jesus' death (as *the payment of a debt*), is being overcome. Nevertheless, that Jesus died *for us* will always be a central part of authentic Christian faith. What are the elements of a balanced picture?

We must avoid three mistakes commonly made in interpreting the meaning of Jesus' death. The first one sees Jesus' significance solely in his dying for us so that the resurrection is reduced to nothing more than an appendage to Christ's life and an extrinsic validation of Christian faith. The second mistake is to so concentrate on his resurrection that Christ's death has no significance in itself and merely sets the stage for the crucial event of his resurrection. The two events must be understood together. The third false start is to fail to see the death and resurrection of Jesus as the culmination of his life and his mission. *All* of Jesus' activity was salvific, and the events must be understood in terms of one another.

The key to understanding Jesus' death and resurrection is to see these two events in the context of his mission—the mediation of the coming of the reign of God. Indeed, all that Jesus does and suffers must be understood in the light of this event. It is the key to understanding him.

THE NEW TESTAMENT UNDERSTANDING OF JESUS' DEATH

Let us start with the question of how the contemporaries of Jesus would have viewed his death.

The people would have viewed it not merely as their leaders' rejection of Jesus but as *God's* rejection of him. For a *powerless* man to claim the messianic role was itself a *prima facie* case against him, and that he had been successfully executed would have been conclusive evidence against him. He could not be the messiah if he could be executed.

For the *early Christians*, then, there is a scandal to be overcome, namely, that Jesus, whom they affirmed to be the Christ, was executed. This is the scandal of the cross. There is no question what enabled the early Christians to interpret the death of Jesus differently than their contemporaries did; it was their experience of Jesus as "risen." But to render Jesus' death more understandable, they looked back to the figure of the Suffering Servant of Isaiah, chapters 40–55 (Deutero-Isaiah). They understood Jesus in terms of that mysterious figure, who preaches to Israel, is rejected, and then executed, but whose sufferings are accepted by God as redemptive. This interpretation of Jesus as the Servant of the Lord, the *Ebed Yahweh*, was woven into the tradition about him, especially the account of his actual sufferings.

There was no "philosophical" attempt to explain *why* Jesus suffered. There appears to have been a school of thought in Israel in the time of Jesus which believed that anyone who kept the law would suffer for it (E. Schillebeeckx, *Jesus*, pp. 282–291), but there was little speculation *why*. *Paul* refused to explain the *why* beyond his statement in 1 Corinthians 1:18, 25: "For the word of the cross is folly to those who are perishing but to us who are being saved it is the power of God. . . . For the foolishness of God is wiser than men, and the weakness of God is stronger than human strength."

The *Gospels* also accept the ambiguity of Jesus' suffering. They no more try to explain it theologically than Deutero-Isaiah tried to explain the sufferings of the *Ebed Yahweh*. Rather they deal with it by going on to say "but he rose from the dead." His resurrection enabled them to *accept* his death—they never really claim to *explain* it. Thus, the *New Testament* prefers short kerygmatic statements as its theology of the death of Jesus, such as the following:

> *1 Cor 15:36* Christ died for our sins in accordance with the Scriptures.

> *Rom 3:25* Whom God put forward as an expiation by his blood.

> *Rom 4:25* Who was put to death for our trespasses and raised for our justification.

These *pre-Pauline* credal statements express well the character of the earliest Christian "theology" of the death of Jesus.

ANALYSIS OF THE NEW TESTAMENT ACCOUNTS

In discussing the New Testament understanding of the death of Jesus, we must take the expressions in the context of the time. For instance, a common mistake in the past was to attribute to words like "expiation" or "ransom" a meaning derived from the study of world religions or even simply what they meant in ancient Greek religion. These notions have their genuine background in *biblical* thought. Secondly, we must again acknowledge the peculiar nature of the apocalyptic language in which the meaning of the death of Jesus is expressed. Apocalyptic language is not "steno-language," that is, it does not point to a single meaning. It is "tensive," elastic language, pointing to a range of meanings. Therefore we must interpret such phrases as:

- "He died for our sins."
- "He died because it was his Father's will."
- "He died because God willed it."

While these statements express a fundamental truth, they are marked by the categories of thought present in first century Palestine. We must separate *what* is being said from *how* it is said if we are to retain the vitality of the message. While Rudolf Bultmann's proposal of a radical demythologization of the Gospels appears to empty them of their eschatological content, certainly most biblical scholars today agree that some demythologization is necessary. Statements made in one culture must be reinterpreted for people living in another culture. This is necessary in any case simply because reading and hearing always involve interpretation. The Gospel statements about the death (and the resurrection) of Jesus were formulated in a culture where people commonly used *apocalyptic* language and ideas. This must be taken into account.

Two parts of the New Testament are especially relevant here. We will discuss the passion narratives and the predictions of the passion.

a. THE PASSION NARRATIVES

- It is a widely held opinion that the first part of the Gospel stories to be put into their present form are the accounts of Jesus' last days. Although there are differences among these accounts because of the use of special traditions and the varying theological intentions of the Gospel writers, there is relatively more agreement in the four accounts than in the rest of the Gospel.
- The early Church seems to have had a special interest in what happened in these final days of Jesus' life and solid traditions to consult. There are many indications that the passion tradition always ended with a brief mention of the raising of Jesus. In other words, the first traditions never just described the death of Jesus but always culminated with the message of his resurrection.
- From a literary standpoint, the passion narratives are the tightest parts of the Gospels. The story flows along without the breaks that we find in the accounts of Jesus' ministry. It is not episodic, that is, it is not constructed of distinct blocks of incidents (pericopes).

• All this gives scholars confidence that the actual events are reflected accurately in the accounts, but (again) not with a modern reportorial accuracy. The accounts are *stylized* and there are theological concerns behind the stylizing. First, the evangelists wanted to show that Jesus was completely obedient in everything to the will of his heavenly Father. The death of Jesus is not an unfortunate accident but takes place within God's saving action and is part of salvation history. Second, they wanted to show that Jesus, despite the brutalization he endured, went freely, even triumphantly, to his death, and that human beings were not the ultimate determinants of his destiny but that he is exercising a sovereign *obedience to the mission* assigned him by his Father. The responsibility of the human actors is present but understressed. The authors achieved their aim by using the language of Deutero-Isaiah and Psalms 22 and 69. In this way they surpass the horror of the crucifixion and portray a drama of a mysterious divine action. What must have been an especially gruesome instance of inhumanity becomes a drama of strange dignity; an episode of meaninglessness becomes full of meaning. But the Gospel accounts present this as the fulfillment of divine plans. And we have to ask what *that* means. Did God "decree" the death of Jesus? What is the influence of apocalyptic thought here?

b. THE PREDICTIONS OF THE PASSION

The second part of the New Testament that is relevant here is Jesus' predictions of his death. In each of the Synoptics, three times Jesus is presented as foreseeing, with increasing detail, the passion and death of the "Son of Man." Jesus never explicitly identifies himself in these predictions as the Son of Man, but it is clear from the context that the evangelists are having him talk about his own death. Thus Mark 8:32: "And he began to teach them that the Son of Man must suffer many things, and be rejected by the elders and the chief priests and the scribes, and be killed, and after three days rise again. And he said this plainly." What is the conventional scholarly opinion of these "predictions"? It is "almost universal" (Kasper) that these statements are "kerygmatic" rather than historical reminiscences. That is, in their present form they are announcements by the early Christians of the central event of faith. This is not to say that Jesus did not foresee and interpret his death (cf. below), but, in their present form at least, these passages are held to have originated in the primitive Christian community in Palestine. Scholars acknowledge that they are very early.

Why do they not trace them to Jesus himself, especially if, as many hold, Jesus could have foreseen his end? The evidence against their being predictions normally cited is that they are too detailed, that they use the phrase Son of Man as a title (which many scholars feel comes from the early Palestine community and not Jesus), but especially that the behavior of Jesus' disciples at the time of his death would be incomprehensible if Jesus had predicted his death and resurrection in such detail. Clearly the judgment that these are kerygma and not prediction depends on a number of presuppositions, especially about the nature of the Gospels.

INTERPRETATION

How are we to interpret the message of the New Testament on Jesus' death? Especially, what does the New Testament mean when it says the Son of Man "must" suffer? The Gospel accounts present Jesus' death as an event in a divine "plan." The Greek word *dei* ("must") appears constantly in the accounts. What does the "must" mean? Does it mean the history of Jesus could not have been otherwise? How would it then be a real human history? What happens to the freedom of the human agents, including Jesus himself, if events *had* to happen the way they did? Does it mean that God desired the death of Jesus regardless of the outcome of his mission? That the "must" is to be taken as predetermined necessity imposed on history by the divine will has led believers down through the ages to regard the death of Jesus as the central concern of God. They have imagined God the Father sending his Son to die as his central or even sole task. The consequences of such a view are sometimes unfortunate: (1) If combined with a crypto-*tritheism* which understands the three "persons" of the Trinity on too close an analogy with human persons, God the Father becomes an ogre. (2) If death is Jesus' real task, what is ours as his followers? (3) How does one make sense of all that went before Jesus' death, his effort to mediate the transforming gift of God's forgiving love, his preaching and miracles, and his effort to gather Israel? Is it merely to incite his own execution? In short, if the death of Jesus is purely and simply willed by God regardless of the outcome of his whole activity, what was Jesus doing? His life begins to lack any coherence and, worse yet, any real connection with a truly human life.

Yet we must not underestimate the difficulty of this question. First of all, the understanding of the meaning of Jesus' death which, in some form, has been widely communicated, namely, that Adam's sin incurred a debt which Jesus' death pays, has the virtue of being easily understood. Furthermore, while it led often to the deleterious effects mentioned above, especially a misrepresentation of God as Father, nevertheless Christian piety was also able to draw from it genuine nourishment. But, finally, the most important thing is that we must be faithful to the revealed meaning of the death of Jesus as contained in the New Testament. A beginning is made in understanding the New Testament here by pointing out that "must" here means, at least, *divine* predetermination. The "must" is not announcing a blind fate, but a *divinely* ordained necessity. And, as we have seen, what is divinely ordained is never merely God acting without reference to a human response, because a human response is precisely what the divine initiative seeks. We must also recall that imagining "God's plan of salvation" as one whose *stages were fixed* from all eternity and had merely to be fulfilled in the course of history is part of Jewish apocalyptic, and apocalyptic is a *genre*, the package not the contents. Apocalyptic is not "steno" language but "tensive" language, that is, it is not merely descriptive but symbolic. If that is so, the question is: Are we bound to see Jesus' death as the result of a divine plan unfolding in predetermined stages? Can we translate apocalyptic statements into that thesis without further ado? (Consider what happens when one does that with the apocalyptic Book of Revelation.) Should we not understand the apocalyptic view within the *prophetic* tradition that envisioned a genuine human input into history—precisely in response to prophecy? Since many people believe in the "divine plan" theory of their own lives, this is a relevant question. For them "divine plan" means that human history, and indeed their own personal histories, are governed by a divinely decreed *scenario*. God is envisioned as a playwright, the human person as an actor. One can recite one's lines well or ill, but one cannot change the fundamental plot. The same is true of history. It unfolds according to "dispensations," epochs, which are fixed and controlled by God. Such views reduce human responsibility considerably. They are reinforced by a similar interpretation of Jesus' death, an interpretation which fails to distinguish the influence and nature of apocalyptic in the gospels. If we can separate mentality and message (and we have been doing that all along), and take into account the apocalyptic form of expression, we can point to some basic positions in the New Testament view of the death of Jesus that seem to be essential.

1. Jesus' death is understood by the New Testament within the context of his mission. On the one hand, the New Testament does not

diminish Jesus' mission in order to concentrate on his death. His death is not an isolated event to which independent significance is attached but is understood in the light of his mission. The New Testament presents the death of Jesus as the intensification of Jesus' proclamation that the reign of God is at hand, indeed as an event within that event. Is the "must" of Jesus' death, then, a "must" which flows out of Jesus' fidelity to his mission? Given his mission, which was decreed by God, would his death participate in the divine plan as the consequence of his mission?

2. All New Testament interpretations of the cross relate it to salvation. Never is it considered a mere tragedy without value or meaning. It is always treated as a salvific event. The precise *way* it is salvific varies, for the New Testament does not have just one theology of Jesus' death and, indeed, does not have a highly developed soteriology (theology of redemption) in any case. Nevertheless, the death of Jesus participates in the salvific action of God unleashed in Jesus' preaching and prophetic acts. Is the proper way to see it as a prophetic act? Is the death of the eschatological prophet itself an acting out of his message? This would not entail that Jesus initiated his own death but that it was accepted by him as the consequence of his message.

3. None of the New Testament witnesses assumes that salvation is automatically assured by faith in the death of Jesus. Faith is not a kind of magic. As much as anything the death of Jesus is a *pattern of life* for believers, an example which summons them to imitate it. One must, in one's life and death, let go of oneself into God, as Jesus did. "Taking Jesus as one's personal savior," if it relieves one from the necessity of doing what Jesus did, would not be truly biblical. Historical-critical studies show this was the preaching of Jesus himself. In accepting the offer of salvation present in his proclamation, one also accepted the necessity of "following" him in all that that might entail, even the loss of one's life in order to save it. Jesus' death is a living out of his own message. It is not just something that happens to him; it is the embodiment of his message that one can and must give one's life over completely to God's call.

What conclusions can we draw from this analysis? If we take into account the nature of apocalyptic expression, what picture emerges? As we have seen, the Bible shows God's activity as "planned" but not in the sense of a *scenario*, and even apocalyptic language as tensive, symbolic language cannot be used to support a strict scenario view of history. To say that God is Lord does not mean that God dictates history but that history is embraced by God's initiative. In turn, God's initiative seeks a human response, allows itself to be determined by the human response, and incorporates the human response into a new initiative. To see Jesus' death as preordained, a predetermined event, occurring because God decreed it, is to make a mockery of human responsibility. It ignores the way the Bible consistently portrays God working. There God's action always takes the human response seriously and does not plunge ahead with a set plan while ignoring the real contribution of human good and evil to history but, indeed, precisely seeks the proper human contribution.

So what does it mean to say Jesus "must" die? It means Jesus had to die not regardless of the human reaction to him but precisely because of it. The initiative of God met human resistance, and the bearer of God's initiative had to die because he proclaimed God's offer to people who regarded his message as unacceptable. It is a "must" created by the intransigence of the divine initiative and the hardness of the human heart in its response to that initiative. In the unwillingness of Jesus to be deterred from his mission, the unconditional eschatological character of God's saving offer is acted out. The death of Jesus, then, is a prophetic act. It is an action which embodied his message. His mission was to preach and effect the inbreaking of God's unconditional love. His message was rejected. What was forced on him by that rejection was the choice of abandoning his mission or embodying his message in an action which, paradoxically, would become the perfect expression of his message. His willing acceptance of the death imposed on him by his fidelity to his mission in the face of rejection became the occasion for vindication of his message. In refusing to abandon his mission he lived his message even in death. He went to this death believing he embodied God's eschatological initiative to save and awaiting a new initiative.

HISTORY

What are the facts concerning Jesus' death? Although the Gospels are faith proclamations, they also contain historical information. Scholars have long held that the accounts of Jesus' final days were the first part of the Gospels to be given continuous form and that their fundamental historicity is well established. Nevertheless, there are debated questions even here. One which is not debated by biblical scholars is *whether* Jesus died. The most radical critics of the historicity of the Gospels, for example, the Bultmannians, do not regard it as worthy of discussion. They would agree with a mainstream Catholic scholar like Walter Kasper when he says: "The execution of Jesus on a cross is among the most securely established facts of his life" (*Jesus the Christ*, p. 113). They leave it to amateurs in the field (Robert Graves, D.H. Lawrence) to call the death of Jesus into question.

SOME GENUINE QUESTIONS: WHEN? HOW? WHY?
WHEN?

According to all four Gospels, Jesus died on a Friday (because in each account the next day is a sabbath) of the week of the great Jewish feast of Passover. However, there seems to be a discrepancy between John and the Synoptics on whether the day of his execution was the day of Passover itself. Passover always took place on the 15th Nisan (roughly March-April). The Synoptics say that Jesus died on Passover itself, because he was arrested *after* he had eaten the Passover meal, which was celebrated in the first hours of the Jewish day (which runs from sundown to sundown). However, according to John, it was on the day of preparation for Passover that he was executed (19:14), and that Gospel adds the detail that when the Jews took Jesus to Pilate, they did not enter the procurator's headquarters lest they be defiled by contact with pagans and be unable to eat the Passover. So, John places Jesus' death on 14th Nisan—the day on which the Passover lambs were sacrificed in the temple. In addition, John describes the Last Supper as a farewell meal, not a Passover supper. In John Jesus dies at the same time the lambs are being killed in the temple in preparation *for* the Passover which will begin in a few hours when the sun sets. Since part of the clear intention of John is to present Jesus as the true Passover Lamb, the question arises whether the theological intention has overridden historical concern here. But the Synoptics had their own theological themes. Did the Synoptics want to set the Lord's Supper over against the Passover *as the new meal of the new community?* While attempts have been made to reconcile the two accounts (for example by saying Galileans ate the Passover a day early or measured the day from sunup to sunup), most scholars feel a choice must be made. Jesus was executed under Pontius Pilate who was procurator of Judea from 26–36 A.D. John the Baptist began to preach in the fifteenth year of the reign of Tiberias (October 1, 27 A.D.—September 30, 28 A.D.), and Jesus' ministry follows John. So the earliest date of Jesus' ministry is 28 A.D. In the years 28, 29, and 32 neither the 14th nor 15th Nisan fell on Friday. The years 35 and 36 seem to involve too long a public ministry for Jesus if he began to preach in connection with John's ministry. Fixing the date any more exactly is complicated by the fact that the Jewish calendar was a lunar calendar and that the start of a month was dependent on the visual sighting of the new moon. Also, to coordinate their lunar calendar to the solar cycle they used leap *months*. This means that we cannot be sure *to the day* when Passover occurred. In the years around the year 30 A.D. the following years could have had the 14th or 15th Nisan occur on Friday: 30, 31, 33, 34. A number of factors point to 30 or 31 (there are indications Paul was converted before 33 A.D.), and 30 rather than 31 for both the 14th and 15th Nisan could have fallen on Friday that year. The 14th is more probable (astronomically), and since it seems unlikely that Jesus would have been executed on the Passover itself, some scholars favor April 7, 30 A.D. as the most probable date of Jesus' death.

HOW?

Jesus died by crucifixion. This was a Roman form of execution reserved for slaves and rebels. It was not used on Roman citizens (who were beheaded). The note of degrading a false claimant's pretensions to power was intentional and designed to deter imitators. The question of the form of Jesus' execution is important, for it points to the nature of the charge against him.

WHY?

Here we encounter a difficult question, one that still affects Jewish-Christian relations. If Jesus was crucified, then he was executed by a *Roman* authority. Jesus' "crime," at least in Roman eyes, was sedition. He was, or was perceived to be, a threat to Roman authority. Had he really committed an offense against the Roman empire? There is no real evidence (apart from the fact that he was executed for the crime) that he committed such a crime. Why, then, would the Romans, who showed no interest in him before the final hours of his life, put him to death? What conspires to get him executed is the *political* and *religious* situation in the Palestine of his time. The death of John the Baptist sheds some light on this. In his *Antiquities* the Jewish historian *Josephus* says that Herod Antipas had John imprisoned because he was afraid his preaching would lead to an uprising. John was imprisoned primarily for *political* reasons—because a movement was forming around

him, and the king regarded this as *politically dangerous even though it was
not a political movement.* We know that Palestine at the time was turbu-
lent. These same forces seem to be at least partly responsible in Jesus'
case.

Jesus had to deal with this volatile socio-political climate from the
beginning of his ministry. If his preaching was successful, if he gained
followers, opposition to him would grow simply because such move-
ments were dangerous in an occupied country. The Romans would not
be able or willing to distinguish a religious from a political movement,
if indeed that distinction had validity in first century Israel. If Jesus
sought "the restoration of Israel" even as a primarily religious event,
it would have had consequences for the society of the time. The Romans would quell any movement that threatened the peace. While
they normally left subject peoples to follow their own religion, they
knew the potential explosiveness of Judaism. In addition, the Jewish
establishment would fear a Roman reaction. The political situation was
such that Jesus, like John the Baptist, would be viewed by both the
leading Jewish circles and the Roman governor as a threat to the civil
order.

But Jesus was not merely a victim of a volatile political situation.
He had challenged the established religious order in a dramatic way.
He undercut the security of people concerning where they stood with
God and called for an acceptance of salvation as the unconditional love
of God. He made claims explicitly or implicitly to be the definitive mediator of God's will for Israel. He attempted to convert Israel, to
"gather" it in preparation for the coming of the Gentiles—a ministry
which he did not clear with the religious establishment. His understanding of the reign of God and his relationship to it, and especially
his claim to underived and absolute authority, were simply more than
the religious elite of his time could accept. It challenged their position.
Jesus' radicalism, the claims implicit in his message, his threat, growing
out of that, to the status quo, also brought about his execution. His
claims amounted to the religious crime of blasphemy and false prophecy if they were not true. The penalty for the latter was death.

Jesus' arrest must have been organized by the dominant groups
among the priestly caste (Sadducees, then, rather than Pharisees, although this latter group was also represented in the Sanhedrin) under
the authority of the Sanhedrin. There was probably no formal trial,
merely a hearing to decide a charge. Could the Sanhedrin execute?
The Sanhedrin could not execute for political crimes. The martyrdom
of Stephen (Acts 7) shows they could execute by stoning for heresy,
however. This leaves some doubt, then. If the Sanhedrin did not want

to execute (or perhaps could not), a charge was needed which would mean something to a Roman political administrator. This was found under the label of "King of the Jews," that is, Jesus was presented as claiming the most political of the messianic titles. This was not sheer trickery. Jesus understood his mission to be the restoration of Israel. That had real implications for the established order of things. But over and above that are the claims *about* himself implicit in his activity. *Apparently* Pilate was reluctant. *Possibly* public opinion pressured him, although that seems a later addition. Indeed, the way in which Jesus was arrested (and perhaps that the Sanhedrin preferred the Romans to be responsible for his death) points to some popular support for Jesus.

HOW DID JESUS UNDERSTAND HIS DEATH?

This has always been considered one of the most difficult questions about the historical Jesus. A review of the debate should help. Bultmann held we do not have the data to answer the question. Among important contemporary critics, the influence of Bultmann is still strong. Some hold that Jesus would have been baffled by his own death, that he would not have anticipated it and would not have been able to view it as bearing on his mission. Such critics hold necessarily then that Jesus in no way saw his death as salvific. And, indeed, it is hard to see how it could be if Jesus does not think it was.

The chief exponent of this line of thought is the Protestant scholar Willi Marxen, who holds that it is historically probable that Jesus did not understand his death as salvific (*Der Exeget als Theologe. Vortrage Zum Neuen Testament,* p. 165). Marxen's view is not based solely on his judgment that the *eucharistic words* (which, if "authentic" in the form we have them, would show that Jesus foresaw his death and regarded it as salvific) are from the early community. His main argument is: How could Jesus have foreseen his death and still have continued to direct his effort at preparing Israel for the *eschaton?*

There is a mistaken impression that this view has entered into *Catholic* scholarship through the Catholic scholar A. Vögtle. For instance, in his influential *Jesus the Christ* (p. 115), Walter Kasper says that Vögtle "more or less" adopted Marxen's view. It is important to point out that Kasper misrepresents Vögtle here. In reality, what Vögtle shares with Marxen is the view that one probably cannot use the *eucharistic words* to establish Jesus' view of his death. This in itself needs to be examined, but in any case it does not amount to Vögtle agreeing with Marxen that Jesus did not see his death as salvific. Vögtle authored the articles entitled "Jesus Christ" in the two important theological encyclopedias, *Sacramentum Mundi* and *Sacramentum Verbi*. Both show that he believes that Jesus "certainly" saw his death as salvific (see *SM*, "Jesus Christ," p. 179, *SV*, "Jesus Christ," p. 424). So in fact, Marxen and Vögtle represent the two radically *opposed* views.

This debate about how Jesus viewed his death goes back as far as William Wrede and Albert Schweitzer. Wrede undoubtedly discovered something—that *Mark* was an *author* and *theologian* and not merely a collector and historian. But because Wrede thought the picture of Jesus as hiding his messiahship did not derive from Jesus himself, he concluded that Jesus did not understand his ministry as messianic. Hence he would not view his death as salvific, as playing a part in the coming of the reign of God, but merely as the unexpected termination of an unmessianic ministry. Albert Schweitzer saw things differently. He believed that messianism was implied by the eschatological nature of Jesus' preaching, that is, that the very preaching of God's definitive saving act amounted to a claim to be messiah. Furthermore, he saw that within the apocalyptic view, the coming of the kingdom is preceded by *the time of tribulation*. In Schweitzer's view then, suffering and death would not only have been foreseen by Jesus but positively evaluated as an element in the coming of the kingdom and forseeable as part of his own mission. Schweitzer went on to say that not only would Jesus have forseen his own death, he would have provoked it.

Bultmann adopted *Wrede's* view, and Marxen represents it in contemporary scholarship. *Schweitzer's* view is represented by various authors such as Jeremias, C.H. Dodd, W.G. Kümmel and most recently, directly against Marxen, Heinz Schürmann. Sometimes the argument turns on judgments concerning the historicity of given words of Jesus, e.g., Jeremias, Schürmann, J. Blank in *The Common Catechism*. Sometimes the whole picture of Jesus is evoked, e.g., Kasper, 116–119. B.F. Meyer, *The Aims of Jesus*, 216–219, combines both approaches.

The Common Catechism (J. Blank) is echoing Albert Schweitzer when it says that logic would have *forced* Jesus to foresee a violent death.

In a sense, the conflict was inevitable. Looked at in this way, Jesus' violent death on the Cross merely expresses the inner logic of his message and his attitude. Jesus appeared in the name of God as a champion (proclaimer and bringer) of radical salvation, radical love and radical humanity, in a world which constantly contradicted them. It is the fate of the "ab-

solutely good" person, the man who loves utterly, that, even
if he does not condemn others, he exposes the less good and
less generous, but deeply religious, by his very existence—the
fact of his being as he is and not different, and uncovers false
positions and the real conflicts and alienations (p. 158).

Or, as *The Common Catechism* goes on to say, "the presence of absolute
goodness provokes extreme reactions: spontaneous trust and love or
deadly aggression. Before the scandal of Jesus hanging on a cross, you
have the *skandalon* (the stumbling block) of Jesus the bringer of unconditional love." There is a unity to Jesus' person and work which
means that his death must be understood not as inscrutable fate but as
the consequences of who he thinks he is and what he thinks his mission
is. It seems probable that he could have avoided it. That he did not
indicates that he saw it as *part of* the coming of the reign of God.

Did Jesus *explicitly* attribute salvific value to his death or did he
merely accept it as the unavoidable consequence of his mission and in
this sense "God's will?" According to Karl Rahner, it is not necessary
to establish that Jesus explicitly attributed "representative expiation"
to his death. He maintains (*Foundations of Christian Faith*, p. 248) that
it is historically well established that Jesus "faced his death resolutely
and accepted it at least as the inevitable consequence of fidelity to his
mission and as imposed on him by God," and that is sufficient to give
Jesus' death the moral character necessary for it to be truly salvific.
Thus Rahner goes on to say it is not necessary to establish in what sense
the pre-resurrection Jesus explicitly ascribed a soteriological function
to his death beyond the fact that Jesus resolutely faced his death and
accepted it as imposed by his mission.

Rahner is undoubtedly correct. But can we go further and assess
the "authenticity" of the eucharistic words which attach an *explicit* soteriological function to Jesus death? This is an important question for
pastoral reasons. It is important to assemble all the possible evidence
that sheds light on how Jesus understood his death in order to call into
question soteriologies among Christians which separate Jesus' death
from his mission, and thus do not see his death as an expression of
God's *love*. It is very easy to fall into the pattern set by *popular adapta-
tions* of Anselm of Canterbury's satisfaction theory of redemption.
These incorporate a soteriology in which the main notion is that there
is a *debt* in justice to be paid and Jesus' death is demanded in order to
pay the debt, with the emphasis on the *brutum factum* of the death. A
number of things are wrong with this view. First, it makes "justice"
(understood in a non-biblical sense) not love the ultimate category in

describing the God-humanity relationship, something which renders Jesus' own message questionable. Second, in a minimalistic form, it would hold that Jesus could accomplish our redemption by a purely external act which he himself could be bitterly rejecting. His death could be something *imposed on him* and not part of his surrender to God and his mission.

Theologically, to be salvific the death of Jesus must be a *moral act*. It must be something he accepts as part of his call. Would that be hard for a man who thought he was mediating God's definitive saving act? Jesus would merely have had to believe his own message to see his death as salvific. Jesus' mission was to preach that the reign of God as unconditional love was at hand. If death overcame him because he was faithful to that mission, how else could he have understood his death? Jesus would have seen his death as an expression of what he was saying—that men and women can rely absolutely on God's love. In other words, he would have understood God to be asking him to act out his message. He would have seen his death as another, the final, prophetic act, an act of faith, by which God would reveal his unconditional love. This is a prophetic act not initiated by Jesus but accepted by him as God's will, in order that God might clarify once and for all how unconditionally a human being can surrender to, can trust in, God's love. The prophets did not merely speak their messages but lived them out; the eschatological prophet acts his out to the end. Accordingly, Jesus' death would be a representative death for men and women in that Jesus would integrate it into his mission of mediating the coming of God's saving event.

We have examined how Jesus *could have* understood his death. Are there "authentic" sayings of Jesus in the Gospels that actually confirm that Jesus attached salvific value to his death? There are, of course, statements by Jesus in the Gospels in which he predicts his death and interprets it as "representative expiation." But, given the nature of the Gospels, one cannot simply cite these passages to establish Jesus' attitude. What are the difficulties?

(1) Q has no passion narrative and no reference to it. Although Q contains the "death of martyrs" motif and refers it to Jesus, it does not explicitly see Jesus' death as salvific. So the theme is absent from a key early tradition.

(2) The predictions of the passion, as we have said, are generally thought to be kerygma. The behavior of the disciples would be incomprehensible if Jesus had accurately predicted these events.

Nonetheless, many scholars feel that one is encountering the historical Jesus' interpretation of his death in the words attributed to him on the occasion of the Last Supper—the "eucharistic words." C.H. Dodd believed they have the strongest claim to be the very words of Jesus of any in the New Testament (*The Founder of Christianity*, p. 109). Generally scholars do not go that far. The difficulties are twofold: (1) *John* does not have Jesus say the words, although the eucharistic theme is not absent from John (cf. Jn 6). (2) Since whatever Jesus said was incorporated into Christian worship, it would be changed somewhat to embody the theological reflection of the early Christians on the meaning *they* attributed to Jesus' death. That the words *were* changed somewhat is clear because the New Testament offers two different versions:

Mk 14:22–25	Take, this is my body. This is my blood of the (new) covenant which is poured out for many.
Mt 26:26–29	Take, *eat;* this is my body. *Drink of it, all of you;* for this is my blood of the (new) covenant, which is poured out for many *for the forgiveness of sins.*
Lk 22:17–19	Take *this* (the cup), *and divide it among yourselves.* This (bread) is my body.
Other manuscripts read:	"This is my body which is given for you. Do this in remembrance of me. And likewise the cup after supper, saying, "This cup which is poured out for you is the new covenant in my blood."
1 Cor 11:23–25	For I received from the Lord what I also delivered to you, that the Lord Jesus on the night when he was betrayed took bread, and when he had given thanks, he broke it and said, "This is my body which is for you. *Do this in remembrance of me.*" In the same way also the cup, after supper, saying, "This cup is the new covenant in my blood. *Do this, as often as you drink it in remembrance of me.*"

There seem to be two traditions: one behind Mark–Matthew, one behind Luke–Paul. The least we can say about these words is that (1) in every case they are said to have Jesus as their origin (Paul uses a technical rabbinic formula to attribute them to Jesus) and (2) in both traditions the words clearly express Jesus' understanding that his death is a death *for others*. If these words come from Jesus (and important scholars hold that they probably do, at least substantially, e.g., Fitzmyer, p. 56), then there is no solid reason to think that a soteriological intention is not to be traced to what Jesus said over the bread and wine at the "Last Supper." He seems to have understood his death as internal to his mission as the mediator of salvation, as a death for the kingdom of God and those who were open to it.

A second saying attributed to Jesus on the occasion of the Last Supper and widely accepted by exegetes as "authentic" seems to point toward the same conclusion: "Truly, I say to you, I shall not drink again of the fruit of the vine until that day when I drink it new in the kingdom of God" (Mk 14:25; cf. Lk 22:16, 18). Here Jesus appears to express an awareness that his end is near and that his death and the coming of the kingdom are related.

WAS IT A "SACRIFICE"?

Should we continue to use the word "sacrifice" to refer to Jesus' death? Does it convey to us what it did for the early Christians? Of course, since the word comes from the New Testament (especially Hebrews), it should be interpreted against the New Testament concept of sacrifice, not from its use in the history of religions. The Gospels present Jesus' death as a sacrifice without using the word. Furthermore, Jesus himself seems to have understood his death as a sacrifice because, if the eucharistic words are his, he used the *cultic* language of his time, a language of sacrifice.

But this language of cult is foreign to us. So sometimes discussions of the death of Jesus avoid the language of sacrifice. The question is parallel to whether we should continue to use the language of sacrifice about the Mass. It is generally conceded today that the traditional statement that Christ redeemed us by "the sacrifice of the cross" at least needs fuller explanation. The sacrifice of the cross cannot be understood in a *narrow* sense. The salvific activity of Jesus cannot be limited to the three hours of Calvary. That event must be understood against the whole ministry of Jesus. What happened there is the summit of Jesus' obedience to his mission. It is Jesus, following his own message, putting himself unconditionally in God's hands. This tells us also in what sense it is a sacrifice: it is self-surrender, a *self*-sacrifice. It is sacrifice in that it is surrender to God's unconditional offer of love.

Jesus said that God loves men and women unconditionally, and that that love was being offered through him. His faithfulness to his message in the face of human evil left him with the choice of abandoning his mission *or* being executed for it. He chose to be obedient to his mission. The Christian thesis is that God revealed that Jesus was right. God's renewed initiative incorporated Jesus' death in a new event, demonstrating how absolute God's love is. Jesus "had" to die in order that we might know how unconditional God's love is, that even death does not defeat it. Thus, we can certainly speak of Jesus sacrificing himself. It is a very suitable way of talking about a person who gives up his life for others.

Chapter IX

THE RESURRECTION OF JESUS

INTRODUCTION

Intense discussion of the resurrection of Jesus is a striking characteristic of contemporary theology. The controversy parallels the debate
over the meaning of the kingdom of God. For scholars who accept the
Enlightenment view that the world is a closed system merely unfolding
its potentialities as it evolves, a world which God no longer creates,
both the kingdom of God and the resurrection of Jesus must be radically demythologized. The resurrection of Jesus cannot be an event
which happens to Jesus, the result of a new creative act on the part of
God, for that would imply an intervention of God in a closed system.
In this view the resurrection is a *metaphor* for something that happens
to the disciples, an awakening to their fundamental situation as creatures.

On the other hand, scholars who find the Enlightenment worldview unsatisfactory, whose worldview, though modern, is also biblical,
seeing the world as being continually created by God, as something
new in each instance, and therefore open to a startling new exercise of
God's creative power, the resurrection of Jesus can be an *event* which
happens to Jesus. It is this latter approach we will pursue here.

IMPORTANCE

The importance of the resurrection for Christian faith can hardly
be overestimated.

1. If Jesus did not rise from the dead, the *Christian message* is empty.
   That Jesus was risen was the core of the *kerygma*—the central proc-
   lamation of the early Christians. Their fundamental message was:
   He is risen.

185

2. Without the resurrection, *Jesus' message* would be questionable. Christian faith in the full sense is resurrection faith—it is faith that what Jesus said God was—unconditional love—is true. Not even death conditions God's love. Jesus' death could be a great demonstration of Jesus' love for us and of Jesus' love for God, but whether, in fact, he was right about his central concern, about *God's* love, depended on what happened to him—on God's vindication of him, on God's love being unconditional in the face, even, of *his* death. Whether God, as Psalm 2 puts it, "suffered his just one to undergo corruption" is crucial for the entire Christian proposal, because the message of Jesus about God as unconditional love rises or falls with the personal destiny of its proclaimer. If Jesus did not rise, the reign of God did not come. But if Jesus did rise, then the reign of God has come.

3. Without the resurrection *Jesus himself* becomes questionable. The importance of the resurrection is also that it vindicates his claims about himself. Implicit or explicit, they were still extraordinary. The claim of the early Christians that Jesus is the unique Son of God had its basis in Jesus' own claims. But it is common today in both Catholic and Protestant theology to say that the disciples of Jesus did not come to a belief in his divinity until after his resurrection. The resurrection shattered their categories and enabled them, with the aid of the Holy Spirit, to *explicitize* Jesus' implicit claims. An older Catholic theology used the resurrection as a *proof* that Jesus was God, by taking as historically true every saying attributed to Jesus by the evangelists, especially in the Gospel of John, and concluding that if he claimed to be God and rose from the dead, his claim must be true. Today the resurrection is presented not so much as proof of Jesus' divinity but, together with the work of the Spirit, as a *revelation* of it, for as we will see, the disciples' experience of the Risen Christ was pivotal in the development of Christian faith. It made explicit what Jesus would have had to leave implied. The resurrection revealed who Jesus really was, how unconditional the love of God really is, and that in Jesus the kingdom of God came in the form of love, service, lowliness, and then triumph over death. It was pivotal in revealing that God himself was personally present in Jesus.

Thus, the resurrection is not a mere extrinsic validation of Jesus' claims. Besides revealing him it is the event which gave final content to Jesus' preaching. Jesus left it to God to fill in the content of his preaching. He said one could give one's life over unconditionally into God's love. His devotion to his mission brought him to the living out of that message. The resurrection is God's affirmation of the truth of that message.

This is the way the early Church understood the resurrection—as the coming of what Jesus announced, the reign of God. For this reason, the first Christians, in preaching that Jesus is "the Lord," did not base their claim solely on what Jesus did before his death, but on what happened after it. That he rose from the dead and that he was the Lord and Christ was the core of their message. The two beliefs were intimately bound together. The witness to those two propositions was the *kerygma*—the core of the Christian message. The resurrection of Jesus Christ was the pivot of Christian faith, not something peripheral to it.

CONTEMPORARY DISCUSSION OF THE RESURRECTION
THE NEW TESTAMENT EVIDENCE
OF THE PRIMITIVE TRADITIONS
ON THE RESURRECTION OF JESUS

Contemporary theology is very concerned to recover the earliest traditions of the resurrection. Because of the nature of the Gospels, the most primitive accounts are not available to us in a pure form. To get as close as possible scholars distinguish between, on the one hand, *testimonies* to the resurrection in the New Testament and, on the other, the *traditions* behind the testimonies. *Testimony* to the Resurrection exists in the New Testament in two forms:

(1) *Kerygmatic statements*—some of which, as in 1 Corinthians 15:3–5 (Acts 10:40f; 1 Timothy 3:16) speak of "appearances" of the Risen Lord; some of which, as in Romans 1:3–4 and Philippians 2:6–11, speak of the resurrection but without mentioning appearances.

Peter is a central figure in the kerygmatic statements. Apparently in the tradition behind those statements there was no mention of an *empty tomb*.

(2) *"Stories"*—the accounts of the *appearances* of the Risen Christ found at the end of each Gospel (Mk 16; Mt 28; Lk 24; Jn 20–21).

Peter is again prominent; there is mention of an *empty tomb*.

Note: The appearances cannot be harmonized between the two lines of testimony. Nor can one harmonize details within the "story" testimonies. One could also exaggerate discrepancies.

A Kerygmatic Statement

We will examine the most important of the kerygmatic statements:

1 Corinthians 15:3–5:

> For I delivered to you as of first importance
> what I also received,
> that Christ died for our sins in accordance with the Scriptures,
> that he was buried,
> that he was raised on the third day in accordance with the
>   Scriptures,
> and that he appeared to Cephas,
> then to the Twelve.

Analysis:

Paul was handing on something he received. He employed a technical formula (cf. 1 Cor. 11:23–25) used by the rabbis when handing on opinions they did not originate. That this kerygmatic statement did not originate with Paul is corroborated by the fact that it has a non-Pauline vocabulary. "In accordance with the Scriptures" is not Pauline usage. He preferred to use "as God said," "it says" or "as it was written." Also Paul talks about *sin* as a personified power, never "sins." Finally this is the only mention of "the twelve" in the entire Pauline literature.

If this did not originate with Paul, when and where did he get it? How far back and how close to the event of Jesus' death does it take us? Walter Kasper argues that Paul probably received it in 30 A.D., the year he favors for Jesus' death. That, however, would presuppose a rapid expansion of Christianity (something not at all impossible) since Paul would have received it after his own conversion on his way to Damascus to stamp out the nascent heresy. Paul's conversion probably cannot be dated before 31 or 32 A.D. Three places and times are proposed: Damascus (early in the 30's), Antioch (still in the 30's), Jerusalem (well into the 40's). We know that Paul was active in those places at those times. Since Paul goes on to say (v. 8) that Jesus appeared to him *after* the other appearances, the tradition of appearances was probably already in existence when he was converted. This would date the tradition to the period between the death of Jesus and Paul's conversion, so the early 30's.

In this tradition two words are key: *ophthē, egeirein. Ophthē,* "appeared," is consistently used in New Testament accounts of the resurrection appearances. Its background is the Septuagint (Greek version of the) Old Testament. There it is used for theophanies, visual experiences of God, that is, for those occasions when God appeared "objectively," not in a dream or trance, but as a phenomenon encountered in a normal state of consciousness. *Egeirein,* "to rise," means literally to "wake up," to rise from sleep and is thus a metaphor for resurrection.

Finally, we must recall that 1 Corinthians 15:3–5 involves elements of theological interpretation. The passage is certainly not an historical report in the modern sense. It is a credal formula. As a *kerygmatic* statement, it combines references to events and interpretation of the significance of events. The question, then, is: What is "he rose again"—history, or theology, event, or interpretation? There seems to be an intentional paralleling of "he died," "he was buried," "he rose." Does the statement "he rose" indicate an *event* at least analogous to death and burial?

The Gospel "Stories"

The Easter "stories," found at the end of all four Gospels, present their own set of problems. The stories lack the relatively unified character of the accounts of the passion, for instance. A particularly perplexing problem is whether these stories testify to historical events, the finding of an empty tomb or appearances of the Risen Christ, which are the *origin of* the Easter faith, or whether they are a *product of* an Easter faith. The majority view is that they testify to an "ignition event" or events, and are not a consequence of faith. They record the origin of belief and are not merely the consequence of a belief already present. The minority opinion is that the Easter stories are not historical in purpose, that they originated in the theological and apologetic needs of the early community. Their purpose would be to demonstrate the meaning and especially the corporeality of the resurrection. In other words, the stories are far more theology than history. (Among Catholic scholars, who nevertheless do not deny the bodily, personal resurrection of Jesus, this view is followed by R. Pesch and E. Schillebeeckx.)

Analysis:

All four Gospels include accounts of Jesus' appearances, but there are *discrepancies* among them. It is impossible to harmonize them; on the other hand the discrepancies are sometimes exaggerated. We could probably harmonize:

1. "the visit of women to the tomb" as to
                     (a) time,
                     (b) individuals involved,
   but,   (c) the visual phenomena are difficult to reconcile,
                     (d) the conversations are somewhat difficult to harmonize,
   and   (e) the reaction is significantly different.
2. With regard to the appearances, the problem is that they are so different in time and place, and they cannot be matched easily with the appearances in 1 Corinthians 15:3-8.

Finally, it is important to note that most scholars believe the original Gospel of Mark did not include an appearance, that is, that Mark 16:9–20, where there *is* an appearance, is a later addition. That does not mean that the author knew nothing of the resurrection, for he has Jesus give a summary of the passion and resurrection three times (chapters 8, 9, 10), and Mk 16:7 clearly anticipates an appearance in Galilee. But if Matthew and Luke are dependent on Mark at this point, then the character of Mark 16:1–8 is crucial. According to W. Kasper (following the analysis of M. Brändle), this pericope is in "no way an historical account." This appears to be an exaggeration. Why does he say it? (1) The reason for the visit to the tomb is improbable (to anoint a body over thirty-six hours dead). (2) The project lacks plausibility—who would open the tomb? (3) Everything points toward a narrative constructed to set in relief the words of the angel—"He is risen." That is, the kerygmatic intent is overriding. (4) The silence of the women is a (the!) *Markan motif.* Yet, as Kasper himself admits, to say that the "story" is theology is not to dismiss an historical core, because if the tomb were not empty, the fact could easily have been verified. In fact, the historicity of the empty tomb tradition is widely accepted by scholars. The women would be going to perform the final religious act—the pouring of aromatic oils on the body of Jesus. A body in a rock tomb at the elevation of Jerusalem in April (Jn 18:18 indicates cold weather) would not necessarily decay rapidly; a group of women could roll a circular stone away from the tomb entrance; the preaching of the resurrection would have been out of the question if the body were still in the tomb. The question, then, is better phrased: Were there appearances at the empty tomb?

Conclusions

Obviously, discrepancies in the Easter "stories" have caused considerable divergence of opinion among biblical scholars. A *common* opinion is that behind these two types of testimony there are two separate traditions that date to the earliest years of the Christian community, and both fuse history and theology. The two traditions are the empty tomb tradition and the appearances tradition. A proposed reconstruction of the empty tomb tradition (J. Schmitt, *The Concise Sacramentum Mundi*, Resurrection IB) before the addition of theological elements is that on the morning of the third day (so about thirty-six hours after Jesus' death) certain women, among whom was Mary Magdalene, set out for the tomb. While they were still at a distance from it, they saw that the stone had been rolled away from the tomb entrance. Hastily they returned and told the disciples what had happened. At this news some disciples ran to the tomb. Unlike the women, they actually entered the tomb (a semi-underground chamber) and were confused to find it empty. At one time some scholars maintained that the tradition of the empty tomb was the only tradition, and that the tradition of the appearances grew up only later. This is the importance of establishing the date and reliability of 1 Corinthians 15:3–5.

1 Corinthians 15:3–5 points to the existence of the tradition of the *appearances* of the Risen Christ at an early date. If it developed out of the empty tomb tradition, it developed quickly—even immediately. But it seems to be independent, even Galilean in origin. It tells of appearances of the Risen Christ which include both a *seeing* and a *hearing* of him. Some scholars hold that 1 Corinthians 15:3–5 points to experiences closer to the apparition to Paul on the road to Damascus than the fully developed appearance stories in the Gospels like that of the disciples on the way to Emmaus. The *Gospel* appearance accounts are (individually and collectively) "recognition scenes" or "mandate scenes." That is, two elements are regularly present: (1) at first Jesus is not recognized and then is; (2) those who see him experience a mandate to proclaim him alive. Although it is the appearance stories and not 1 Corinthians 15:3–5 which point to these phenomena, scholars regard this data as reminiscences of actual experiences, not the least because Paul himself based his ministry on such an experience. The appearance may have been distributed unequally over a relatively long period of time, perhaps even up to three years (the limitation of appearances to forty days that we find in Luke seems to stem from Luke's own theological

concerns) and, insofar as places are mentioned at all in the text, they take place in Galilee (and perhaps Jerusalem). Some exegetes maintain flatly that the appearances tradition is originally Galilean, while the empty tomb tradition would necessarily originate in Jerusalem.

If the earliest traditions are so relatively simple, why are the Gospel "stories" accounts so elaborate and so diverse? In order to adapt these events to the mentality of their hearers and to theologize, and to emphasize the actuality of the message, especially the "bodily" character of the resurrection, the early preachers interpreted the events with the aid of themes drawn from Jewish anthropology and, especially, the Old Testament. The angel at the tomb, for instance, functions in the classical role of *angelus interpres*, a literary convention in which the central message of the author is put in the mouth of a divine emissary. Or, the developing insight of the early Church was not only attributed to the Risen Christ working through the Spirit but to the Risen Christ in a given appearance. Thus the early Christians took the missionary mandate which *is* found in the oldest tradition and expanded it. In Matthew (28:19) the appearing Risen Christ commissions the disciples using a full Trinitarian baptismal formula. In adapting the tradition, the early Church was simply doing what it thought it was supposed to do—on the one hand, be faithful to the tradition, on the other, adapt it to its own current needs. In the process, the two traditions tend to merge in the Gospel stories. Mark 16:1–8 speaks of an empty tomb in Jerusalem and appearances in Galilee. Matthew and Luke speak of an empty tomb and have appearances in Jerusalem (Matthew: as the women are on the way to the disciples; Luke: in the neighborhood of Jerusalem and then in the "Upper Room"). John has the appearances right at the empty tomb. The Markan appendix (16:9–20) also has appearances at the tomb (to Mary Magdalene) and in the upper room.

THE EVOLUTION OF THE THEOLOGY OF RESURRECTION IN THE PRIMITIVE TRADITION AND THE NEW TESTAMENT

Our analysis allows us to separate out the theological reflection of the early Christians and the evangelists on the meaning of the resurrection.

THE PRIMITIVE TRADITION

As we have seen, what we find in the New Testament represents the end product of a development. The event, while it had the capacity to shatter one's pre-conceptions, nevertheless would be interpreted according to the categories of thought and the worldview of the people who experienced it. Since the people who experienced the resurrection were Palestinian Jews, the theology of the primitive traditions reflects their unique worldview:

(1) They viewed the resurrection as the culminating word, the eschatological word, of God, to his people. The resurrection of Jesus gave Jesus' message its final content. *The kingdom of God had come*—the new age had dawned. It signaled the dawn of the eschaton, the breaking-in of the *new creation*. The world was in a radically new situation—death, the ultimate enemy of humanity, had been conquered and so the forces of evil had been dealt a mortal blow. In other words, the *reign of God* announced by Jesus, had now come *in power*. Because of the influence of apocalyptic, the coming of the reign of God and the end of time were not distinguished. The end was near. Jesus would return soon. Thus, they prayed: *Marana tha!* "Lord, come!"

(2) The resurrection *vindicated* Jesus and his message. The earliest tradition presented the resurrection as the *response* of God to the submission of Christ on the cross and a validation and completion of his message. It was even presented as a *reward* to Christ for his obedience, but it was pre-eminently *a deed of the Father,* the earliest language speaking not of Jesus *rising,* but of God *raising* him. By this he was "*made* Lord and Christ," the definitive mediator. The resurrection of Jesus was seen as his "exaltation" to the right hand of the Father, where he shares in divine power. "Exaltation" is interchangeable with "resurrection." Sometimes it is a *consequence* of the resurrection, and sometimes a replacement of it. In the primitive tradition the resurrection-exaltation-ascension is one event. Exaltation was a ready-to-hand concept in Judaism. Elijah, Enoch, Baruch and others were spoken of as "exalted" to be witnesses at the last judgment. It expressed the belief that a human being is to play a part in the final judgment. Since Jesus' resurrection inaugurates these events, he *even now* is Lord, or ruler. The present position of Jesus as ruling was expressed using the psalms, especially Psalm

110. He shares God's power, and is in the divine dimension. Since God is not elsewhere but present, Jesus is not elsewhere but present. "Jesus is now with us in God's way" (W. Kasper).

The language of the primitive tradition can mislead us because it is not the language of the doctrinal tradition. It is the way people express their beliefs who think in terms not of *what* things are but in terms of what they *do*. They think "functionally," not "ontologically." In saying that Jesus was "*made* Lord and Christ" they are not saying that he was not the Messiah before and has only now become Messiah, or not Lord before, but has been divinized. Their entire context is different. They are saying that Jesus, by virtue of his exaltation to the right hand of the Father, reigns—he exercises the definitive reign of God. He does what God does. He is God's anointed one, the Messiah, the Christ, and now he reigns. They thought he was Messiah before his death, and so they are simply saying that by his resurrection, Jesus now *fully* exercises his power as God's anointed one. And so he is the Lord, because he does what God does—he reigns.

(3) The primitive tradition's theology of the resurrection holds that by his resurrection God had established Jesus as redeemer. It is only "in his name" that one can be saved. And the resurrection is part of the redemptive process. That is, the redemption of the world is not effected by just the death of Jesus, but by his death and resurrection. The raising of Jesus from the dead is the cause and beginning of the "new heaven and the new earth."

THE NEW TESTAMENT WRITERS

What the New Testament says about the significance of the resurrection is continuous with the primitive tradition but draws it out. Again the Old Testament was the decisive influence, not Hellenistic religious philosophy. The New Testament authors were theologians whose concepts were derived from the Old Testament and the Jewish thought of the time, including apocalyptic.

First of all, they draw out what was *implied* in the early tradition, namely what happened to Jesus as a human person: by his resurrection he underwent a total transformation, while at the same time remaining human. He became a life-giving Spirit, but without ceasing to be human and therefore without ceasing to have some sort of bodily existence. Paul struggles with the data in 1 Corinthians. He says a risen person has a *soma pneumatikon*—a spiritual body (1 Cor 15:44). Hebrew that he was, he believed that for a human being to be at all was to be bodily, at least in some way. Greeks that we are, we are accustomed to distinguishing and opposing body and soul. We have a tendency to identify ourselves with that which transcends materiality (soul). We speak as though our body is something which we "have," and which does not constitute us as persons. All this reflects our Greek heritage. The Hebrew view of the human person is not without support in modern thought. For the Hebrews a person, to be a person, must be related to the world, and the body is the "in-the-worldness" of the person. For them a person without a body is unthinkable. The body is the way the person *relates,* and without relationships—to God, other persons, the world—there is no human person. The body is the possibility and the means of communication, the way in which one relates and thus is human. For Paul the body is where the relationship to God is manifested. The body, thus, can have a variable character. A spiritual body is a person directed by the Spirit, a person imbued with the Spirit. A *soma pneumatikon,* then, is a total human person in the dimension of God, but who is also in relation to the world.

Thus, for Paul, to say Jesus is resurrected is to say Jesus as a whole person is with God. But being in the dimension of God does not mean being removed from the world. It means being *related to* the world in a new way—as one who is with God. This is why Paul can see a real continuity between Jesus as a resurrected body, the Church as the body of Christ and the Eucharist as the body of Christ. By virtue of the resurrection, and the response of individuals to it, the Lord is present with his disciples in a new way and they relate to him in a new way. (This is a crucial moment in the "extended foundation" of the Church. The community was founded in stages corresponding to the entire activity of the earthly and exalted Jesus. Foundation stones were laid in his ministry, the gathering of disciples, their being commissioned to preach, the meals [especially the last one], and the sharing of *exousia* [authority, power], with the twelve. The Easter appearances grounded the restoration of the community after the failure of the disciples to follow Jesus. Jesus is present in a new way, embodies himself in the community itself. This community is where Jesus dwells. Therefore it is where reconciliation with God, the forgiveness of sins takes place. The Lord is bodily present in its worship.)

Finally a word on the role of the resurrection as *soteriological.* Why, for the New Testament, does the ministry, death and resurrection of Jesus *save?* Simply because in them, in their actual occurrence, a *new world dawns.* What happens in Jesus is the coming of God's reign. It is the eschatological event. He is the "first born from the dead." In other words, what happens to him creates a new situation, the restoration and transformation of the creation which had fallen through sin. The resurrection of Jesus is the "proleptic" end of the world, that is, the anticipation and principle of the reunion of creation with its creator. Nevertheless, the kingdom still comes to the extent that men and women open up to it. Jesus does not launch an inevitable process that operates irrespective of human response. New creaturehood arrives when we give ourselves to the reality made present in Jesus' life, death and resurrection.

Thus the resurrection is not an event for Jesus alone. If the primitive tradition saw Jesus as the source of the redemption of the world, the New Testament spells out what that involves. The resurrection of Jesus is the prototype and cause of the resurrection of creation and history. Jesus is the New Adam, the source of a new humanity, "the *first* born from the dead." And the Spirit which effects this transformation is already at work. Through the Spirit, the Church is already in some sense the body of the Risen Lord. Finally, the whole of creation is seen as being oriented toward this transformation. Romans 8:19–23 would be typical of these beliefs (but the same thought is present in Ephesians and Colossians):

> Indeed, the whole created world eagerly awaits the revelation of the sons of God. Creation was made subject to futility, not of its own accord but by him who once subjected it; yet not without hope, because the world itself will be freed from its slavery to corruption and share in the glorious freedom of the children of God. Yes, we know that all creation groans and is in agony even until now. Not only that, but we ourselves, although we have the Spirit as first fruits, groan inwardly while we await the redemption of our bodies.

THE HISTORICAL QUESTION

Having explained the levels of development in the New Testament testimonies to the resurrection, we are in a position to discuss what happened.

METHODOLOGICAL CONSIDERATIONS

1. *The Right Starting Point.* Just as theology sometimes lost the original context of Jesus' miracles when it debated them with people who

saw them as "God's interventions in the laws of nature," so the proper starting point regarding the resurrection is not to see the question of the resurrection as simply a problem of *fact*. Proceeding that way, theology tried to *prove* the resurrection. That is, it tried to *prove* the central object of Christian *belief*. The resurrection is credible (and we will give some reasons why), but it is a mistake to think that the central belief of Christianity can be established as a fact. Easter is not a fact to be cited as evidence; it is itself the most important *object of faith*. By its very nature as faith, Christianity cannot ground itself in a pure fact that would enable it to by-pass its essential character as faith!

To concentrate on the historical question misses what the New Testament wishes to accomplish, the making present to the believer of the risen Christ. Without denying that, for moderns, concern for the historical question is probably inevitable, for believers what is more important is the New Testament's power to shed light on the life of faith—not the mere factuality of the resurrection but its *significance*.

Bultmann, of course, took this to the extreme. He minimized the factuality of the resurrection primarily because he did not think there is an importance in knowing "facts" in religion, and such knowledge can be simply a screen for not really responding in faith. Karl Barth also stressed significance over fact, but Bultmann went too far even for him. He concluded that for Bultmann Jesus is risen "only in the kerygma." Bultmann affirmed the accuracy of Barth's analysis. For Bultmann the *kerygma*, preaching, is the eschatological event; to believe in Christ in the kerygma is the essence of Christian faith. The difficulty with Bultmann's position, of course, is that the central content of the kerygma was: Jesus is risen. The kerygma itself seems to refer to an event other than itself. This demands some historical discussion, therefore.

2. *A Fundamental Problem.* The New Testament presents the event as something that has no analogy in history. It is just not another event. It is presented as transhistorical, as something which effects Jesus as the Crucified One but takes him out of the space-time continuum, the conditions of materiality that we know and that history can deal with. It is not that history can say nothing about the resurrection—about the attitude of the disciples, what they say, what they believe—but the restraint of the New Testament about the event itself, the refusal to speculate about the nature of a resurrected person must be respected. The core of the event is that it takes Jesus out of history or, better, positions him with respect to history in a new way. This means that the resurrection cannot be discussed as just another historical event.

3. Over the centuries a number of alternative hypotheses have arisen:

- removal of the body (the Talmud, Reimarus)
- substitution (Koran: Simon of Cyrene actually dies)
- trance (not real death) (D.H. Lawrence, Robert Graves, H.E.G. Paulus)
- "Evolution" (James Fraser, History of Religions School)
- "vision" (hallucination) (D.F. Strauss, Celsus)
- merely a change in the disciples (Bultmann, Paul Winter)

Three of these *alternative* hypotheses that have some currency today are: (1) "Evolution" = spontaneous, not necessarily malicious, myth-making, (2) "vision" = hallucination, (3) that the New Testament accounts indicate merely a change in the disciples.

SOME HISTORICAL POINTS

Historical discussion of the resurrection, as we said, faces a fundamental difficulty. The resurrection is not an historical event in the normal sense. The New Testament does not present Jesus coming back to the life he had before he died. The resurrection is not the resuscitation of a corpse. It is an event which takes Jesus out of, or, better, positions him differently with respect to space and time. It has no analogy in our experience. Nevertheless, some historical investigation and conclusions can be made.

1. The actual *death* of Jesus is not really questionable. That he merely appeared to die is an old discredited thesis which is periodically revived, but there is not a serious scholar in this field today who would argue it. As a matter of fact, besides the fact that there is not a shred of evidence for it in the only documents that give us historical information about Jesus, the New Testament, in his own time no one questioned that Jesus died. Those who propose the "swoon" theory do so not because of hard evidence, or indeed any evidence at all, but because they have already decided that resurrection cannot happen. Also they exhibit remarkably simplistic understandings of what resurrection means, often equating it with the resuscitation of a corpse.

2. The situation of the disciples. The picture in the Gospels stands up under critique. The disciples of Jesus failed him. The early Church would have no interest in gratuitously slandering its own leaders. Probably no one except some women disciples were faithful during the

passion (only Luke, as is his custom, has the men disciples look in any way involved—23:49). As a group, Jesus' disciples appear crushed and confused, disillusioned by the death of Jesus, fearful for their own safety. Furthermore, while the Gospels have Jesus predict his resurrection in detail, the *details* are universally held by exegetes to be supplied by the early Christian community. He probably predicted his death and vindication but not in detail. Even had he done so, the disciples did not expect him to rise because they never really faced the probability of his death. Their behavior would be incomprehensible if they had. Also, while belief in resurrection was common among the Pharisees, it was a belief in a *general* resurrection at the final judgment. There was no belief in a single individual, let alone the messiah (who would not die), rising from the dead before the last judgment.

3. Jesus' burial. This is part of the bedrock of the earliest tradition. The burial is associated with the name of a man, Joseph of Arimathea, who was not a member of the circle of closest disciples. It is thus an event with a wider audience than Jesus' immediate companions, who indeed apparently did not participate at all. Finally, when the apostles began to preach that Jesus was resurrected, no one denied that he died or was buried. The Talmud accepts the death and burial. It confirms them, in fact, when it says the disciples stole the body.

4. The tradition that the tomb was found empty by women is a solid part of the early tradition. The Gospel accounts are unanimous that women discover the empty tomb. A legend or fraud would not have made women the initial witnesses, because under Jewish law they were not competent witnesses. Furthermore, apostolic preaching in Jerusalem would have been impossible if the tomb were not identifiable and verifiably empty. Again, the rabbinic literature did not challenge the tradition of the empty tomb. It says that the disciples of Jesus stole the body, but that in itself is recognition that the tomb was empty.

5. The appearances. There are discrepancies in the appearances stories, as we have seen. The place, the number, the sequence and some circumstances of the appearances are uncertain. A small minority of Catholic scholars, for example, E. Schillebeeckx, agree with a line of thought developed by the Protestant scholar Willi Marxen. Marxen proposes that Jesus' mission was taken up by his disciples, and the appearance stories are really intended to legitimize their endeavor. Thus, they do not describe an ignition event but are a way of conveying the authority the early Christians felt they had received to preach. A similar view is held by the Catholic exegete, Rudolf Pesch. He actually goes farther than Marxen in trying to dispense with the "occurrence" character of the accounts. For Pesch, accounts of appearances are

really interpretations of the permanent validity of Jesus' claim. The earthly Jesus is the basis of resurrection faith—and the appearances are merely a metaphor for his permanent validity. The vast majority of Catholic exegetes disagree with Pesch. For them, that a number of people had visual and not merely internal spiritual experiences of the Risen Christ is indisputable. Why would people who never expected Jesus to die and were shattered by the event continue the mission of Jesus—and *what* mission? That the appearances were not purely internal or a mere metaphor for a new understanding of Jesus is supported by the transformation that took place—in the case of the disciples, from disillusioned, frightened men into preachers of the Risen Christ at the risk of their lives, and in the case of Paul, from a non-believer and a persecutor to an apostle who would make the resurrection of Christ the core of his message. One must ask: What validity did Jesus' message have if there was no event beyond his death? Furthermore, while "resurrection from the dead" meant far more for first century Jews than merely the resuscitation of a corpse, they had a much more (not less) "physical" conception of resurrection than we do. The New Testament account of Jesus' resurrection presupposes the Old Testament understanding of resurrection and that understanding did not use the term as a metaphor but as the actual resurrection of the body *from the grave*. The Hebrew notion of resurrection was not merely of the soul's continued existence. Nor was it merely a metaphor for the continued existence of a person or his teaching as a memory. To see the appearance stories as metaphors for a change in the disciples involves denying that the authors mean what they say. It also means the people most qualified to understand the Gospel stories, the early Christians, badly misunderstood them. Finally, to say "seeing Christ risen" is really a metaphor for the disciples finally coming to understand what he was about, and taking up his mission, ignores that there is no cause for either if there was no experience. Why now would the disciples understand Jesus when they had not understood him before? Why would they take up preaching which would have been discredited by his death? The Jewish theologian Pinchas Lapide insists that only an experience of Jesus as personally alive accounts for the transformation of the disciples. The real question is not whether there were experiences of seeing Christ, but what caused them.

Could the appearances have had a psychological cause? Are they merely subjective? This is the decisive question, and it has become more important because of the growth of our knowledge of human psychology. What can be said? Nineteenth century criticism explained the appearances as the psychological effect of the Easter enthusiasm or as an "evolution." The notion that Jesus has risen "evolved" out of the enthusiasm that arose from the finding of the empty tomb. But present scholarship tends to see the traditions of empty tomb and appearances as unconnected in their earliest forms. Furthermore, an empty tomb is an ambiguous sign. What existed was disillusionment. Easter faith did not yet exist. Would an empty tomb start the disciples hallucinating? Indeed, there is some evidence that they had returned to Galilee and taken up their former occupation and that it was in Galilee that the appearances began. There is also evidence that the crucifixion of Jesus was such a scandal that some of his disciples could not believe or had great trouble believing in the experiences of the others. This does not indicate the existence among the disciples of a burning expectation of Jesus rising which would result in a wish-fulfilling hallucination. To say that Jesus had prepared, or even had hypnotized, his disciples to expect his resurrection is to ignore the virtually unanimous opinion of New Testament exegetes that the "predictions" of Mark 8, 9, and 10 do not derive from Jesus, at least in their details.

Furthermore, could visions of purely subjective origin adequately explain the complete change in the disciples, their unshakable certainty and their readiness for sacrifice? The conviction that Jesus had risen was the foundation of the rest of their whole lives, and it was easy to see that their saying that Jesus rose would bring them to grief. (This has been the standard objection against Reimarus too—why invent a fraud that was bound to endanger your life?)

The *character* of the appearances experiences also argues against a purely subjective cause. The New Testament knows about purely internal psychological phenomena. For instance, Paul said that he had had visions (2 Cor 12:1–9). But he distinguished them clearly from his one and only experience of the Risen Christ (on the road to Damascus) which he listed along with the appearances recounted in the tradition found in 1 Corinthians 15:3–5 and not among his visions. It appears he intended to present the appearances mentioned there as parallel to, and therefore having something of the character of, the death and burial of Jesus. In the New Testament generally, the appearances of the Risen Christ are consistently presented in an objective manner, and when purely subjective visions (Acts 10:9–11) occur, they are labeled as such.

Another objection to a purely psychogenic explanation is that appearances took place even to groups, once to more than five hundred people together, and at least once to an opponent—Paul. Certainly in Paul's case, and probably in other cases, at least when the appearances began, they occurred to persons who were not looking for them. While some sort of openness to them seems to have been required, that open-ness hardly constituted an anticipation, or an auto-suggestive longing. The appearances are not described as merely internal experiences, but *as events* that happen to people and are not generated from within. Fi-nally, the word *ophthē* does not denote an interior vision or trance but an *"appearing to."* It is true that the Old Testament did narrate internal experiences as events. However, first century people could distinguish internal and external experiences and had the vocabulary to describe them differently.

We have examined the historical aspect of the resurrection in or-der to establish its nature and credibility. Nevertheless, we do not wish to *prove* the resurrection. One can "objectify" the appearances too much. They have an "occurrence" character, but that in itself involves *personal encounter.* They are essentially revelations by God to individ-uals (all but one of whom, Paul, knew the earthly Christ) in which God reveals his glory in the Risen Christ. The appearances are theophanies, and theophanies require personal encounter. The interpersonal char-acter of the appearances is seen in the greetings, blessings, conversa-tion, comfort, directives, and calls to mission that accompany the appearances. As interpersonal, they appeal to faith, and some sort of openness to them is required. On the other hand, one must recall the disciples' state of mind. They are not, at least initially, waiting for Jesus to appear, and they are to a certain extent overwhelmed by the ap-pearances which cannot be conjured up, controlled, or programmed.

But do not the accounts emphasize the tangible, objective char-acter of the appearances? In fact they do and at times (Jn 20:27) touch the limits of the theologically possible. The body is almost no longer a transformed body, but a resuscitated corpse. This "realism" of the sto-ries seems to want to *emphasize* but not invent (1) the *identity* of the one revealed with Jesus, and (2) the *corporeality* of the resurrection. John himself noticed that this tendency to bring the Risen One back to the conditions of mortality could be misleading, so he added to the story of Thomas, "Blessed are those who have not seen but believe" (20:29). In fact, even those who first preached faith were not dispensed from the necessity of faith. A totally uninvolved observer probably would have experienced nothing. It was a believing-seeing of something *re-vealed.* While we can say with Kasper that "Faith did not establish the reality of the Resurrection . . . " (that is, faith in God as unconditional love did not lead to a *deduction* that Jesus was risen), "but the reality of the Resurrected Christ obtruding in the Spirit upon the disciples es-tablished faith" (*Jesus the Christ,* pp. 139–140), nevertheless an open-ness to this gift was essential. There was a personal encounter with

Christ as the Risen Lord in the glory of the Father. This is not an experience vouchsafed to us who did not know the earthly Jesus. Our faith rests on the testimony of those who knew the earthly Jesus and recognized him in the Risen Christ.

Certainly all this does not prove beyond a reasonable doubt that Jesus rose from the dead. It is not that sort of event. Faith in the resurrection is a classic instance of faith itself. Faith is not the result of a sheer exercise of historical reason by which one moves through a series of irrefutable premises to an undeniable conclusion. Rather, people believe because what their investigation reveals somehow has credibility and clicks with their human experience. The data are "signs"—they point, open up the possibility of conscientious belief. They do not coerce. On the one hand it is unreasonable and inhuman to simply adopt as true some arbitrary worldview because one needs something to make sense of one's experience. One should not invent truth simply because one needs some truth to live by. If the world is absurd, it would be more proper to simply acknowledge that and not talk about truth, for if the world is absurd, anything and nothing is true.

But in important areas of life reasoning can take one so far and then one must make a leap. Then, what is merely credible, when surrendered to, begins to light up one's existence from the inside and becomes self-authenticating—that is, one recognizes the truth of it in living it. But that requires that one have had certain experiences. For the resurrection to make sense, it must not be unhistorical, but at the same time it must correlate with experiences such as death, separation, the absoluteness of love, and the intimations of immortality in those experiences, and the *hopes* that they give rise to. But the basic motive "of credentity" (why one actually *decides* to believe) in the resurrection is knowledge of God. The God of Jesus is the God of faithfulness. God has implanted hope in us. It is incompatible to affirm on the one hand the unconditional nature of God's love and on the other that these hopes have nothing to do with that love. In the end the Spirit which engenders this hope in us is the ground of our belief in the resurrection.

IMPLICATIONS

Suppose the resurrection is true, in the sense that Jesus of Nazareth, a body-person, entered into a transformed state following his death and in a continued personal existence continues to be an effective presence in history. What does it say about human life? For this belief to mean something, one must have a basic trustfulness in the meaningfulness of existence as a whole. If one does not trust that life has meaning, the resurrection would not make much sense, but then nothing else does either. In that case the only truth is death—the ultimate affirmation that it was all absurd anyway.

But what is the resurrection when looked at from a full faith? It is a call to accept one's full humanity and to hope for full human fulfillment, the fulfillment of the whole person, a person who does not merely temporarily "have" a body but is essentially a body-person, a person who is a body. What the resurrection tells us is that what happened to Jesus was not the annihilation of his humanity, but its fulfillment in a transformation. Obviously we have no experience of such a thing. We cannot really understand what this involves. We know that it is not the mere resuscitation of a corpse, but an event in which the whole person is transformed. The limitations of time and space are overcome, but one's integral humanity is not left behind. When we say "bodily" resurrection, we simply mean that the whole person is brought to fulfillment. Just as we cannot divide ourselves into an ever-valid "spirit" and a merely provisional "body," the resurrection says that we are and will in some sense *remain* body.

Moreover, the resurrection is not just something that happened to Jesus. It is *the* proposal of Christians concerning the fundamental meaning of existence. It is the revelation of the goal of God's action in history. It means that death is not the final word, and that what God "saw" in the beginning, that matter is good, remains true and that the good creation is headed for transformation.

It also means that what we are here and what we do here is not something left behind. Resurrection is the transformation of who we are and what, empowered by God's love, we have made of ourselves. What one will be by virtue of resurrection is the fruit produced by a lifetime of one's choices to love or not love, a process of self-creation which has its source in God's love.

But we must not be individualistic. More than merely a proposal about *my* possibilities, resurrection is a proposal about *our* possibilities where *our* includes (because we are matter) not just human beings as strangers in a cosmos but human beings as the meaning and summit of a cosmos. Resurrection is not a proposal for how *I* get *out of this world* into a better one. It is a proposal about the ultimate meaning of *this* world and not merely in some remote future but *now*.

There are various alternative proposals to the meaning of human existence. Which one one adopts will depend very much on one's experience. If one's experience of human life is that it is fundamentally meaningless, this proposal, the Christian proposal, will not seem credible. But most people experience their lives as full of meaning, but a meaning which remains ultimately mysterious and unattainable. Resurrection is the Christian proposal about what that ultimate meaning of human life might really be.

Appendix 8:

THE EMERGENCE OF THE CHRISTOLOGIES OF THE EARLY CHURCH

INTRODUCTION

We have seen that Jesus did not make himself the center of his own preaching. But as the Christ, the Anointed One, the eschatological mediator of salvation, and especially as the Risen One, Jesus became the center and object of early Christian faith. The focus shifted from the preaching of Jesus about the reign of God to preaching about Jesus as Lord, Christ, Son of God and mediator of the reign of God. We will give an account here of this development.

CLAIMS

Jesus claimed to have an intimate knowledge of God's attitude toward men and women. He preached that the reign of God was coming as an act of forgiveness, and that God's love was being offered without discrimination to all of Israel and through Israel to the rest of the world. He preached that this was happening now, that the decisive moment in human history had come. His message was not the product of scholarly study of the tradition, or inspired speculative thinking, or even a prophetic call. It apparently was born of Jesus' own underived knowledge of God with whom he claimed to have a unique filial relationship. In his ministry, as a sign of the inbreaking of God's salvific love, he healed the sick and possessed. His message and manner amounted to the claim that through him definitive salvation was being mediated to the world. Jesus of

Nazareth claimed to be the definitive mediator between God and the world.

METHODOLOGICAL REFLECTIONS

Despite Jesus' identification of his cause with God's, the movement from the pre-Easter understanding of Jesus to the post-Easter understanding is not merely a process of making explicit what Jesus left implicit. It is that, but it is also more. An *event*, the Easter experience of the disciples, provides the bridge.

The Easter experience is the foundation of New Testament Christology. We begin, then, not in the customary way, that is, by tracing the emergence of the Christological titles. Instead we will trace the evolution of reflection on the resurrection itself. Since the Easter experience triggered the growth of Christology, it provides the key to the evolution of thought about Jesus. This corresponds better to the mentality of the earliest Christians. As we will see, they did not look at Jesus *metaphysically*, that is, by asking who Jesus (ultimately) was, but rather *functionally*, asking instead "What does the Risen Christ do?" The Easter experience provided the answer. Moreover, there is a second factor at work in the development of the earliest Chris-

tologies: the experience of the Spirit dwelling in the early Christians as God's eschatological people. The result is that this period of the Christian understanding of Jesus has always been regarded as part of the Christ event and its understanding of Jesus as normative.

We must acknowledge, of course, that the Gospel traveled quickly through different cultures, all of which contributed to the evolving understanding of Jesus. The primitive, functional question yielded in time to more ontological concerns. There were significant differences among the cultures of the Palestinian Jewish Christians, the Hellenistic Jewish Christians, and the Hellenistic Gentile Christians (although some scholars doubt the presence of a purely Gentile Christian community before the second century). Another factor in the evolution of the first century Christologies was the ongoing tension between "Church" and "synagogue," between Christianity and Judaism.

We must, furthermore, come to grips with the fact that there are *different* Christologies in the New Testament. Some are "low," such as the Christology of the Letter of James which mentions Jesus only twice (as "the Lord Jesus Christ"—1:1; 2:1); some are "high" (like the Gospel of John); and still others, like Paul, are soteriologically centered and not *directly* concerned with Jesus' "ontological" status.

In this investigation we must also be aware of our tendency to think of ideas as developing in an evolutionary fashion, with less development giving way to more development. It is just as likely that Christology did not develop in a straight line and that a low Christology could emerge in one place *after* a higher Christology had developed in another place.

Finally, we must keep in mind the early Christian communities' explanation of their beliefs, namely that they were not merely remembering a dead and gone Jesus of Nazareth but that the Risen Christ continued to speak to them through his Spirit. The modern concern to sanction or decry the development of the Christologies of the first century churches usually abstracts from that claim.

ANALYZING THE SOURCES

We begin with an observation. In his letters, the earliest New Testament documents, Paul does not concern himself with the life of Jesus. Rather he writes about the Risen (contemporary) Lord. His epistles are minimally concerned with the teaching and events of the life of Jesus before he died. What about the Gospels?

At first glance their focus appears to be different. The life and teaching of Jesus seem to be precisely what they are concerned about. But a distinction between the concerns of the epistles and the Gospels could be overstated. One cannot say, for instance, that the subject of the letters is the "Christ of faith" and the subject of the Gospels is the "earthly Jesus," for in fact, as we have seen, the Jesus of the Gospels is already the Risen Christ. The Gospels were written to mediate the presence of the exalted Lord, not just recall Jesus as a figure of the past. The Gospels are faith proclamations. They present, as an object of faith, not the pre-Easter Jesus but the Risen Lord. So the difference between the letters and the Gospels is not which Jesus Christ they proclaim but the approach they take to proclaim him. In Paul, Jesus is the Son of God as risen, as exalted to heavenly power (Rom 1:3–4). In Mark, on the other hand, Jesus is designated Son of God at his baptism (Mk 1:11). The creed quoted by Paul in Romans divorces the earthly stage (and the "Son of David") from the heavenly, post-Easter stage of the Son of God, while Mark's Gospel does the opposite, concentrating the dignity of the Son of God in the earthly, pre-Easter history of Jesus.

What does this difference indicate? Reflection on Jesus

took two paths in the early Church, both of which start from the same place—the Easter experience of the Risen Lord—but then proceed in different directions. The difference corresponds not to *earlier* (Paul) and *later* (the Gospels) stages, but to how reflection on the resurrection proceeded *outside* (Paul) and *inside* (the Gospels) Palestine. It is true that the Gospels as we have them are the end product of a development, are later than the letters of Paul and were probably composed outside Palestine for non-Palestinian audiences. Nevertheless, the Gospels betray a genuine concern that Paul did not have—for the teaching of Jesus and the events of his earthly life—which roots the Gospels in the primitive Jewish Christian church of Palestine. It is true that we do not have a pure picture of the Christology(ies)/resurrection faiths of Palestinian Jewish Christianity because we do not have a purely Palestinian Jewish Christian Gospel. According to some scholars, Mark comes closest, while others believe Matthew does, but even these betray a *Hellenistic* Jewish Christian influence. However, because we know more today about the differences between Palestinian and Hellenistic Judaism, the Palestinian layer in the Gospels is becoming more available to us.

THE CHRISTOLOGICAL THINKING OF PALESTINIAN CHRISTIANITY

Let us summarize present scholarly thinking on the earliest Christian faith. The event of the resurrection, while it obviously dramatically rearranged the preconceptions of the disciples, was necessarily interpreted according to the worldview and categories of thought of the people who experienced it. When we explore the *significance* of the resurrection for the earliest Christians, since the people who experienced it were Palestinian Jews, we find that:

(1) They viewed the resurrection as the culminating word, the eschatological word, of God to his people. The resurrection of Jesus filled in the content of Jesus' preaching. The kingdom of God had come, the new age had dawned. The resurrection of Jesus was the sign of the dawning of the *eschaton*, the dawn of the *new creation*. For them the world existed in a radically new way. Death, the ultimate enemy of humanity, had been conquered and the forces of evil had been dealt a mortal blow. In other words, the *reign of God* announced by Jesus had now come *in power*. From this they drew the conclusion so common in the early Church: The end is near and Jesus will return

soon. Thus they prayed: *Marana tha*. "Lord, come!" Jesus is addressed in prayer as Lord and petitioned to return soon.

(2) For the Palestinian Jewish Christians the resurrection *vindicated* Jesus because it vindicated his message. As a result, preserving and adapting his message became important. It is probably out of this concern that "Q" developed.

(3) The earliest tradition presented the resurrection as the *response* of God to the submission of Christ on the cross and a validation of his message. It is even presented as a *reward* to Christ for his obedience, but it is pre-eminently *a deed of the Father*. The earliest language does not speak of Jesus *rising*, but of God *raising* him. The resurrection is seen as Jesus' "*exaltation*" to the right hand of the Father. By it he is "*made* Lord and Christ," and thus he shares in divine power (this is also said outside Palestine and indeed becomes the characteristic emphasis in the Pauline churches). "Exaltation" is roughly interchangeable with "resurrection." Sometimes it is a *consequence* of the resurrection, and sometimes it replaces it. The resurrection is interpreted as the installation of Jesus as Messianic *Son of God* and as his enthronement as *Kyrios* (Lord) equal to God. In this interpretation, Old Testament "kingly" messianic prophecies

such as 2 Samuel 7:14, Psalm 2:7, and Psalm 100:1 played a key role.

Above all, for Palestinian Jewish Christians Jesus was the *Messiah*, the anointed one (Greek: *christos*), the mediator of definitive salvation. The title *Messiah* had no fixed content in Judaism. The Palestinian Jewish Christians claimed it for Jesus, and it became the most frequent way of designating Jesus' *function*. When it was used later by Greek speaking Christians, it ceased to designate a function and became a name. The Palestinian profession of faith of Jesus as the Christ, a functional statement, became in Hellenistic circles a proper name, Jesus Christ, as we see in Paul.

To buttress their claim that Jesus was the Messiah, Palestinian Jewish Christians presented Jesus as *Son of David*, appealing to his ancestry (cf. the *Palestinian* kerygmatic formula preserved in Romans 1:3). This was not due to interest in or even knowledge of his ancestry but to the technique of proof from prophecy. It really just expresses a claim that Jesus is the Messiah. Because of its obvious connection with Palestinian concerns, this title would disappear as the Church became more Gentile, although it is still an important title in Paul who, as a Jew of the diaspora, is a bridge.

At this early stage of the developing faith, resurrection-exaltation-ascension is one thing (cf. Jn 20). Exaltation was a ready-to-hand concept in Judaism—Elijah, Enoch, Baruch, and others were spoken of as exalted, meaning that they would be witnesses at the last judgment. Exaltation expressed the belief that a human being would play a part in the culminating eschatological event of judgment. This event was thought to be near at hand, for Jesus' death and resurrection had initiated the eschatological age. The primitive community, according to the most probable meaning of their prayer, "*Marana tha*, Lord, come," prayed for the coming of salvation not directly from Yahweh but from Jesus, to whom the heavenly title *Kyrios*, Lord, was applied. This indicates a belief that Jesus shared in God's power to save. Whether or not Jesus had referred to himself as the *Son of Man*, the primitive Palestinian Jewish Christian community saw him that way. He would *return* from his exaltation as the "one like a son of man" (Dan 7) to render judgment.

The language of the Palestinian Jewish Christian community can mislead us because it is not the language of the doctrinal tradition. Two thousand years and a vast cultural gap separate us. As I mentioned in Chapter IX, the earliest Christians expressed their beliefs in terms of what things *do*, not in terms of what they *are*. They thought "functionally," not "metaphysically." In saying that Jesus was "made Lord" they did not mean that he was not the Messiah before and has now become Messiah, or that he was not God before and has been divinized. They were not talking about Jesus' person but about his function. They meant that Jesus, by virtue of his exaltation to the right hand of the Father, reigns—that he exercises the definitive reign of God (through the Spirit he has sent on the community). He does what God does. He is God's anointed one, the Messiah, the Christ, and now he reigns. By his resurrection, Jesus now *fully* exercises his power as God's anointed one. And so he is the Lord because he does what God does. They do not distinguish between "nature" and function. What things do *is* their nature. Very quickly, *before* the actual writing of the New Testament, the implications of this view of Jesus were spelled out by *Hellenistic* Jewish Christians on the basis of the Old Testament. The early Palestinian community would not have rejected this development toward a clear understanding of the divinity of Jesus. They simply did not think in those Greek categories. What is significant is that they prayed *to Jesus* as *Lord,* that is, they worshiped him.

(4) Finally, the primitive tradition's theology of the resurrection held that by his resurrection Jesus had been established *Re-*

deemer. It is only "in his name" that one can be saved. While it is true that Palestinian Jewish Christianity emphasized Jesus' role as *teacher,* the belief that Jesus was a Redeemer did not first arise only in Hellenistic Jewish Christian circles. The resurrection was a redemptive event, a making new of the world. The raising of Jesus from the dead was the cause and beginning of this new creation and depended on his voluntary surrender to his "Father's will."

CHRISTOLOGICAL THINKING OUTSIDE PALESTINE

Both the Gospels and epistles preach that the resurrection of the crucified Jesus is God's salvation. Yet outside Palestine, concern focused on what happened to Jesus—his exaltation as Lord and Christ by his resurrection. In this circle, the resurrection is a heavenly legal act. Not Jesus' *history* but his *present status* is the focus of attention, not the confirmation of Jesus' earthly career but what happened because of his death and resurrection. This is the path taken outside of Palestine, and it is enshrined in Paul's letters.

Another characteristic of Christological thinking outside Palestine was the use of titles for Jesus. Thus the frequency of titles in the letters of Paul is significantly greater than in the Gospels, although standard New Testament scholarship has often sought the Christologies of the Gospels by concentrating on the relatively infrequent titles found in them. For instance, the central title *Christ,* which is rare in the Gospels and where it does occur derives from a later stage of the tradition, is found everywhere in Paul and plays a central role. Outside Palestine (that is, in Hellenistic Jewish and Gentile Christianity) the Jewish term Messiah was applied to Jesus but given a content from the fate of Jesus. Jesus, precisely as the "cursed one," is the Christ. His messiahship operates not in power but in weakness, for in his death God shows his love for us (Rom 5:8).

A second favorite Pauline title for Jesus was *Lord,* which Paul used to convey two associated meanings, that of Jesus' unique authority, and the close relationship to Jesus of those who are able to call him "Lord." As we saw, the Aramaic equivalent of Lord was applied to God in Palestinian Judaism. It was also applied to Jesus in the prayer *Marana tha,* an act of worship of Jesus. The use of the Greek *kyrios* in the Judaism of the diaspora and primitive Hellenistic Christianity exactly parallels this. But in Hellenistic Christianity the use is also broader. In the Pauline churches "Jesus is Lord," that is, he is the exalted Lord of all the principalities and his name as Lord "is above every other name" (Phil 2:9–11).

Son of God is a third prominent Pauline title for Jesus. Its original meaning (Rom 1:4; cf. Mk 1:11) was "God's plenipotentiary," his representative, but it also connotes Jesus' filial obedience. Jesus is the Son of God in the second sense, especially in his death (Rom 8; Gal 2). Just as it is excessive to read into this title at this point the fully developed dogma of the later Church, it is incorrect to reduce the content of the title to a mere figure of speech. Paul's use of the title is not yet fully ontological; he is using it "functionally." Yet he uses it to express his belief that in Jesus God is at work in an absolute way. The evolution of the later doctrine is not a misunderstanding of Paul but an elaboration of the basic mystery he was trying to convey. Paul's *Christology* is largely a *soteriology*. The later Church would recognize more clearly the ontological basis of soteriology. Nevertheless Paul himself had already started in that direction. According to many scholars, in adopting the primitive Christian hymn found in Philippians 2:6–11, Paul is already hinting at the pre-existence of Christ. According to other scholars, in speaking of Jesus as "the Son himself" in relation to "God the Father" in 1 Corinthians 15:24–25, Paul has progressed from a purely functional horizon to an ontological one. Finally, in Romans 9:5, the better reading of the Greek text has Paul simply call Jesus "God." The Deutero-Pauline Letter to Titus calls Jesus "our great God and Savior" (2:13).

To conclude this brief sketch we return to the Gospels, for although they incorporate the Palestinian tradition, in the form we have them they derive from Hellenistic Christianity. Thus the title *Son of God* here (Mk 1:1; 15:39) probably expresses a belief in Jesus' divinity. For that matter, some scholars hold that even the title *Son of David* (Mt 1:1) does this. Certainly the baptismal formula employed by Matthew at the end of his Gospel (Mt 28:19) has reached this stage. Finally, the Prologue of John clearly expresses Jesus' divinity, and near the end of this Gospel Jesus is recognized as "Lord and God" (20:28).

Chapter X

THE TRINITY AS THE SUMMARY
OF THE CHRISTIAN ANSWER
TO THE GOD QUESTION

GOD-TALK

All religious traditions recognize that to really conceptualize God is impossible. If God is the absolute, that which is the source of its own existence, then God does not depend on anything outside God and is not limited in any way. If God is without limitation, only something without limitation could comprehend God, that is, only God is adequate to understanding and saying what God is. As a matter of fact, that is one way of saying what God is—an infinite act of understanding, understanding itself. Aristotle understood the ground of all things in this way—as pure thought thinking itself. According to Bernard Lonergan, it was also Thomas Aquinas' preferred understanding of God. God, for Thomas, was *ipsum intelligere,* understanding itself or pure understanding, in which the act of understanding and the understood are the same thing. Yet because this one reality is infinite, it is essentially mystery to all but itself.

While the biblical religions subscribe to the thesis of the incomprehensibility of God, they also make cautious attempts to speak about God. As we saw earlier, people in cultures affected by biblical religion have inherited a concept of God as one who hears, responds and acts. Within our acknowledged limitations, can we develop this understanding further? For instance, is God a person? The Bible never actually calls God a "person," but it does speak of God constantly in personal categories. Like a person the God of Israel has a personal name, Yahweh, and by that name God is revealed, as a subject, as an I. Yahweh enters into personal relationships. However, when God is said to be personal, the term must be used "analogously," so as not to connote any limitations in God. When we say God is a "person," we run the risk of understanding God as different from us by degree, rather than in kind. For this reason, some theologians are reluctant to call God a person, preferring instead to describe God as personal being.

The obvious conclusion from this is that if human speech about God is possible at all, it must be analogous. It will always labor under the limitation that any words we use are derived from experience of the finite world and can only partly express the reality of something which is not part of that world, which "transcends" the world. On the other hand, human speech is not totally inadequate; if the world is and God is, they have some sort of common ground (although, for example, John Macquarrie does not even wish to say God "is" because it makes God sound like a being alongside other beings). To say that the world is, and that God is, is not to say that they are in the same way, but it does say that they are and not that they are not. There is at least that analogy between God and the world. Furthermore, God seems to have thought that human language could say something about God because God adopted it as a means of speaking to us. Human words became the vehicle of God's revelation of God, and ultimately *the* human Word, Jesus, became the definitive revelation of God to us. In Christ, humanity and human speech became the grammar of self-revelation God uses, so we have warrant for *some* human discourse about God.

Is God a "*he*"? One cannot acknowledge that God transcends materiality and attribute sexuality to God. Accordingly words such as "Father" and "he" are metaphors. There are times when the biblical God demonstrates qualities customarily thought to be more characteristic of women so that the metaphors "Mother" and "she" would better convey what God is like. Because we will discuss God as trinitarian, and the traditional language of trinitarian theology refers to God as Father, Son and Holy Spirit, we must at least begin with those metaphors. In general, however, when we speak of God as one, we will use a form that best captures the primary biblical understanding of God, including God's character as mystery. We will call God "the Transcendent," and when a pronoun is required, to maintain the mystery of God, we will refer to the Transcendent as "it" rather than "he" or "she."

While *philosophy* may have something to say about the Transcendent, the historical revelation of the Transcendent cannot be superseded by the assertions of philosophy. Catholic theology has had a tendency to supplant what the Transcendent says about itself in salvation history and especially in Christ, with philosophical speculation. Philosophy can aid, but it cannot supplant. After all, if the Transcendent is personal, we can only know it if it reveals itself. Self-revelation is the condition of anything personal being known. The normative data about God cannot be what the human mind generates, but what God has chosen to reveal.

GOD AS AGAPE

So rather than using philosophical categories and saying that God is pure thought thinking itself, or a supreme Being, or even Being Itself (all of which have their value), we begin with what Scripture says God is. The First Letter of John (4:8) says that God is love. Is that just a pious way of speaking? Is love merely an attribute of God or can we really say that, in its innermost reality, the Transcendent is, precisely, love? Christians have always understood the statement to mean the latter. The Transcendent is love not just in relation to us, but in itself.

In the course of Christian history, the belief that God is love has often drifted into the background as other characteristics such as God's justice or power have taken precedence. But we never read in Scripture that God *is* justice, or *is* power; we read that God is "just," and "powerful." In fact, God's justice is merely an aspect of God's nature as love, for the biblical "justice" (*sedekah*) often means "merciful love." The New Testament equivalent of the Old Testament "justice" is "grace," which connotes love. It is true that the constant love of God for men and women entails, also, "judgment" (separation from God) when it is rejected, but God's justice does not stand in opposition to God's love—it is simply the effect of God's love.

There are many kinds of love. What kind of love is God? The Greek word used in 1 John 4:8 is *agape*. The word expresses that God does not love out of desire or need—the Transcendent's love is not *eros*. Its love is not an appetite for self-fulfillment, but a love which overflows from the superabundance of love that God is. Nevertheless, because it is real love, it does seek the response of the beloved, a response created and evoked by the love itself.

God's love for the world must not be thought of as a natural, necessary movement toward creatures, or otherwise God would be indigent and dependent, not truly transcendent. Some theologians do wish to present God as needy. Some "process" theologians contend that God needs completion, that human beings play a role in making God. If this makes God *eros* and not *agape*, it is questionable. The classical view, that God does not love out of need but out of God's own fullness, and that God is a movement of love independent of the world, a world it has no need of, preserves God's character as *agape*. The biblical position is that out of love for the world the Transcendent gave itself to the world, in an act of pure gratuity. Of course, since there is no time in God, we must recognize that it is a world which God has "always" willed and as such is not an after-thought but a world whose existence is a part of God's eternal being. Furthermore, we must acknowledge that the classical view was strongly influenced by Aristotle, for whom God's principal attribute is unchangeability. For Aristotle, God is pre-eminently *apathos*, non-suffering (and *monos*, alone). Suppose God is not *apathos* (and *monos*) but *sympathos* (and *relational*). And suppose that God, not out of need but out of abundance, *freely decides* to risk, to become indigent, to suffer with, then maybe there is a process in God. But it would be a process rooted entirely in God's abundance being freely bestowed, in *agape*, not *eros*.

THE TRINITY

If, as the classical approach maintains, the Transcendent is love and does not need creatures to be a lover but creates creatures because it is a lover, what does God love "before" creatures exist? The "before" is in quotes because there is no before and after in God. Time begins with creation, with matter in motion, so strictly speaking there is no time when God was not loving his creation. But the intent of the question is clear: "Before" there was something which is not God for God to love, what was God loving? Is God's love objectless "until" there is a world to love? "Was" God radically alone (*monos*)? Or "was" God enjoying a giving and receiving of love that is part of God's very being? If God is love, is there a giving and receiving of love that *is* God? Are there relations *within* God? Is God relations?

That there are personal relations within God cannot be deduced simply from the realization that the innermost nature of God is love. That there are personal relations within God can only be known if God reveals it. Has God revealed it, and, if so, how was it revealed?

The New Testament reveals a fundamental awareness that God is Father, Son and Holy Spirit. This is clear especially (but not exclusively) in such formulas as:

2 Cor 13:14   The grace of the Lord Jesus Christ and the love of God and the fellowship of the Holy Spirit be with you all.

Mt 28:19   (where Jesus is represented as telling his disciples to) "Go, therefore, and make disciples of all nations, baptizing them in the name of the Father and of the Son and of the Holy Spirit."

How did this development occur?

THE TRINITY IN THE OLD TESTAMENT

There is, of course, no explicit knowledge of the relational nature of God in the Old Testament. Indeed, in a world of polytheism, it was precisely the *unitary* nature of God that needed to be stressed, along with God's transcendence of and dominion over the world (including its very origin and continued existence, that is, its created character).

However, as we said in Chapter IV, the understanding of God as the God of the covenant was a fruitful source of theological understanding. The God of the covenant is hardly Aristotle's "supreme substance." The covenant theology of the Priestly writer displays a bold application of the insights of the prophets concerning God. An understanding of God as love was emerging and being applied already in the Old Testament.

Certainly the God of the Old Testament is not static, but essentially creative. Some scholars, a minority to be sure, believe that the name that God reveals to Moses on Sinai, *JHWH*, normally translated "I am who am" or "I am who I am," really should be translated as "I cause to be . . . " or "I bring to pass . . . " Even those scholars who do not translate it that way acknowledge that the Hebrew verb "to be" (*hyh* or *hwh*) does not connote static unchanging existence, but dynamic, active existence. The God of the Old Testament is revealed not as one who simply is. God's first words are creative: "Let there be light" (Gen 1:3). The God of the Old Testament is, in and behind other images, a God who is dynamically loving. The question is: Does this loving take place only *ad extra*, to objects which are not God? Does God have to create in order to have an object of love, or does God create further images of the object God does love?

Late in Old Testament times, there were the *beginnings* of an attempt to capture a "diversity in the unity" of God in the place assigned to "the angel of the name." In some heterodox Jewish sects this angel became a divine *hypostasis* (something standing on its own) called "little Yahweh" (apparently standing for the outgoing aspect of God, in contrast with God's hiddenness and transcendence). In the later literature of the Old Testament, we encounter the well-known hypostatizations of wisdom (*sophia*) and the word (*logos*). This prepared the ground for the Christian understanding of God by providing the vocabulary the first Christians used to articulate their experience. Also present was the notion of "the Spirit of the Lord"—the means by which God enlivens, moves, and creates. Thus, even in the Old Testament, the unity of God is not identified with a static uniformity. As Abraham Joshua Heschel has pointed out, the Old Testament is hardly an endorsement of philosophical monism, or a belief in an aloof, uninvolved God. Rather it is a theology of the divine *pathos*.

THE TRINITY IN THE NEW TESTAMENT

Why did the first Christians describe God in triune terms? Because of their *experience*. Following the resurrection, they experienced Jesus as the Lord and they experienced themselves as enlivened by his Spirit, as a permanent divinizing presence in the world. They experienced the Son and the Spirit as sent by God as *Abba* (Father), and they experienced themselves as related to God as "Father," in Jesus as "Son," through the indwelling of the "Holy Spirit." Jesus himself, as well as late Old Testament conceptions, provided them with a way to articulate their experience. Comparing their experience with Jesus' speech, they understood there to be a relationship *within* God. In other words, they did not understand the one God to be merely *acting* in different ways but of *being* in different ways; that is, that God is constituted by internal personal relations, and these were being revealed in God's historical action. Of extreme importance here is their eschatological sense: in the Christ event (including the permanent gift of the Spirit) God's definitive saving act was taking place. In this act God was revealing God's inner self. The definitive act is a definitive revelation of its very nature because the act is self-giving. Even in the Old Testament the belief was implicit that the way God *acts* in salvation history really reveals how God *is*, for God is faithful, trustworthy. Now, in Christ and the Spirit, God is acting definitively. In other words, the first Christians' eschatological sense told them that they could trust their experience to embody the *definitive* revelation of God.

Were they in any way prepared for this? As we said, the doctrine of the Trinity is not explicitly revealed in the Old Testament. Rather, the oneness of God is the cardinal point of Old Testament faith. There would have been no point in simply *saying* God was relations before the actual *eschaton* had arrived. As Karl Rahner has said: " . . . as long as God's self-communication in Jesus Christ was not yet an irreversible reality and the Spirit of God was not yet a triumphant eschatological manifestation but merely an offer, the revelation of the Trinity would have been word of a reality entirely outside the historical realm as such of man" (*The Concise Sacramentum Mundi,* p. 1755). But as we saw, the Old Testament does provide some preliminary *preparation* for the doctrine. The basic notion of God as *hesed* and *emet* is "on the way" toward seeing God as internally related because it sees God as unconditional love. And the Old Testament also provided some useful concepts for the early Christians when it spoke of the "*Word* of God" going forth in history, or the *Wisdom* of God as an indwelling gift, or of a personified *Spirit* of God.

But only in the New Testament does the real data for a belief in the Trinity appear, for only in the events it recounts is the gift of God's self complete. When the New Testament speaks simply of "God," it means the same as the Old Testament—the God who is at work in history. But following Jesus, the New Testament calls this God "Father," and sees Jesus as his Son and says he sends his Spirit. Normally the New Testament shies away from calling Jesus "God" (*theos*) precisely because this would confuse him with the "Father." There are places in the New Testament where Jesus is called "God" (certainly Jn 20:28; Tit 2:13), but the normal New Testament pattern reflects a consistent *distinction.* Yet, there is no question that the New Testament authors thought of Jesus as divine. He is not some sort of created intermediary between God and the world. It took time for his full status to be understood, but that an awareness of his divinity was present in the first generation of Christians is revealed in the statement of the early Church that "Jesus is Lord." "Lord" was used by the Old Testament to circumvent using the sacred name—Yahweh. Using it of Jesus was equivalent to saying that he is in some sense equal to the one who rules heaven and earth, for it was a term used in Palestinian Judaism for Yahweh. Jesus was seen as the presence of the reign of God, of the lordship of God. When they said he is Lord, they meant that in Jesus the lordship, the reign of God has come. There was a *functional* note to calling him "Lord"; he exercises divine power. It is a much-debated question among New Testament scholars if within the New Testament there is a movement from a functional to an ontological Christology. Many scholars claim that in Paul and John—and Paul begins to write within twenty years of the death of Jesus—Jesus is seen as the *pre-existent* Lord. Perhaps it is sufficient for our purposes to say that the *grounds for* an ontological Christology are laid in the New Testament.

The New Testament authors also clearly refuse to see the Holy Spirit as a cosmic or religious power acting as an intermediary between God and the world. The spirit is "sent," missioned as the Spirit of God and/or Christ. This is the Spirit *of God.* Again, in the native soil of Christianity the uppermost concern was *function,* not *nature,* so it is not surprising that the New Testament speaks more of the Spirit's function in our salvation than of its nature. This is true of the Old Testament too; there the Spirit of God is God working in history to save Israel. But when the New Testament speaks of the Holy Spirit, it sees some sort of distinction between the Father and the Spirit. The Father and the Son *send* the Spirit. Where did the New Testament community see the Spirit as active? First of all, *in the work of Jesus* himself (Jesus is the Messiah, the one *anointed* by the Holy Spirit) and, in continuity with that, *in the community which Jesus founds.* So the Spirit anoints Jesus and the Risen Christ sends the Spirit to anoint the Christian in the community, precisely in the event by which the Christian enters the community—baptism. The early Christians experienced a definitive presence of God as enlivening Spirit. They were new creatures because the Spirit had been poured into their hearts (Rom 5:5).

Paul especially gives testimony to this experience, but it is difficult to discern exactly what "Spirit" meant for Paul. He calls the Spirit both the Spirit of God and the Spirit of Christ, and speaks of Christ giving the Spirit. Yet at times, Christ and the Spirit seem to be one principle of activity. Paul does not use the developed concept of the later teaching of the Church; he is more concerned with the function of the Spirit than its nature. The reader must infer the Spirit's nature from its function and combine this with other texts of Paul such as 2 Corinthians 13:13 which clearly show that he thinks of God as triune. One sees *by implication* that the Spirit is personal.

In the Gospel of John the personal nature of the Spirit is more explicit. John speaks of the Spirit as "another advocate or comforter" who will be with the disciples as Jesus was. The parallelism seems to indicate that John thinks of the Spirit as personal, as Jesus is a person.

When one undertakes to distinguish three "persons" in the New Testament doctrine of God, one should not start from the modern notion of person. Possibly one cannot clearly distinguish Father, Son, and Holy Spirit to fit that notion. Yet some sort of distinction must be made to respect the data in the New Testament, because the three titles are not used interchangeably. Furthermore, the New Testament speaks of relationships between Father, Son, and Spirit, and there can be no relationships if there are no distinctions between the entities related. On the other hand, there is a *unity* among the persons that simply is not found in other personal relationships. Jesus is the presence of God the Father for us, but is still not the Father, and the difference is not just due to his created humanity. The Spirit is the Father's gift of himself, yet he, too, is not the Father. The Spirit is the Spirit of Christ, but ultimately not Christ.

One thing the New Testament authors do not try to do is explain their experience rationally. They simply express it.

THE CHURCH'S DOCTRINE

On the basis of the New Testament and amidst much controversy, the Church gradually clarified its belief about God as triune. Through a series of general councils it stated that the one God exists in three persons who are equal, co-eternal, and omnipotent. The doctrine avoids two extremes: on the one hand *tri-theism*, and on the other *modalism*. God is not to be conceived as so radically three that there are really three Gods (tri-theism), nor does talk of Father, Son and Spirit merely refer to modes or ways in which the one God manifests itself but would not refer to any real relatedness within God (modalism). The councils intended to say that there is one God who is internally related. The Father is God as having no principle of origin. The Son is "begotten" of the "substance" of the Father, but this is an eternal generation—"begotten not made" (against Arius). That is, the Son does not come into existence, but he is not his own origin like the Father. On the other hand, the Father is Father because of the Son, that is, what the Father is is eternally established by the existence of the Son. The Spirit is not begotten but "proceeds" from the Father and the Son *as from one principle*. (The "proceeding" of the Son is called *generatio*, "begetting," that of the Spirit, *spiratio*, "breathing.")

Thus, the relations in God are such that the divine persons are constituted by the relations. The "persons" are not really distinct from the essence of God—such that there is God and then three divine persons. Nor are there three persons in the sense of three distinct centers of freedom and.knowledge. There is only one God, one will, one intellect, but precisely the activity of God as one will, one intellect, results in internal relatedness. God is one, but God is also internally related so that each of the persons is God or, better, the "persons" are the three ways in which the one God is.

"The persons are not divided in being or in operation." That is, the three persons are one God, and it is the one God who acts. The persons do not act independently as three human persons would; on the other hand, the one God does not act as a monolith, but in accordance with God's identity as three persons. To say that the Father creates is not strictly true if it means that Son and Spirit do not. We "appropriate," or assign, characteristic functions to the different persons according to their relations, yet there is a oneness in all their operations. While it is clear that only the Son became human, even that can be misleading if it is not seen as the work of the Father and the Spirit. The "persons" have different roles in creation and salvation, but it is always God as three persons who is acting.

Another important point is that the Holy Spirit is not presented in the New Testament as something one experiences as an object—as something or someone at the other end of an experience. Rather, the Holy Spirit is God as present *in* the Christian—as that which *makes possible* the experience of God as Father and Jesus as Son. Thus, we do not experience the Holy Spirit as something to which we relate, as a Thou. Reflectively, we can make the Spirit a Thou and pray to it, but it is significant that there is far less prayer *to* the Holy Spirit than to the Father or Christ in the Christian tradition. The Holy Spirit is the ground which makes an experience of Christ as Son or God as Father possible. Spontaneously, the Christian experiences the Spirit not as an "other" but as united to one's own self.

It is not surprising, then, that we have not made the Holy Spirit an object of theological reflection the way we have made God as Father or God as Son objects of reflection. The Holy Spirit is experienced by the Christian as what makes such reflection possible. In Scripture, the Holy Spirit does not reveal itself as an "I" the way Yahweh did in the Old Testament or Jesus did in the New Testament. For instance, Scripture never presents the Holy Spirit as speaking on its own, but always through people. It reveals itself not as something or someone to be encountered, but as what makes encountering possible. The divine person, so to speak, "closest" to us is the Holy Spirit, and it is so close to us that it cannot be discerned as a self separate from the self of the Christian. One experiences the Spirit as the horizon in which the Son reveals the Father, as the power to recognize the Son as the expression of the Father. Our capacity to experience the Spirit is different from our capacity to experience the Son because Jesus, as a concrete human person, can be an object for us. We do not have that relationship to the Spirit. We experience the Spirit in experiencing Christ, as the ground of that experience, as what makes that experience possible. That is how close the Spirit is to us and that is what makes it impossible to make an object out of the Spirit.

So how do we experience the Spirit? The Spirit lets itself be experienced not as another but in what it does in us, especially as community, for the Spirit is the principle of unity in us (as it is the principle of unity between Father and Son). Our experience of the Spirit is always an experience of God's presence in people, including ourselves, which means that experience of it is always going to be affected by the human condition, including our sin. As a result, our experience of the Spirit is always somewhat ambiguous. This is compounded by the fact that its function is to act as the principle of unity among persons. The Gospel of John speaks of Jesus sending the Spirit to do this. On the cross he "gives up his spirit." Apparently this image has a double meaning. "Then he bowed his head, and *delivered over* his spirit" (19:30) means, surely, he died, but it also seems to be the evangelist's way of conveying the Spirit's coming upon the community as the result of Christ's death. Just as the community, the Church, is symbolized by the blood (Eucharist) and the water (baptism) from his side (Adam-Eve) so he endows the Church with his Spirit. Thus the New Testament Church understood itself as *constituted by the Spirit,* not in the *ad hoc* manner the Spirit came to the prophets, but as the community constituted by the definitive, permanent, sending of the Spirit. As the permanent bearer of the Spirit of God, Jesus communicated the Spirit to them, not as separate individuals but as community. The Holy Spirit was thus the Spirit of Jesus, constituting them the body of Christ. If we think in terms of salvation history, the death of Jesus begins the time of the Holy Spirit—but the Spirit is not a substitute *for* Jesus. As *his* Spirit, it is *his* presence.

CONTEMPORARY DISCUSSION OF THE TRINITY

In recent years the realization has grown that the dogmatic definitions of councils are more open-ended than they seemed to an earlier age. The councils used terms that sounded like terms from Greek philosophy—*hypostasis, ousia*—but they did not use them philosophically. For instance, at Nicea the Son was said to be consubstantial (*homoousios*) with the Father. But, according to a scholar like Bernard Lonergan

the Nicene concept of consubstantiality does not go beyond the dogmatic realism that is contained implicitly in the word of God. For it means no more than this, that what is said of the Father is to be said also of the Son, except that the Son is Son and not Father (*The Way to Nicea,* p. 130).

The conciliar definitions are very minimalistic, precisely because key terms are left open.

This, among other things, has led to more discussion of the Trinity. This discussion immediately encounters a basic problem which runs through theology because of its history. Medieval theology aspired to be systematic. Theology is made systematic by the introduction of a coherent set of *philosophical* categories into properly theological data. Aquinas, for example, used Aristotelian philosophy (with additions from Jewish and Arab philosophers). The difficulty is that Aristotle derived his philosophical categories from analysis of *nature*. These categories were elaborated for a metaphysics of *pre-personal* reality. But their use in theology is problematic because theology ultimately deals with reality that is pre-eminently personal. When the medievals talked about *grace*, for instance, it became, so to speak, "thingified." They talked about "created grace" and "uncreated grace" as though they were things. But what is "uncreated grace"? It is simply God. What is "created grace"? The likeness of God in free, personal creatures through God's love for them.

It is true that in discussing the Trinity theologians were drawn (as early as Augustine) to *human consciousness* as the best analogue for God's interior life, which is a good start because human consciousness is personal. But Trinitarian theology failed to do justice to the truly personal character of God's interior life because, to a great extent, it used pre-personal categories to analyze human consciousness.

It should come as no surprise, then, that contemporary discussion is concerned with reworking the classical tradition by using categories derived from personal relationships. Theologians still talk of God in terms of consciousness, but they now discuss consciousness in categories derived from personal relationships, rather than pre-personal reality. But this effort has only just begun. Two proposals by Karl Rahner are the center of debate.

SALVATION HISTORY AS REVELATION OF GOD'S BEING

Rahner's first proposal, which has received wide acceptance, is that we must not be Trinitarian in doctrine but philosophical monotheists in practice. He asserts that we must take seriously that the Transcendent acts in history according to the way it *is in itself*—that it is loving toward us because it is love in itself. Applying this to the Trinity, Rahner insisted that the "economic Trinity" (the Trinity as revealed in salvation history or the "economy" of salvation) *is* the "immanent Trinity"—it is how the Transcendent is in itself. This means that God acts in history according to God's own internal relations, and that the roles of the "persons" within salvation history are not arbitrary but flow from the relations which constitute the Trinity. God communicates God's self to the world precisely as God is. A movement away from an "apathetic" God to a "sympathetic" God is apparent here. Rahner is saying that God does not just act *on* history as an undifferentiated, external, unitary agent, but that God really makes a gift of *self* to the world God creates. And precisely because it is God's self that is given, God's presence in history is Trinitarian—God is there precisely as God is in God's being. God's gift of self is triune because God is triune. This means that what the Father does in history, what the Son does in history, and what the Spirit does in history, follow from what they are in the Trinity, although every act is somehow an act of the one God.

Rahner believed that there is a significant loss for the life of faith when Christians are *theoretically* Trinitarian but practically only monotheists, for then spirituality does not exploit the fullness of revelation. He urged that, over against the traditional theological position that (1) the Trinity acts as one principle and so only by "appropriation" (to accommodate our finite minds) do we assign different functions to the different persons, and (2) the conclusion from this, that anyone of the three persons could have become human, we must return to a salvation history approach to the Trinity. This is the import of his insistence that the economic Trinity *is* the immanent Trinity. In contrast to the position that the relations of the persons within the Godhead have no intrinsic bearing on the salvation of human beings, Rahner held that God saves by communicating himself—and thus the Transcendent communicates itself as it is. We know how the Transcendent is in itself precisely because it has given itself to us as it is. Or to put it another way, salvation history *is* the Transcendent giving itself, communicating itself, outside itself just as it communicates itself inside itself.

The corollary of this is that the Second Person, the Son, becomes human and not the Father or the Spirit. The Second Person *is* God as expression. In Christ the Transcendent does outside itself what it is always doing inside itself. As it expresses itself inside as the Son, so, when it expresses itself outside, it does it as the Son. Likewise, the Spirit is given to humanity to integrate it into the divine life because that is precisely what the Spirit is—the bond between Father and Son, the shared love. The principle of unity *within* the Trinity, the Holy Spirit, is the principle of unity of creation *with* the Trinity.

Rahner's point is that we should take the New Testament way of speaking seriously and realize that it is not merely accommodating God's activity to our finite minds. In Paul, and especially in John, the

New Testament expresses the notion that in salvation history there are two *missions*—there is the sending (mission) of the Son from the Father and there is a sending of the Spirit from the Father and the Son. Rahner says that the first is a mission in the modality of *truth*. In virtue of God's truthfulness (Hebrew: *emet*) God gives himself to humanity in history, making us an offer of intimacy and friendship. This is the mission of the Son. Then, out of love, God creates in human beings the ability to respond to the offer of friendship. This is a mission in the modality of love, the sending of the Spirit.

Thus, when the New Testament talks of the Son as the truth and the Spirit as love, it is describing God's internal life, not merely "accommodating" God's mystery to our minds. The principle that underlies this conclusion is that the Transcendent's action within itself and outside itself is love, genuine bestowal of self. The Transcendent is love. It does not merely give *things*. It gives *self*. Furthermore the Transcendent's *being* is to give itself and it thus reveals its inner life in the way it gives itself.

THE CRITIQUE OF "PERSON" IN CONTEMPORARY TRINITARIAN THEOLOGY

A second aspect of Rahner's Trinitarian theology involves a consistent critique of the use of the word "person" to indicate what there are three of in the Trinity. This criticism is paralleled in Protestant theology by Karl Barth and in Anglican theology by John Macquarrie. Although this proposal has not received as much support as the first, a review of the discussion is useful.

According to Rahner, we think of a person as a distinct center of knowing and loving based in a distinct existence. But there are not three of those in God. In God there is only one essence, hence one absolute self-presence. Also, because there is only *one* self-utterance (the Logos does not utter the Father, it is uttered), "there is properly no mutual love between Father and Son, for this would presuppose two acts" (*Trinity*, p. 106).

So in Rahner's view any attempt by Christians to refer to members of the immanent Trinity as "persons" is misleading because persons involve separate consciousnesses, numerically distinct psychological centers of operation. But the unity of God's essence means there is only one will and one intellect in God, which, indeed, themselves are not distinct, and would be identical with God's being. So Rahner proposes to substitute for "person" the phrase "distinct manner of subsisting." The one God subsists in three distinct interrelated modalities; the Father, Son and Spirit are the one God *each* in different manners of subsisting. The "threeness" of God—the *otherness* within God—is that God subsists in different ways.

The reserve with which Rahner's proposal has been met centers on whether, in backing away from tritheism, he has fallen into modalism. The original modalist, Sabellius, said that the distinction in salvation history between Father, Son, and Spirit does not reflect a real distinction in God. Those are simply the ways the one God *appears* to us. God is revealed in three different *personae* or masks. Clearly Rahner is not a Sabellian modalist, for true Sabellianism proposes no genuine self communication in God, which is precisely what Rahner sees as the ground of salvation history. But what happens if we abandon the traditional language? If we abandon "person" in discussing the immanent Trinity, then should we not abandon it in discussing the economic Trinity? But if we do that, do we not run the risk of a popular modalism?

Walter Kasper criticizes Rahner's proposal to drop person from the theological vocabulary because, he says, Rahner understands "person" in an antiquated, individualistic way. It is true that what "person" eventually came to mean was not its meaning when the dogma of the Trinity was being worked out. The "modern" concept of person as a distinct center of existing, knowing and willing is not what was meant by the term *hypostasis* (Latin *subsistentia*). But, Kasper insists, there is a "post-modern" understanding of person (coming from German Idealism) that is appropriate for Trinitarian theology. As Kasper points out, paraphrasing Hegel, to be a person in any real sense one must abandon isolation and particularity, enlarge oneself toward universality, and, by giving up abstract personality and becoming absorbed in what is other than oneself, acquire concrete personality. The person therefore is a reconciliation of universality and particularity and thus the realization of the essence of love. For as Hegel says, "love is a distinguishing of two who are nevertheless not distinct for each other." For Hegel, love is "distinction and the cancelling of distinction" (Kasper, *Jesus the Christ*, p. 184). The abstruse Hegalian language is pointing to a fact that can be verified in experience: To truly be a person one must escape from isolation and enter into relationships. To be a person in the *concrete* sense is to be in relation to other persons. A radical individualism is the very antithesis of true personhood.

Kasper's proposal is that, rather than capitulating to the defective "modern" notion of person and eliminating it from Trinitarian theology, we should redefine "person" in the light of our experience and

Trinitarian theology. He says the post-modern (Hegelian) understanding of person amounts to a paraphrase of the traditional definition of the divine persons as subsistent relations and also it is the best
justification for describing them as persons:

> If . . . we abandon the term "person" and speak instead of
> modes of being or subsistence in Trinitarian doctrine, an ab-
> stract concept of being is made ultimate and supreme, al-
> though the whole point of Trinitarian doctrine is to say that
> reality as a whole is profoundly personal or interpersonal in
> its structure (ibid.).

Kasper's point is that an understanding of person must include,
as constitutive of the person, the aspect of relationship. A person is not
merely a center of existing, knowing and willing which *then* relates; a
person is essentially related. One becomes a person by relating. To be
related is constitutive of a person as person. In this sense, "person" is
perfectly appropriate and indeed indispensable for capturing precisely what the dogma of the Trinity wishes to express, namely, that
the divine essence is essentially relational within itself. The persons of
the Trinity are subsistent relationships, which means that *Being itself* is
essentially relational, interpersonal, and loving. Thus, for Kasper, to
speak of God as modes of being or subsistence is to speak of God in
pre-personal concepts. It gives ultimacy to concepts that conceive of
being in a pre-personal way when precisely what the dogma of the
Trinity implies is that Being itself, the ultimate reality, is personal, and
that Being is creating beings in order that it might enter into relationship with what is created.

Whatever the final fate of Rahner's second proposal, his insistence
that the economic Trinity *is* the immanent Trinity has received wide
acceptance. It means that God the Father communicates *himself* to the
world as Son and Spirit. That is, the sending or missions of the Son
and the Spirit are the way God is. Salvation is the Transcendent doing
"outside" itself what it is always doing "inside" itself.

Rahner sees the two missions as the *one* self-communication of
God to the world, but, as we said, under different modalities. The essence of the mission of the Son is the communication of the *truth,* but
truth in the full sense of lived truth, as irrevocable reliability. The essence of the mission of the Spirit is that God imparts himself to his
creation without self-seeking, as overflowing love, as *agape.* As committed to *revealing* and *saving,* the essence of the mission of the Spirit
is the communication of love. Thus God enters into history the way

God is, in the two basic modes of the divine self-communication within God, those of truth and love. In *history* there are *two* moments of God's self-communication. God communicates himself to the human nature of Jesus as the Word, and God communicates himself to the Christian as the Spirit. The first "mission" gives historical expression to God's truth about God; the second gives historical expression to the love which exists between the Truth and its origin. The distinction should not be seen as a separation. These are *moments* in the one self-communication of God.

But if the Transcendent is really communicating *itself,* then the missions *reveal* that within God there is a procession of Truth in which God as origin and as unoriginated ("the Father") *expresses* his own Truth ("the Son") and is received as love. The love is the Spirit. The "Father" communicates "himself," utters himself and this constitutes the Son. The reception of the Father as love in the Son is the Spirit. But since this is self-communication within God, God *is* these communications. The distinction between the origin and the originated is not a distinction between separate substances which come into a relation but between the terms of a relation which constitutes the Being of God. Within the one God, because God as unoriginated (the "Father") not merely expresses "himself" but communicates himself, there are relations and the terms of the relations are distinct. But the relations are the very essence of God.

Accordingly, when we say that there are three persons in God, we are saying that the persons are not distinct substances the way we are, but *terms of relations* within God. There are not persons who *have* relationships—the persons *are* the subsistent relationships. Here personhood is perfect. As unoriginated, the Transcendent gives expression to itself but, in expressing itself, *gives* itself and is received in what is constituted by its giving itself. The very being of God is giving, self-communication, love, *agape.* God *is* this dynamic activity. The ultimate reality, Being itself, *is* personal self-communication.

THE HOLY SPIRIT

Another theologian who thinks that traditional discussion of the Trinity has taken place in inadequate categories is Heribert Mühlen. He points out that the inadequacy of the Scholastic (Aristotelian) categories is particularly acute when discussing the Holy Spirit. The personal reality of the Holy Spirit is affirmed by the doctrine but not well accounted for in the theological reflection on the doctrine. Mühlen wants to abandon the language which presents the Spirit as an impersonal efficient cause in favor of terms which capture the Spirit's personal character. A problem arises immediately. Mühlen himself has pointed out that the Holy Spirit is not experienced the way we experience another person but as that which relates us to the Father and Son. The Spirit, as the expression of the bond between Father and Son, performs the function in believers of uniting them to God. How would this be expressed in personalistic terms? Using the traditional notion of the persons as subsistent relations, Mühlen calls the Father the subsistent I-Relation, the Son the subsistent Thou-Relation, and the Holy Spirit the subsistent We-Relation. As was said above, to be a person is to be related. While it is too much to say of finite persons that they go in and out of existence dependent on relationships, nevertheless, we can say they are more or less persons depending on their relationships. With God the relationships are permanent, constitutive of the very identity of the persons—"subsistent." The Father is not first a person who then is related to the Son as Father. His fatherness is constitutive of his personhood. The relation is subsistent. To give this traditional doctrine a personalistic cast Mühlen points to a phenomenon of human language, namely, that in their use personal pronouns are always relational. Even though the pronouns refer to separate individuals, within the mind of the speaker, they always imply a relation to another. In other words, even in human discourse to say "I" always involves addressing a Thou. If I refer to a third party, I use he or she, but it is inevitable that I relate the third party to the discourse created by the use of I and Thou. He or she is in the third person precisely because he or she is not the speaker or the addressee.

Mühlen uses this analysis of our language to clarify our thought about the Spirit. He points out that when we say "we," two persons are not standing over against one another, facing one another, as it were, but rather next to one another and facing in the same direction. They speak from an antecedent union. Yet the We-relationship is the perfection of the I-Thou relationship. In the We-relationship the I-Thou relationship turns outward. The I and Thou become a principle of activity not solely toward one another but beyond one another, together.

What Mühlen sees in the structure of human *discourse*, he applies analogously to the Trinity. His distinctive contribution is that the Holy Spirit is treated as a truly personal reality, but not as an I or a Thou. The Spirit is the We-relationship of the I-relationship (Father) and the Thou-relationship (Son). Moreover, the inseparability of the personal pronouns in discourse (there is no I without a Thou implied or expressed) captures better what the tradition has always asserted, namely, that the three divine persons really are "terms of subsistent relations" (in the relationship A = B, A and B are the "terms" of a relationship of equality), are distinct from one another as terms of relationships, but also are "constituted by" their relationships.

Thus there is in God (God is) one consciousness, one self, which is shared by the Father, Son and Spirit in three distinct, but related, ways. The Father as the subsistent I-relation is conscious of himself, first of all, as the first person, that is, as the one who is underived and without origin from another. But just as there is no I without a Thou, the Father implies the Son. Without the Son to address as Thou, the Father would not be an I. Just as the Son is constituted by relationship to the Father, the Father is constituted in his personhood by the Thou who is the Son.

It may help if we relate what Mühlen is saying to the traditional language. The theology of the Trinity characterized the Son as the Word, following the Gospel of John (1:1). The medievals customarily said that as Word the Son is the expression of the Father, that is, in knowing himself the Father gives perfect expression of himself in the Word. But they also consistently said that not only is the Word an expression of self-knowledge and therefore known, but that the known is loved. As perfect self-expression the Word *is* what the Father is (except Father, for that is precisely what the *expression* involves), so the expression participates in what the Father is and is therefore personal and therefore loved. The medievals also said that the person so constituted would fail to be person if he did not respond and relate to that which engendered him, loved him. For both reasons, according to Mühlen, it makes sense to call the Son the subsistent Thou-Relationship.

It is at this point, with reference to the Holy Spirit, that Mühlen makes his contribution. He points out that at two general councils of the Church—Lyons II in the thirteenth century and Florence in the fifteenth century—the assembled bishops affirmed that the Holy Spirit proceeds eternally from the Father and the Son not as two principles or sources of activity, but as one, not in virtue of two "spirations" but in virtue of a single spiration. Mühlen says this is what the pronoun "we" points to—it is used when two persons act as a single principle. The Spirit therefore can be described as the subsistent We-relationship in which Father and Son act as one principle. The personhood of the Spirit is precisely the personhood of an I and Thou acting as a We. The Spirit is "one person in two persons." Although traditional discussion of the Spirit recognized that the Spirit was the "result" of one spiration, it was content to speak of the Spirit as the mutual love between Father and Son. Mühlen, however, goes further: The Spirit is precisely the person constituted by the I and the Thou as a single principle of operation—a We.

In his book *Die Veränderlichheit Gottes als Horizont einer Zukünftigen Christologie* (1969), Mühlen's reflections on the Trinity are applied to the question we began this section with: Is God *apathos* or *sympathos*? His Trinitarian conclusions lead him to criticize "the classical conception of God." By "classical conception of God" he means a God who is "unchanging." According to Mühlen, the notion of God as unchanging is a theological, not a conciliar, doctrine. Thus, he says (his "minimalistic" reading of the meaning of the Councils echoes Lonergan's) the fathers at Nicea meant by the term *homoousios* only to affirm that Jesus was of the same being (*gleichseiendlich*) with the Father. They did not specify what the being or nature of God is. They may have *thought* in terms of a single substance, but their explicit affirmations at Nicea were limited to a rejection of the Arian position, that is, they were only affirming what Arius was denying, that Jesus was divine and not merely a creature.

According to Mühlen, at Chalcedon the underlying assumption that God's nature is one (*monos*) indivisible "substance" resulted in a confusion. Because they unreflectively thought of the divine reality as a single unrelated substance the bishops affirmed that the Son "suffers" (is *pathos*) only in his human nature. God remains untouched by participation in human history. What happens when a fully Trinitarian conception of God comes into play? Can we continue to represent God as *apathos*? Mühlen's point is that Scripture and Trinitarian doctrine itself both require us to see the ultimate reality as personal, interrelating Being, not a simple undifferentiated substance. In Scripture God's nature is unchanging not in the sense of an indivisible divine substance, but rather in terms of God's constant fidelity to his promises. When, therefore, John has Jesus say "I and the Father are one" (10:30), we should not interpret the statement metaphysically as though it connotes the unity of Father and Son in a divine substance. Instead, it refers to the *quality of the interpersonal relationship* existing between Jesus and the Father. Father and Son constitute a community. This, Mühlen says, is what *homoousios* means when we transcend the pre-personal *presuppositions* of the fathers of the council. Two things follow. The essence of God is not immutable substance, but *community*. Thus Mühlen presents the Holy Spirit as the personification of the divine essence as community. The Spirit is the communitarian reality of God in person. But the Spirit then is the We relationship in God, the outward movement of the Father and Son as one principle, but as self-giving community. The tradition, at its best, did understand God as essentially self-giving, self-communication. Thus Mühlen's second point: the divine nature *consists* in the giving *away* of one's own (*Weggabe des Eigensten*). The Spirit is the personification of the united giving of Father and Son within, and then outward from the Godhead. God *is* this dynamic, self-giving process which is of its very essence not *apathos* but *sympathos*.

THE BIBLICAL GOD

It is not difficult to see that contemporary discussion of the Trinity is engaged in trying to answer the most fundamental theological question, the question we asked in the first section of this book, the God question. We have sought an answer to this question in the biblical tradition. It is time to summarize our findings.

The biblical God, at least the God of the Old Testament, is often presented as a God of *power*. The God of Israel is a God of power; Yahweh is a creator God and the Lord of history. But the God of Israel is not someone who *dominates* men and women. Yahweh wants something from Israel that cannot be attained by domination, for love cannot be extorted. The *Shema*, the prayer of the devout Jew, expresses well the relation of the true Israelite to his or her God. "Hear, O Israel! The Lord your God is one Lord and you shall love the Lord your God with your whole heart, your whole mind, your whole soul." It is true this is a commandment and does sound as though God is demanding love. But the Old Testament does not portray the Lord as demanding it for himself. God urges Israel to love because it is good for Israel, and commands Israel to love because love is Israel's destiny. The biblical God calls Israel to a *partnership*. It is true it is an unequal partnership. God is God and Israel is his creature, and there is an infinite difference. But the true greatness of Yahweh is that he does not cling to the difference.

In Jesus, God's offer of intimacy reaches its definitive stage. We have seen that Jesus' use of *Abba* in addressing God is more than just a way of speaking. It says something about who God really is. God as "father" is a true father whose whole goal is to nurture his child to maturity. As creatures we will always be dependent on God. But as free creatures we are called to responsible partnerships with our creator. Thus, to say that we are dependent on God is not to say that we are not free or that God is an obstacle to our freedom. It is precisely true freedom that God wishes to bestow on his people. The biblical God does not treat his people as a puppet but as the partner in a dialogue—the purpose of which is the growth of that people.

In Jesus, the dialogue reaches its eschatological stage. It is accomplished by God's "humility," by God's emptying of himself into history. The Christian understanding of God as Trinity is really an expression of this event and its foundation in God's very being. According to the contemporary Protestant theologian Jürgen Moltmann, the doctrine of the Trinity is

> nothing other than the conceptual framework needed to understand the story of Jesus as the story of God. The doctrine of the Trinity is the theological short summary of the story of the passion of Christ. With it we grasp the story of the passion of Christ in the story of the divine passion (*Jewish Monotheism and Christian Trinitarian Doctrine*, Fortress, 1981, p. 47).

In the view of the Catholic theologian, Walter Kasper, the Trinity is the Christian form of speaking about God. A truly Christian answer to the God question would have to be Trinitarian. What in the end does the doctrine say?

The doctrine of the Trinity says this: Ultimate reality—Being itself—is love. Ultimate reality is not *something that* loves; the very essence of Being itself *is* loving. The ground of being is not a static, impervious, self-absorbed "substance" but a ceaseless personal creativity whose very essence is communication of self, emptying of self, full bestowal of self. Being itself is kenotic, that is, self-emptying, self-giving. In the ultimate reality loving is not subsequent to being. Being itself *is* free conferral of self. It *is* largesse. It *is* grace. The very stuff of God is self-giving. God *is* this communication of self in love.

Being itself, then, is relational. It is unoriginated giving, the joyful pure reception of the gift, the movement outward from this I-Thou in a We. That which truly is, that which is its own ground, does not *have* relations. It *is* relations. The oneness of ultimate reality is not the static oneness of solitariness, but the joyful oneness of a union so profound that there is no distinction in being. The oneness of God is the perfect union of a love which *is* the partners to the union. The oneness of God is the oneness of a "we" so united that there is no distinction in being between the I and the Thou.

What has all this to do with human existence, which is so fragmented, so threatened by personal and social disunion and by the ultimate disintegration called death? There is certainly a marked contrast between the unity of Being and the disunity of beings. We cannot but ask: Are beings destined to share in the unity of Being? Could Being create beings and this creation not be, in its origin and destiny, an expression of what Being is—love, personal self-giving, the oneness of union based on loving self-giving?

The doctrine of the Trinity asks us to believe that in the end reality begins and ends in love. Our nerve fails us. How can we really believe that, even if we want to? Is that not wishful thinking? But is it easier to believe that Being is in the end blind, unconscious, and impervious cosmic debris? Apparently some people who encountered Jesus of Nazareth felt that in him and in the Spirit he sent, they had encountered the heart of reality. As unoriginated, creative love, it had loved a universe into existence. As the expression and mediation of love, it had entered that universe as a person. As the bond of unity, as the principle of union, it remained in this world as the eschatological gift. The Christian doctrine of the Trinity says God is what God does—love. It says further that we are the objects of this love that is God. Nothing can separate us from this love, except our refusal to accept it, because for God to cease loving us would be for God to cease being God.

To understand the Christian mystery and to be accurate about God, we must take our beliefs seriously. The doctrine of the Trinity encompasses the two central Christian beliefs—what God has done, and what God is—and grounds the former in the latter. God is an infinite act of love. Salvation history is God being God, now not within, but without. The exuberance of God, joyful and complete within itself, now bursts forth in creation, into the coming-to-be of that which is not God. The love that is God creates an object of love which is not God. But love is not mere positing of the other. It is union with the other; it is communication of self to the other. In Israel this love begins to communicate itself, seeking union with the beloved. In Christ this love is personally present in the mode of the beloved, as "flesh." In the Spirit God's communication of self is complete, creative of a community that is the continued presence of the Father and Son in history, the "we" of the community mirroring the "we" that the Spirit is.

The community is the place where God's self-communication in history reaches its eschatological stage. But the community does not exist for its own sake. It is the instrument of the Spirit, whose function in history is the same as it is within the divine life—union, oneness, "we"-ness. Moved by the Spirit, the community seeks the unity of God's creation. It seeks, not through dominance but *kenosis*, self-giving, to reveal to the world its true identity as the object of God's love, to be an instrument of reconciliation of creature with creature and creation with Creator. To be a Christian is to live in this community, and to build it up in love in order that it might build up the world in love. It is to seek to hasten the day when God is all in all.

EPILOGUE

Theology aspires to say something about God. But theology has an ulterior motive. It seeks to serve faith. It tries to say something about God so that men and women might know God better. It would be nice to think that this book helped someone to know God better; but if it did, it was simply because the reader already knew God, and this book helped to clarify that experience. Theology cannot "deliver" God; it can only deepen what one already knows.

Perhaps theology can also point to where God can be found. The biblical witness is consistent in indicating that God is found only if one is willing to be called forth, away from the familiar and expected, the comfortable and reassuring. God refuses to be domesticated. God challenges. Love always does. Thus the Father's love for Jesus manifested itself as an absolute challenge.

God's challenges are tailored to individuals. Love is like that, too. It respects the identity of the beloved. But there is a common element in the diverse calls. Every call is a call away from self. It is a call toward solidarity with others. The biblical God hides among the others, has lost himself in the others, especially among the dispossessed of the earth (Mt 25), and demands that we seek him there.

This is not an arbitrary challenge. It could not be otherwise. God is love. God is self-sharing. To know God means that we must become what God is: self-sharing, ec-centric, self-less. This is the condition of union, for love can only be received by returning it.

God has become incarnate in Jesus. This man from Nazareth is the Father's perfect self-expression. In Jesus, the men and women of first-century Palestine encountered unconditional love enfleshed. They were surprised where they found him. He was not among the rich and powerful. He was not with the revolutionaries or the religious elite. He was not with the theologians. He did not exclude anyone from his companionship, but he had a preference. He preferred to be with

237

the "lost sheep of Israel," the sick, the blind, the hungry, the ignorant, the sinners, the powerless, the victims—in a word, what both he and we call "the poor."

But is it so surprising? Where else would one expect to find unconditional love except among those who need it most?

SELECTED BIBLIOGRAPHY

Bornkamm, Günther. *Jesus of Nazareth.* New York: Harper and Row, 1961.

Brown, Raymond E. *The Birth of the Messiah.* New York: Doubleday, 1977.

Collins, Raymond F. *Introduction to the New Testament.* Garden City, N.Y.: Doubleday, 1983.

Ellacuría, Ignacio. *Freedom Made Flesh.* Maryknoll, N.Y.: Orbis, 1976.

Ferner, Johannes, and Lukas Vischer. *The Common Catechism.* New York: Seabury, 1975.

Fitzmyer, Joseph. *A Christological Catechism.* New York: Paulist Press, 1982.

Gutierrez, Gustavo. *A Theology of Liberation.* Maryknoll, N.Y.: Orbis, 1973.

Kasper, Walter. *Jesus the Christ.* New York: Paulist Press, 1976.

———. *The God of Jesus Christ.* New York: Crossroad, 1984.

Kümmel, Werner. *The New Testament: The History of the Investigation of Its Problems.* Nashville: Abingdon, 1972.

Lohfink, Gerhard. *Jesus and Community.* Philadelphia: Fortress Press, 1984.

Lonergan, Bernard. *Method in Theology.* New York: Herder and Herder, 1972.

———. *The Way to Nicea.* Philadelphia: Westminster, 1976.

Meyer, Ben F. *The Aims of Jesus.* London: SCM Press, 1979.

Murray, John Courtney. *We Hold These Truths.* New York: Sheed and Ward, 1960.

O'Brien, Niall. *Revolution From the Heart.* New York: Oxford University Press, 1987.

O'Collins, Gerald. *Interpreting Jesus*. New York: Paulist Press, 1983.

———. *The Resurrection of Jesus Christ*. Valley Forge, PA: Judson, 1973.

Pannenberg, Wolfhart. *Jesus-God and Man*. Philadelphia: Westminster, 1968.

Rahner, Karl. *Foundation of Christian Faith*. New York: Seabury, 1978.

———. *The Trinity*. New York: Herder and Herder, 1970.

Schnackenburg, Rudolf. *God's Reign and Kingdom*. Montreal: Palm, 1963.

Sobrino, Jon. *Jesus in Latin America*. Maryknoll, N.Y.: Orbis, 1987.

Van Roo, W. A. *The Mystery*. Rome: Gregorian, 1971.